WELCOME

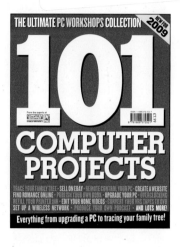

Whether you work with a behemoth of a machine stuck in the corner of a room, a compact laptop or something in between, the modern-day computer is a versatile, powerful and fascinating piece of equipment. The sheer number of things it offers the potential to be able to do is genuinely extraordinary.

However, just because a computer can do a lot of things, that doesn't mean that the average PC in our homes actually does. And that's generally because, sometimes, we need an extra push or a helping hand. Fortunately, that's where we come in.

This book gathers together 101 different projects and tasks you can undertake, mostly with nothing more required than your existing computer. What's more, it covers a range of expertise, so whether you want to upgrade your motherboard, record a podcast or trace your family tree, there's help and guidance right here, all explained in straightforward, no-nonsense language.

We hope that something in here inspires you to try something different using your computer. Do get in touch and let us know you get on.

Us? Well, this very book that you're reading now began when we ourselves sat down, determined to try something different with our own computers. We only hope you have as much fun as we did!

The 101 Computer Projects Team
101projects@dennis.co.uk

101 COMPUTER PROJECTS

EDITORIAL
Editors
Simon Brew, Steve Haines
Sub-editors
Gareth Beech, Anthony Enticknap, Janey Goulding, Rob Woodcock
Art Editor
Khoi Kieu
Cover
Bill Bagnall

PROJECTS WRITTEN BY
Martin Anderson, Aaron Birch, Gaye Birch, Simon Brew, Martyn Carroll, Jason D'Allison, Barry de la Rosa, Sarah Dobbs, Anthony Enticknap, Chris Finnamore, Karl Hodge, James Hunt, Joe Lavery, David Ludlow, Jim Martin, Mark McKay, Mark Oakley, Kat Orphanides, Ian Osborne, Mark Pickavance, Kevin Pocock, Jenny Sanders, Stuart Smith, Alex Watson

ADVERTISING
Julie Price
ads.shopper@dennis.co.uk

INTERNATIONAL LICENSING
The content in this bookazine is available for international licensing overseas. Contact Winnie Liesenfeld +44 20 7907 6134, winnie_liesenfeld@dennis.co.uk

MANAGEMENT
Bookazine Manager
Dharmesh Mistry (020 7907 6100)
dharmesh_mistry@dennis.co.uk
Publishing Director
John Garewal
Operations Director
Robin Ryan
Group Advertising Director
Julian Lloyd-Evans

Circulation Director
Martin Belson
Finance Director
Brett Reynolds
Group Finance Director
Ian Leggett
Chief Executive
James Tye
Chairman
Felix Dennis

A DENNIS PUBLICATION
Dennis Publishing, 30 Cleveland St, London W1T 4JD. Company registered in England. All material © Dennis Publishing Limited, licensed by Felden 2008, and may not be reproduced in whole or part without the consent of the publishers.

Dennis Publishing operates an efficient commercial reprints service. For more details, please call 020 7907 6640.

LIABILITY
While every care was taken during the production of this bookazine, the publishers cannot be held responsible for the accuracy of the information or any consequence arising from it. Dennis Publishing takes no responsibility for the companies featured in this bookazine.

Printed by BGP, Bicester.

The paper used within this bookazine is produced from sustainable fibre, manufactured by mills with a valid chain of custody.

ISBN 1-906372-52-7

WHAT'S INSIDE

INTERNET

HARDWARE

SOFTWARE

INTERNET PROJECTS

There's a wealth of projects you can tackle with the help of the internet, and we've got lots of tips and advice to get you started. Whether you're tracking down distant relatives, finding romance or selling your possessions, there's plenty you can do!

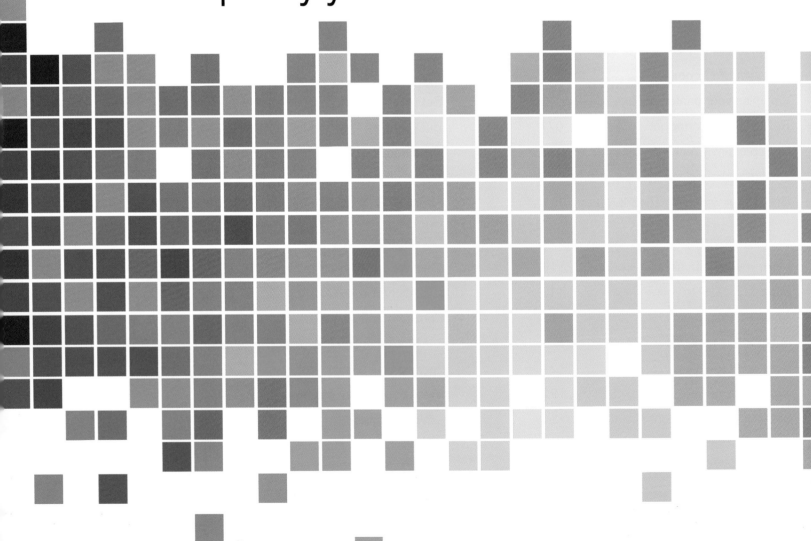

 PROJECT 001

 DIFFICULTY LEVEL HARD / INTERMEDIATE / EASY

TIME REQUIRED 2 HOURS

Trace your family tree

Want to trace your ancestors online? Here we show you how to begin

RESEARCHING YOUR FAMILY tree online can be a rewarding hobby, but where do you start? For the sake of this project, we'll assume that you have already spoken to living relatives, and thus been able to trace your ancestry back three or four generations, although what we'll be talking about can help cover a few more recent gaps, too. But we'll also go back further than living memory allows.

A great source of information is the National Archives (*www. nationalarchives.gov.uk*), which stores and maintains UK government records, including really interesting and valuable census information. In the UK, a census has been taken every ten years since 1801, though there was no census in 1941 as it wasn't really practical during World War II. The first four surveys, from 1801 to 1831, contain very little personal information. From 1841 onwards, however, the names of everyone in a household or institution were recorded for posterity as well.

Census records are kept confidential by law for 100 years, so the earliest census you can access is the one carried out in 1901. The earliest accessible census dates back to 1841. You can search the 1901 census information using a person's name, an address, a place name, an institution or vessel. Note that searches available vary in the earlier, 19th century surveys. Searching the archives is free, but

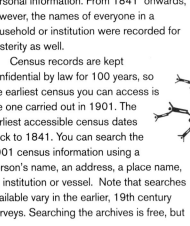

actually reading one of your hits costs money. Not a fortune, but be careful only to check out the people and places you really need to see.

Of course, having used the free internet searches to familiarise yourself with what you're looking for, you could then visit the archives in person to check them out, which is free. Its postal address is The National Archives, Kew, Richmond, Surrey, TW9 4DU.

Remember, a census is crammed with useful information, much of which can open other areas of research. For example, a census entry tells you what your ancestor did for a living and where they lived. This could give clues about their social status. Any census taken after 1851 will offer information on where an individual was born, which immediately offers an opportunity to find out more about the preceding generation. You may only know what your great grandfather's parents were called, but by tracing their place of birth, you know where to look for their own parents.

But there's more to online research than The National Archives. Friends Reunited, the popular service used to reacquaint yourself with old school chums, has a sister site, Genes Reunited. It currently boasts over eight million members, and this can prove incredibly useful. After all, your extended family covers hundreds of people, and it might well be that a distant relative you didn't even know existed is already working on it. You can also team up.

By typing the name, date of birth and place of birth of a member of your family (or at least as much information as you can provide), you can search Genes Reunited's database of

MILITARY HISTORY

If you have an ancestor who has served or you think might have served in the military, there's a great resource to be found at *www.nationalarchives.gov.uk/militaryhistory*.

A database of everyone who earned a campaign medal in World War 1 is now online, as are the British Army Pensions Records of soldiers discharged on account of sickness or injuries sustained during

the war. You can also search for individuals according to when and in what branch of the forces they served.

Accessing some of the information found on this site incurs a charge, but you can glean a decent amount for free, as well as gaining interesting pointers about where to look next and which documents it's worth your while buying.

The National Archive has an online record of everyone who earned a medal in WWI

Searching for a person in the 1901 census, which you can find online

A marriage register sourced offline. Online searches might help you find where to look

Could Genes Reunited help find your ancestors?

Do your relatives turn up in other people's family trees?

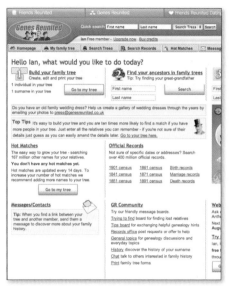

Finding your roots using the Genes Reunited website

Family Tree Searcher collates results from nine different websites

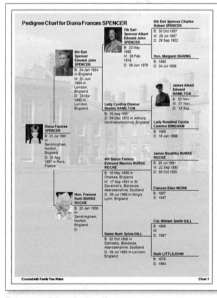

Princess Diana's family tree

online family trees, created by members who wish to research their ancestry, just like you do. If you find a family member in someone else's family tree, you can contact the person behind it and team up, sharing information and greatly expanding what you know about your own ancestry. Be careful, though – not everyone researches their information as thoroughly as you might do your own, so it's always worth checking before adding a branch or two to your own family tree in this way.

Perhaps best of all, Genes Reunited offers a search engine which offers results from numerous online sources, such as census information as discussed earlier, the Registry of Births, Deaths and Marriages and military records of deaths in both World Wars. Because much of the content of search results originates in The National Archives, you have to pay to view information gleaned in this way through Genes Reunited. Once again, the search results are free, but accessing the details costs. At the time of writing, you can spend £5 on pay-per-view credits which last seven days, or get six months' unlimited access for £34.95.

Of course, Genes Reunited isn't the only site which offers combined search results.

Over at Family Tree Searcher (*www.familytreesearcher.com*), you can do an ancestor search that covers nine different sites dealing with family trees. It's a US-based site so expect a little bias, but the searches function worldwide. It's an excellent resource if your family tree extends outside the UK, especially if there's an American branch somewhere along the line. There's some interesting advice on starting and developing your family tree too, with tips and tricks for absolute beginners, free advice to make your searches on the Internet more productive, and helpful testimonials from other users.

Something else you might not want to miss is the application Family Tree Maker 2008, a piece of software that 'combines the convenience of online research with the efficiency of a desktop family tree tool'. It has incredibly low minimum specs, demanding only Windows XP or Vista, a 500MHz Pentium II processor or better, 256MB of RAM and 400MB of hard disk space. Basically, if you've got a PC capable of accessing the internet, it will should run it. Read more and buy online at *www.tinyurl.com/65yad3*.

Naturally, there's far more to online researching of your family tree than we've

outlined here. There are more sites, more resources and more services than we could ever hope to list in this brief guide, but we hope we've provided enough to whet your appetite and to get you started. The more you find out about your family, the more you'll find there is to learn. ■

INTERNET

PROJECT
002

DIFFICULTY LEVEL
HARD
INTERMEDIATE
EASY

TIME REQUIRED
15
MINUTES

Set up your own blog

Unleash your inner Bill Bryson by starting your own online blog

YOU CAN START a blog, or weblog, from any computer, so long as it has internet access. And it's a very quick job.

If you are familiar with HTML and know how to upload content, then setting up a site specifically to host a blog is one option. For most of us though, a far simpler option is to sign up to a free blog publishing tool. There are many tools that can be sourced on the internet, and one of the most popular is Blogger (*www.blogger.com*), run by Google. Free to use, it offers a variety of layouts and styles, and is simple to get to grips with.

Before using Blogger, you need to sign up for an account by giving your email address, and choosing a username and password. Having signed up, you're then asked to decide on a name and address for your blog, with the address ending in a standard file extension (*blogspot.com*). For the blog's web address, choose a name that's appropriate, easy to type in and simple to remember to encourage people to visit it. The desired blog address may not be available (this can be checked via the Check Availability hyperlink), so a creative, unique address will work best here. You're more likely to click on *101projects.blogspot.com* than *lotsofthingstodowithyourcomputer 8241.blogspot.com*.

Once you've chosen a blog address, hit Continue. You now need to choose a design template from the available options. This can be customised at a later date and there are a large number to choose from, which should suit most people's tastes.

It's important at this point that you give some thought as to the content of your blog. Whether it's a daily diary, examples of your writing or a pictorial-based blog, you need to make sure that the chosen design and layout of the blog site will be appropriate for the content.

Blogging has become increasingly popular, and it's simple to get started

Having picked a design template, you can than input and post your first entry. Inputting text is simple, and if you have an understanding of HTML, you can edit it manually while posting if you wish. But you don't need to if you don't want to.

There are also other options to italicise or embolden copy, insert block quotes and add web links. Text can also be checked for spelling mistakes, and corrections are automatically saved as you type, ensuring that any copy will not be lost in error. Images and videos can be added via clicking on small icons at the top of each new post. Finally, posts can be previewed, so that you can see how any text will appear online. This is important, as any errors will make the blog look unprofessional.

Once you're happy with the post, you then click on Publish Post at the bottom left of the screen, and it will be published instantly online for other web users to view.

Now that the first post is online and the blog is up and running, you shouldn't be afraid to alter things. One of the great things about blogging is that it's an ever-evolving process. If you want to add or change content, edit posts, remove them or start all over again, you can do so via the Edit Post hyperlink, found within the Posting section of the blog. ■

PERSONAL PROFILE

Another important area of the blog is the personal profile. In Blogger, the User Profile box lets you include any details about yourself that they want visitors to see, alongside any photos you wish to publish. It's all accessible via a form that pops up when clicking on Edit Profile on the your dashboard (essentially the blog's home page), and is a great way to personalise the blog a little.

Set up an online photo album

Upload your photos to the internet so the whole world can see them

WITH SO MANY social networking sites now in existence, it's easy for anyone to make themselves known to all and sundry online. This isn't a phenomenon limited to blogs though, and if you're a budding photographer, getting your best shots onto the internet is now just a few mouse clicks away, with absolutely no need to write a single line of HTML programming code. All you need to do is sign up with an online photo album service, and you're all set to share your images via the internet.

There are a number of such services online, but one of the best and most popular is Flickr. Owned by Yahoo!, it's free, and as long as you have a Yahoo! account, you can upload images to your own personal web album. Visit *www.flickr.com*, and once you've registered, you can upload photos and videos, which other users of the service can then rate and comment on.

Another well known online album service is Google's Picasa Web Albums. This free

Flickr is a popular image-hosting site and features a strong community

service can be used entirely online, or integrated with the downloadable Picasa image-organising application: available from *picasa.google.com*. The downloadable method makes it easier to manage large number of photos, and we've covered this in the Picasa example here.

1 To set up your web album with Picasa, first go to the library and select the images that you want to upload: it's quicker to hold Ctrl and click each image. Now click the Web Album button. You'll need to log in with your Google account, which is the same as your Gmail account if you have one.

2 If you don't have a Google account, then you'll need to register for one. Once you've done this, you're required to activate your Web Album, and agree to the terms and conditions.

3 A dialog box will open up. In this, you can set the name of the album, as well as an optional description and information about the location where the photos were taken. Specify the size of the uploaded images and then choose whether you wish the album to be public or private.

4 The transfer process will then occur, and your photos will be uploaded, and resized depending on your chosen settings. Once this is done, you'll be able to view your new online album.

One of the main advantages of Web Albums is that you can have more than one album, and upload additional photographs to current volumes. ■

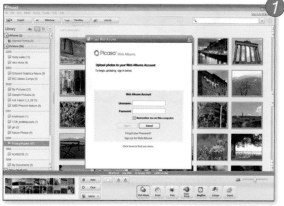

LIGHTBOX WEB GALLERY GENERATOR

Create your own animated web albums

If you'd rather create your own web album but don't possess the know-how, you could make use of an application such as Lightbox Web Gallery Generator (*pranas. net/webgallerycreator*).

This simple and free tool can easily create a fully-functional image gallery

with impressive animated image frames. Simply specify the folder containing the images to insert into the album, and it will then generate all of the code and the web pages needed. These can then be uploaded with ease, all without the use of a single HTML/CSS editor.

Set up your own Yahoo! Group

Create your own online community with Yahoo! Groups

YAHOO! GROUPS IS a free service that enables you to set up space online where people who share interests can store and access messages and photo albums, and create calendars of events, conduct polls and e-mail everyone involved in one go. Groups are an easy alternative to creating and maintaining a site along with a discussion forum, and require no programming or scripting knowledge.

Groups can be made of members who are fans of the same actor, author, athlete, band or TV show, or have circumstances in common, like becoming a parent, combating illness, or sharing hobbies. They can be widespread and far-reaching, across your country or even the globe. Or, they can be more focused on your local community, and if you wish, you can limit membership to your friends or family, creating a private group.

1 In order to set up a Yahoo! group, you first need to visit *www.yahoo.com* and register for a Yahoo! account. This is the same account used for Yahoo! Games and E-mail,

amongst other services, so you may already have a login. If not, you'll need to sign up.

2 Once you've logged in, select the Groups section and then click the 'Easy as 1, 2, 3, start your group today' link. Select one of the categories from the list, or use the search box. Once you've found the right category, click 'Place my group here'.

3 In Step 2 of Yahoo!'s process you need to describe your group. Proceed down the page, enter a group name, then add the first part of a group email address (they'll always end in @yahoogroups.co.uk). Enter a description for your group and click Continue.

4 To finish, you need to pick your personal email address so you can receive messages. Your Yahoo! mail address should be listed, along with any others you may have, so select one of these. Pick the profile you want other users to see (or create one) and finally enter the CAPTCHA text and click Continue. Your group will be created.

5 You now need to set the finer details for your group, including adding members. To get started, click 'Customize

Your Group'. You'll be taken to Step 1 of 3. Here you need to choose if your group is public or private, how people can join your group and who can post messages. Make your choices and click Next.

6 Next, you'll choose how messages are delivered, whether replies go to everyone or only the message sender and if you wish to use the web features, such as photos, files sharing, calendars and polls. Choose your options and click Next for Step 3. Here you can choose who can view message archives, and set permissions to various group features. Once you've selected your options, click Finish. ▬

ADDING MEMBERS

No group will be of any use unless it has members, so select the 'Invite People' option. You'll see the 'Invite People to Join' window appear. You need to enter friends' or family's email addresses or Yahoo! IDs, with one person per line. Click 'Submit Invite' and you'll send out emails to everyone listed, inviting them to join your group.

Keep up with the news using RSS

Unlock the secrets behind RSS and make the news come to you

RSS STANDS FOR Really Simple Syndication. It's a web-based technology for distributing content to those who don't want to hunt for it. That content might include news, views, scores or blogs.

The range of uses of RSS technology is wide, and growing. To use it, you'll need an RSS-enabled web browser or a specific RSS-feed-gathering tool. The latest versions of Microsoft Internet Explorer and Mozilla's Firefox are suitable for this task, or you could try a dedicated free tool such as Pluck (PC) or a commercial application such as NetNewsWire(Mac).

First, though, you need to locate an RSS feed that contains items of interest to you.

The best places to look initially are news sites and blogs. However, feeds can be found on a wide range of sites – just try any place that has regular updates. They promote RSS either using terminology such as Syndicate this site or RSS feed, or by presenting logos that include XML or RSS in their design. Look out for an orange RSS logo, too.

There are also web locations dedicated to bringing master lists of RSS content together so you can create your own merged feeds such as *www.syndic8.com*. If a site that you visit regularly doesn't appear to have an RSS feed, then it might be worth sending an email to the webmaster asking if this feature is available, or when they might be introducing it.

Connecting to a feed is usually very easy, as you'll only be required to click on an RSS icon or link and then confirm you wish to subscribe.

In Internet Explorer the RSS icon will become highlighted if the page in question has a feed on it, and clicking on the icon will initiate the subscription process. Let's look at an example.

Most popular websites have RSS feeds available; just look for the orange logo

You can access an RSS feed through a web browser such as Internet Explorer

You can customise how many headlines you want displayed on your desktop

Windows Vista has a sidebar gadget that brings the news direct to your desktop

On the BBC News site you can see the RSS logo on the right, next to the words 'News Feeds'. Clicking on it will take you to its RSS page. To subscribe to the feed, click at the top of the page and confirm where in your Favourites you'd like to save the bookmark.

Once you've stored a feed, you can access it through Internet Explorer or, if you run Windows Vista, you can add that feed to the desktop RSS gadget that's part of the sidebar technology included in the operating system.

Using this feature the latest news is brought directly to your desktop. However, these aren't the only ways to read RSS feeds.

In some circumstances you may have to copy a feed location into the address bar of the web browser to get a subscription, but that's not usually required.

Most blogs offer an RSS feed, so if you like to be made aware of new posts, then using this facility can be ideal. Some blogs are actually entirely formed from the RSS streams of other sites and blogs, providing a subject-driven coalition of content drawn together by the blogger. Note that it's generally assumed that if you make an RSS feed of your content available, then you're happy for people to link into that source without requiring any further approval. However, the content itself may still be copyright-protected, even if it's presented as part of another site through the RSS mechanism. ■

RSS FEED-READERS

Most browsers support RSS, but lack the ability to manage and organise large amounts of subscribed content. Feed-reading applications (also called 'aggregators') can be free, shareware or commercial, and enable you to manage many feeds easily. A popular choice is SharpReader, which can collate numerous feeds into a single live list.

Other common feed-reading tools include Pluck, Google Reader, Bloglines, RSS Bandit and BlogExpress. There are many more to choose from, and many are free, or just ask for a voluntary donation.

Avoiding Online Fraud – Mission Possible!

Today more and more people use their computers for pretty much everything – from communicating with friends and family to online shopping, investing and banking. This all makes life a lot easier, yet at the same time we open ourselves up to a host of PC security and privacy related dangers.

Online Fraud

These days, stories of online fraud, identity theft, and phishing scams appear on the news so often that many of us don't pay attention anymore. And that is a big mistake. The Association for Payment Clearing Services revealed that in 2007, banking losses due to online fraud totalled £22.6 million. And there were 20,682 reported phishing incidents in the UK in the first half of 2008 alone. Bear in mind that many people choose not to report the crime.

One software that can protect you from identity theft is **Auslogics BoostSpeed.** Being a useful computer optimization tool, it also includes a number of very useful privacy and security applications. It offers advanced protection where anti-virus software can't help.

Track Eraser

Every time you visit a web site or open a file, a record is created on your computer. If someone gets access to this information, they can find out a lot about you – your browsing preferences, which online stores you use, and maybe even something that can jeopardise your reputation or finances.

Auslogics Track Eraser protects your privacy by removing all the tracks and history from your computer. Run it on a regular basis to not leave any sensitive information behind.

Jessica Dolcourt from CNet introducing Auslogics BoostSpeed.

File Shredder and Disk Wiper

Another source of identity theft are files with sensitive information (bank statements, etc). Simply deleting them doesn't make them go for good. They are only "forgotten" by your system, but in fact remain somewhere on your hard drive. It's quite easy to "undelete" them and use in ways you probably will not be happy about. But if you delete a file, or a folder with **File Shredder**, you can be sure that they will be impossible to recover.

Auslogics Disk Wiper works in a very similar way. It also ensures that files cannot be recovered. While File Shredder deletes the existing files and folders, Disk Wiper ensures that the already deleted files cannot be recovered later by anyone gaining access to your computer.

PC Security

Windows XP and newer versions include services like Remote Registry or Windows Messaging. These services make it possible to access your computer remotely and bombard you with spam. Auslogics PC Security disables these services, protecting you from possible attacks.

No one leaves their house with the front door left wide open. And nobody walks around with their bank account number printed on a T-shirt either. But when it comes to computer security, people are often too careless. Avoid being the next online fraud and identity theft victim by protecting yourself and your computer.

Removing traces of your activity with Auslogics Track Eraser

Disk Wiper ensures that sensitive information cannot be recovered

Plan a journey using your PC

Get yourself going in the right direction quickly and easily

IN THE NOT too distant past, planning a journey meant splashing out on an atlas or a street map, picking through it to find your destination, and then tracing your route with your finger or a felt-tip pen. Regularly-used maps soon got creased and tatty, and having to turn the page in your street guide was a real pain. Not any more. All the modern computer user has to do to plan a journey is point his web browser at Google Maps

Found at *maps.google.co.uk*, it covers a huge portion of the world and is getting bigger all the time. But for the purposes of this guide, let's plan some UK journeys.

First of all, we'll map a motorway drive between two West Country towns. Click on the Get Directions link under the Google Maps logo in the top-left corner. You're invited to enter your starting point and destination. Type Exmouth in the A field and then Penzance in the B field. The site's auto-complete function helps you out, especially where more than one town of that name exists. The pull-down menu under these fields allows you to select a journey either by car or

walking. Let's stick with the car. You can add further destinations or change options, such as avoiding toll roads, and toggling between miles and kilometres using the links found here, but for now, we'll leave them as they are.

Press the Get Directions button, and you're shown the best possible road route from Exmouth to Penzance, with step-by-step instructions and a detailed map.

Note the controls located in the top-left corner on the map. By clicking on the + and - signs on the vertical bar, you can zoom in and out of the map. Alternatively, use your mouse's scroll wheel. The arrows above the + and - let you move or centre the map. Or press and hold the left button, and drag it around with the mouse.

If you're not keen on the route that's offered, you can drag the blue line that traces your path from A to B onto the roads and motorways you prefer to use. The step-by-step directions are updated automatically. When you're satisfied, use the print options to get a paper copy you can take with you on your journey.

Google Maps is great for plotting a route through towns and cities, too. Let's take a trip from Birmingham's New Street Station to the city's Science Museum. First, select Walking on the pull-down menu covered earlier. Now enter Birmingham New Street Railway Station in field A. You're offered several options, the first of which is the correct one – click on it. Entering Science Museum gives you the correct directions straightaway. Press Get Directions, and you're shown the street route you need to follow. You can once again manually zoom in and out, or change your route by dragging the path indicator onto the streets you'd rather use.

We've only scratched the surface of what Google Maps can do here. Experiment with it. If you're visiting several sites in the same town, use the Add Destination link and map them all at once. You can reorder destinations in your list by dragging and dropping them. Use the buttons in the top-right corner of the map for different perspectives, or more information courtesy of Flickr or Wikipedia.

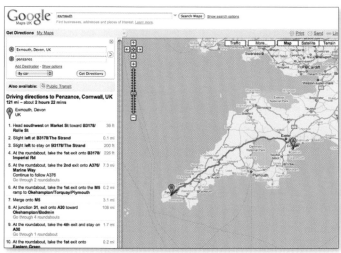

In this example we plan a journey from Exmouth to Penzance

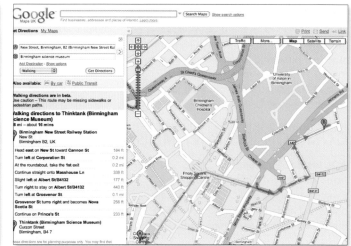

You can zoom in to get a more detailed map view

PLANNING A TRAIN JOURNEY

If you're travelling by rail, check out the Qjump website at *www.qjump.co.uk*. It's a great resource for planning your journey. Simply enter the stations you're travelling between, opt for a single or return journey

and add your preferred times of travel. It then offers you details on the next four or five services leaving after your chosen time.

It's a great resource if you're planning a rail journey, but take care if you're

travelling late in the day. The last service offered might involve starting your journey on a late night train, then connecting with an early morning service, leaving you with a six- or seven-hour wait for your connection.

Chat with friends online

Email's great, but sometimes you want to chat in real time. Here's how

USING AN INSTANT-messaging program can be a quick and efficient way of communicating with someone, be it friends, relatives or colleagues from work. It can also be a fun and effective way to keep in touch with old friends – or to make new ones. It's also really easy, and you can be up and running in a matter of minutes.

There are lots of different instant-messaging programs available, some of which are compatible with one another. Your choice of which to use will probably be influenced by the ones the people you want to talk to use. If they all use Yahoo! Messenger, for example, it probably makes sense for you to pick that program, too. However, once you can use one instant messenger, you can use them all, as they're very similar in look and feel.

The first thing you'll need to do is to sign up for a user account. In the case of Windows Live Messenger, for example, you'll need a Windows Live ID. Signing up for a username or account shouldn't take you more than a couple of minutes. The usual advice for signing up for online accounts applies. Therefore, you should think carefully about whether you want to use your real name (an alias might be a better idea), make sure your password is secure and not easy to guess and, if you're female and wary of online harassment, you might want to choose a gender-neutral ID.

Once you've got your ID, you'll need to download and install your messenger program of choice, and then sign in for the first time. It really is that straightforward!

Next, it's time to populate your contact list. You may be able to import contacts from an existing email address book. Alternatively, you can add contacts manually by typing in the email addresses or usernames of people you know. Your contact list should show you who is and isn't online. If someone's online, clicking on their username will open a window in which you type messages and start chatting to them.

There are a few other considerations worth bearing in mind before you dive in headfirst, though. When chatting online, for instance, people often use apparently nonsensical abbreviations. These are usually shortened forms of common expressions, but they're always evolving, and new ones are constantly being created. To complicate matters, some older expressions have changed in meaning since they were first used. For example, LOL used to mean laughing out loud, but it has since become less sincere and is now used ironically. Intentional misspellings are also common, and some people also like to use emoticons. These are approximations of facial expressions created using punctuation marks, and are often translated by instant messaging programs into either still or

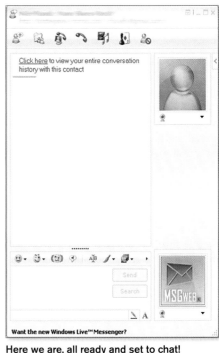
Click here to view your entire conversation history with this contact

Want the new Windows Live™ Messenger?

Here we are, all ready and set to chat!

animated pictures. For instance, :-) represents a smile, while :-(is a sad face. There are umpteen more to choose from!

No list of internet idioms could ever be complete, so if you don't understand something, it's usually best to either ask the person who said it, or quickly type it into Google for an explanation. The bizarre slang of the internet can be intimidating or off-putting if you don't understand it, but don't be discouraged – you don't need to learn another language just to chat online.

Traditional chatrooms used to be the most common method of chatting online, but these have fallen out of favour now. Some websites still provide chatrooms, and using them is generally pretty self-explanatory: you enter a username for yourself and then select a chatroom, often from a list of options. These can be private or totally public, in which case you could be talking to anyone at all and should be extremely careful about revealing any personal details.

Using chat programs is mostly just about common sense; just as you wouldn't hand over your bank details or passwords to a stranger on the street, you shouldn't do so online either. ■

COMMON INSTANT-MESSAGING PROGRAMS

AOL Instant Messenger
http://dashboard.aim.com/aim
Even if you're not an AOL user, you can download and use AIM – it's even been made available as an iPhone application.

ICQ
www.icq.com
One of the first instant messaging programs, ICQ is still widely used today.

Skype
www.skype.com
Skype is best known for its VoIP (voice-over internet protocol) functionality, but

the software also has with the ability to do instant messaging.

Yahoo! Messenger
http://messenger.yahoo.com
Less popular than Windows Live Messenger and AIM, Yahoo! Messenger is associated with Yahoo! e-mail accounts.

Windows Live Messenger
http://messenger.live.com
Formerly known as MSN Messenger, this is Microsoft's instant messaging program, and if you have a Hotmail account, you already have an ID for this one.

Manage your Windows Messenger contacts

Stay organised while chatting with friends and family over the internet

WINDOWS MESSENGER MAY not be the only instant-messaging software application out there, but it's arguably the most widely used. In this project we'll look at how to launch the program for the first time, and add contacts so you can chat online. We've used the Windows XP edition here, but the project works with versions running on other operating systems as well.

First, open your copy of Windows Messenger. If you're using Windows, it will already be installed as part of your operating system. If you're using a different operating system or simply don't have Windows Messenger, go to *www.uk.msn.com* to download it. Click the button marked Start in the bottom-left of your screen. It brings up a window – Windows Messenger is in the left-hand column. Click on it.

A window opens inviting you to Click here to sign in. Click on the link, and follow the .Net passport wizard. If you already have a Windows Live account, sign in using the email address and password with which you registered. If not, follow the prompts to sign up for one.

When you first get started with Windows Messenger, you won't have any contacts listed in your Messenger window. Thankfully, adding friends is a straightforward process. First of all, click the Add a contact link. If you know the email address or username of the contact you wish to add, pick this option and click Next. You're offered the chance to type in your contact's details. Do so and add them to your list. You can then add further contacts, or finish.

If you don't know your contact's email address, opt for Search for a contact, and you can then try to find your friends using other details, such as their name, location, company and more. That said, it's usually easier just to ask them for their email address, as searching for contacts isn't always successful.

When you've added a contact, you're told whether they are online. An online contact is represented by a green icon to the left of their name, while an offline contact has a red icon. When a contact is online, click on their name to open a chat window, from where you can have an instant message conversation. Type in the text field at the bottom of the window, and

press Enter or click the Send button to message your contact. They will do the same, and your conversation is displayed above.

As your contacts list grows, it can get unwieldy if they're all in one long list. Instead, arrange your contacts in groups. You might have a group for your professional contacts, one for your work colleagues and one for your friends. It's up to you.

To add a new group, from the Tools menu, select Manage Groups. From there, you can add a new group, delete one or edit a group's name. You then drag and drop the contacts you want in that particular list into the group. They're still in the All Contacts list too, but you can show or hide groups of contacts by clicking on the chevrons symbol to the left of the group name.

If you wish to delete a group, first delete all the contacts in it by right-clicking on their names and selecting Remove contact from group. When it's empty, from the Tools menu select Manage Groups, Delete a group, [group name]. Alternatively, right-click on the group and select Delete Group from the contextual menu. ▇

Windows Messenger is pre-installed in Windows operating systems

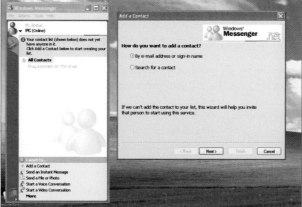

Adding contacts to your Windows Messenger account is a simple process. Simply follow the wizard

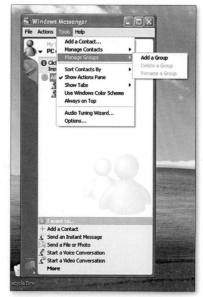

Once you've got more than a few contacts, you'll find it easier to manage them by organising them into groups such as family, colleagues and so on

TRILLIAN AND PIDGIN

Naturally, Windows Messenger isn't the only client out there, so what if you have friends who use a different one? You could do a lot worse than check out a couple of third-party applications, which are compatible with pretty much any instant-messaging client. Trillian supports AIM, ICQ, MSN, Yahoo! Messenger, and IRC. Download it at *www.ceruleanstudios.com*. Alternatively, Pidgin, which is compatible with a large variety of instant messengers, can be found at *www.pidgin.im*.

INTERNET

PROJECT
009

DIFFICULTY LEVEL
HARD
INTERMEDIATE
EASY

TIME REQUIRED

N/A

Advanced Messenger options

We show you to enhance your Windows Messenger experience

IF YOU WORKED through our earlier Windows Messenger project on page 17 (or simply didn't need it), you've now set up your Microsoft instant messenger client and added a few contacts. What next? You know how to chat, but what about the other features and options? In this project we'll take a look at what else Windows Messenger can do.

There are numerous ways you can customise your Windows Messenger experience. From the Tools menu, select Options to open a window. Here, from the Personal tab you can change the font and text size, and also your display name.

Also in the Options window you'll find the Preferences tab. Here you can set up Messenger to suit your specific needs. Uncheck the boxes for options that you no longer want to activate.

By default, Windows Messenger is included in Windows XP and automatically launches when you boot up your computer. If you're an XP user and wish to delete the application from your system, maybe because you never use it or have replaced it with another instant messenger tool, or want to keep it but not have it automatically start with the operating system, then you need to follow these instructions.

Preventing it starting automatically when Windows is booted is simplicity itself. From the Tools menu, select Options to open the Options window. From here, select the Preferences tab and uncheck the top box, the one labelled Run Windows Messenger when Windows starts.

Deleting Windows Messenger is not quite as simple, but not too tricky either. First of all, from the Start menu, choose Control Panel, then Add or Remove Programs. From the Add or Remove Programs window, select Add or Remove Windows Components from the left-hand column. This takes you to the Windows Components Wizard. You can then remove Windows Messenger by unchecking the box as shown. To be honest, it's quicker and easier to simply stop it launching automatically – there's no real need to remove it.

Most of the time, chatting with people on Windows Messenger is great fun, but occasionally you get hassled by someone who, for whatever reason, you simply don't want to talk to. Thankfully, it's easy to block an unwelcome chatter. Just click on the Block icon under the chat window and you need never hear from them again.

You can organise your blocked contacts by going to Tools, Options, Privacy, from where you can block people on your contacts list or unblock people on your blocked list.

Sometimes, a text-only message just isn't enough, and that's when you need an emoticon! Emoticons are those little smiling faces and icons which can add a gesture or tone to an otherwise-bland sentence. For example, if you say something with a smile on your face, why not add a smilie? Or if you type something in jest, add a winking face?

Adding emoticons is easy. Just click on the Emoticons icon under the chat window, and you're presented with a big panel full of selectable smilies and other such pictures. They include a smiling face, winking face, a sad or even crying face, an angry expression, and if you're embarrassed, a blushing face. Non-smilie emoticons include a heart, broken heart, 'idea' light bulb, a kiss and a flower. There are plenty to choose from.

Make sure that you use emoticons sparingly, though. If you use too many at once or use them too often, then they lose their effect. There's nothing more irritating than a chat window crammed with lots of unnecessary emoticons.

If you have a microphone and a webcam installed on your PC, you can initiate camera or voice chats using Windows Messenger. It's easy. In the chat window, click the option marked Start Camera at the top of the side bar. If this option is not there, camera chat is not available at this time.

If your contact accepts the request for camera chat, his or her picture appears in the side bar. To see your picture too, click Options below the picture and select the Show My Video as Picture-in-Picture option. To stop sending your video, click Options, and then Stop Sending Video. You'll still be able to see your contact's video image, but your own will be frozen.

If you want to use voice chat but not video chat, that's straightforward, too. All you need to do is use the Start Talking option instead of Start Camera. ■

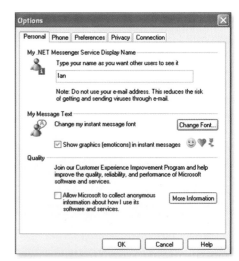

Customise Messenger through the Options window

Uncheck the box to remove Windows Messenger from your computer

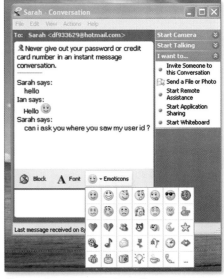

Choose from a range of emoticons

TIME REQUIRED	DIFFICULTY LEVEL	PROJECT	INTERNET
15 MINUTES	HARD / INTERMEDIATE / EASY	010	

Filter out your spam emails

Give junk mail the elbow with message filtering

NO-ONE LIKES junk mail, digital or otherwise. Luckily, while boarding up your letter box is the only way to stop real junk mail from entering your house, on your computer there are far easier methods you can use to limit the amount of unsolicited emails you receive.

One of the easiest ways of achieving this is to limit the type of message that can make it to your inbox. Simply instruct your application to filter out certain keywords or senders, and then any mails that fit your given criteria will automatically be sent to a spam folder, or deleted. That way, you never have to see them. In this example, we'll use Outlook Express, but most email applications feature a similar system.

1 Open Outlook Express and click Tools, Message Rules. You'll see the Message Rule dialog box, which lists your various rules. Click the New button to begin creating a new rule from scratch.

2 The next window is the rule builder. First, select an option from section one. Here we've selected the option Where the subject line contains specific words. Tick this and then click the blue hyperlink titled Contains specific words. In the window that appears, add any individual words you wish to capture, but try to be specific, as common words may filter legitimate mail. Something like Viagra is very common to spam emails. Click OK when you're done.

3 Now select an option from section two of the New Mail Rule window. Choose Move it to the specified folder, and click the blue specified hyperlink in the rule description section. Select an existing folder to move mail to, or create a new one.

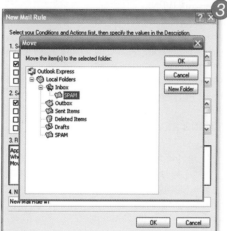

4 Click OK and give the mail rule a name, then click OK again. You'll return to the Message Rules window, and your new rule should appear in the main list. If the tick is in the box next to it, the rule is active. To deactivate a rule, simply remove the tick.

Most internet security suites have built-in spam filtering tools, which work with most mail clients, so make sure you enable such options and configure them to best suit your mail use.

However, even with such measures in place, the best spam filter that you have is your own brain, and the best way to avoid junk mail and spam is to stay vigilant and be wary of email from unknown senders or services. Simply opening an unsolicited email can let spammers know that your address is active, and in worst case scenarios may result in viral infections. If you find yourself in any doubt, junk the junk mail. ■

PLAIN IT SAFE

Email can be received in various formats such as HTML, which is usually the default setting and means more graphical mails can be displayed. This may not sound harmful, and in most cases it isn't. However, some nefarious spammers can actually detect when images in HTML emails are viewed, just as website owners can see a history of visits. This notification informs spammers that someone exists at that email address, and will probably mean more junk mail in the future.

The easiest way to combat this with no extra software is to set your mail client to view all mail as plain text, which trims out all HTML functionality, including images. To do so in Outlook Express, click Tools, Options and select the Read tab. Now, place a tick next to the Read all messages in plain text option and click Apply.

PROJECT
011

DIFFICULTY LEVEL
HARD
INTERMEDIATE
EASY

TIME REQUIRED
15
MINUTES

Control your PC remotely

Take control of your computer from anywhere in the world

YOU CAN'T ALWAYS access your computer when you need it, as it might be in a different part of the building or even on the other side of the planet. That doesn't mean you can't work on your PC as if you were actually sitting at the keyboard, though. All you need is a little software to make the right kind of connection to your PC – and you'll be glad to hear that you've probably got it already.

REMOTE DESKTOP CONNECTION

Microsoft has included the ability to control your PC from another computer in the Windows XP and Vista operating systems. To do this it uses technology licensed from Citrix called Remote Desktop.

Using a PC over a Remote Desktop connection feels remarkably like sitting at that machine. You control the remote PC with the local 'client' PC's mouse and keyboard, and the screen and audio output from the remote PC are channelled through the local 'client' PC's monitor and speakers. The remote 'host' computer does all the work, but the results are displayed on the client machine in front of you. Before you try this, however, you need to be aware of a few limitations to using this type of technology:

● You can't play games or videos stored on the remote PC, because the rate at which

the screen refreshes is too high in applications such as these.

● If you turn the remote computer off from your location, there is no easy way to power it back on again.

● To use this type of connection across the internet, you may need control of both the local and remote broadband routers, or to creation a special Virtual Private Network (VPN).

● To use the host computer you must already have an account set up on it, and Remote Desktop must be configured on the host PC beforehand.

USING REMOTE DESKTOP

1 Go to My Computer and right-click to bring up the Properties dialog box. If you're using Windows XP, select the Remote tab. On Vista you'll find this by choosing Remote Settings.

You can use the Remote Desktop tools built into Windows XP and Vista to control another PC over the internet

2 Once you've enabled the option to 'Allow users to connect remotely to this computer' or the equivalent on Vista, click Select Remote Users, and add those users you'd like to give remote access.

3 You need to allow Remote Desktop through the firewall. Find the firewall settings in the Control Panel. Open the firewall control and select Exceptions. You'll see a list of applications that the firewall lets through. Enable Remote Desktop.

4 To make a connection you need the Remote Desktop Connection tool, which should already be installed on the computer under Accessories. Run this and enter the name of the computer. You'll then be asked for the name and password of an existing user on that computer. Enter these correctly and you'll be able to take over the desktop of that PC.

5 If you want greater control, click on the Options button. You can use the series of tabs here to set the resolution and colour depth of the virtual desktop, vary whether the sound is heard locally and even if the local printers are to be connected to your PC. When you have set up the system to your liking, you can save these settings in an RDP file for future use.

COMMERCIAL PRODUCTS

Getting the free software in Windows to work across the internet can be challenging, but it's not impossible. If you need more advanced features, such as the ability to transfer files between PCs, a commercial remote access tool might be a better option, and they make the process easier, too.

Good examples of these applications are Symantec pcAnywhere, GotoMyPC, Bomgar PC Access, IBM Director and Citrix XenApp. However, there are many more, including many variations on the open-source VNC project, which is available for operating systems other than Windows.

The typical cost of these is between £25 and £60, although it can be made cheaper per PC if you can get bulk licensing.

pcAnywhere lets you control your PC

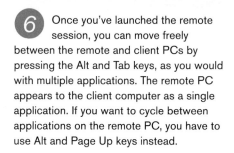

Once you've launched the remote session, you can move freely between the remote and client PCs by pressing the Alt and Tab keys, as you would with multiple applications. The remote PC appears to the client computer as a single application. If you want to cycle between applications on the remote PC, you have to use Alt and Page Up keys instead.

SHUTTING DOWN AND REBOOTING A REMOTE COMPUTER

If you need to reboot the remote PC, you'll find that the usual methods don't work, and Shutdown is missing from the Start menu. To access this facility, use the Settings option on the Start menu and click on Windows Security.

In Windows Vista, this will take you to a screen where you can select Shutdown or Restart from the gadget in the bottom right of the screen. In XP, this will open the Task Manager, where you can find these features under the Shut Down menu.

Both Windows XP Professional and Vista have Remote Desktop preinstalled, but you can use it on every version of Windows from 95 upwards. If it isn't installed on your machine, download the files you need from the Microsoft Download Center at *www.microsoft.com*.

You can also take over the desktop of a PC that uses a different operating system, so an XP machine can take over a Vista Desktop and vice versa. In Vista, you can limit Remote Desktop clients to PCs running Vista by choosing to allow only

Network Level Authorisation when you configure the host PC.

Any security limitations that the host PC enforces on the user are retained, even if the same restrictions don't apply on the client PC. If you're not in the Administrator group on the host PC, for example, you still won't be if you log in from a remote PC.

This doesn't mean you can be relaxed about security, though. Saving the username and password in an RDP file may be convenient, but it isn't particularly secure.

You should also bear in mind that while the machine is being used remotely, no-one can log into it locally without disconnecting

the remote system and user. Logging in will automatically throw off anyone using the machine at the time. The system is strictly one user at a time.

If you use Remote Desktop over a broadband connection and you want to improve its performance, reduce the colour depth and resolution and remove the wallpaper to make it more responsive.

One limitation of Remote Desktop is that it doesn't offer a simple way to transfer files between the host and client computers. This is a facility that many of the commercial applications offer above and beyond what Microsoft has provided for free. ▪

VIRTUAL NETWORK COMPUTING

Some of the commercial remote tools are built around open-source software called Virtual Network Computing (VNC).

What's exciting about VNC is that it's platform independent, which means you can use it to control a computer that isn't running Windows. It's similar to Remote Desktop in that you have a host PC, or VNC server, and a VNC client. This might be a Windows PC, an Apple Mac or a Linux Workstation – installations are available for a wide range of computers. The only downside to this software is that it doesn't offer the most secure protocol, which is where commercial versions have the edge.

RealVNC, for example, offers industry-strength encryption, and comes in free, Personal and Enterprise editions.

RealVNC running two remote desktops on Windows XP, one to an Apple Mac running OS X and another to a Vista PC

INTERNET

PROJECT	DIFFICULTY LEVEL	TIME REQUIRED
012	HARD / INTERMEDIATE / **EASY**	**15** MINUTES

Watch television online

Catching up with the latest TV shows you've missed is easy

IN RECENT YEARS, UK television broadcasters have started to offer on-demand services for users to catch up with TV programmes online. The BBC has developed its much-publicised iPlayer service, and sitting alongside that are similar offerings available from Channel 4 (4oD), ITV (ITV Catch Up), Five (Demand Five) and Sky (Sky Player). Some programmes are free, others have a charge attached, but all the services offer a selection of television shows to watch from their schedules.

Anyone wishing to take advantage of these services can do so using any computer equipped with Windows XP or Vista, plus a broadband Internet connection and Windows Media Player (this can be downloaded from *www.microsoft.com*). Some services also state that they require you to use Internet Explorer as your web browser, so make sure you check for any individual requirements.

Programmes can be watched online either via a streaming service (whereby the programme is shown 'as live') or by downloading them to watch in your own time (if available). As a rule of thumb, downloaded programmes will be of better quality than streamed ones, due to the constraints of watching 'live' video content over a regular broadband connection.

Finding and selecting a programme to watch is simple. Taking the iPlayer as an example, you should search for and click on the programme you fancy watching, and choose whether to stream or download it. If streaming a programme, you simply have to select 'Click to Play', and playback will begin. If downloading programmes, just click on the Download link at the bottom of the selected programme and follow the instructions on how to install iPlayer's Download Manager

The BBC's popular iPlayer service

programme. Once this is installed, you can then download any programmes by clicking again on the 'Download' link.

One aspect of watching television online that you should be aware of is the use of peer-to-peer technology, which is typically used to help speed up programme downloads.

Peer-to-peer refers to a method of transferring files over the Internet by using a number of computers as part of a network. When you opt to download a programme, as well as downloading the necessary file data for your own use, your computer is also used to upload programme data as well, thus helping other users download their shows quicker. You should be aware that peer-to-peer technology can also upload programme file data using your computer whenever you're online, and not just when you're using the on-demand service.

For this reason, anyone watching television online should be aware of any download and upload limits that are set by their internet service provider (ISP), and of the consequences of exceeding those limits.

Finally, digital rights management (DRM) prevents the illegal copying and distribution of programmes. What it means for users is that after downloading a programme, it can typically be stored on a PC for a set amount of time. For example, with the iPlayer, having downloaded a programme, you have a maximum of 30 days in which to watch it. Other services will differ in their terms and conditions, so you should check this out before downloading. ▬

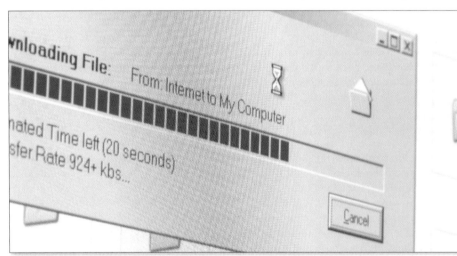

When downloading programmes online, you need to be aware of any download limits set by your internet service provider

THE PROVIDERS

BBC iPlayer – *www.bbc.co.uk/iplayer*. The BBC's free service.
ITV Catch Up – *www.itv.com/catchup*. ITV's free service, offering live and streamed catch-up only, and no downloads.
Demand Five – *demand.five.tv*. Channel Five's on-demand service.
Sky Player – *skyplayer.sky.com*. Free and paid-for (depending on the user's Sky package) catch-up and live TV service from Sky.

Upload your own podcast

Recorded a podcast? Now it's time to publish it and send it into the world

ONCE YOU'VE PREPARED, recorded and edited your podcast, there's only one thing left to do, and that's publish it online. It's easy to forget about this part of the process during the recording and post production stages of putting the podcast together, but if you don't upload the finished effort, no-one will ever get listen to your hard work.

The two options that we look at here are either to upload podcasts to your own website (although this assumes a certain degree of technical prowess in this area), or to use a dedicated podcasting host to do the work for you. For the uninitiated in HTML coding and web hosting, the second option is the best way to upload a podcast, as it takes away the bulk of the hassle.

However, there are many hosts out there all vying for your business, so the first important thing to bear in mind is to choose one that offers the right level of service. Research is key here. Does the host offer the right level of storage? What is its service policy? Is the host's site backup up with around the clock technical support? And, of course, what are the costs involved?

So, when choosing a host for your podcast, you should look for the following:
● A clear explanation of the service provided, including bandwidth usage, costs, and customer service support.
● Simple user interface.
● User recommendations.
● A site forum. This can be invaluable, as you can find out how happy existing customers are and whether there are any issues you need to be aware of.

One host is *www.libsyn.com*, which costs from $5 (around £3.06) a month, with monthly storage packages starting at 100MB of data. That's ample for a podcast.

Once the host site has been chosen, it's time to upload files. If you are uploading to a podcasting host, then the files are uploaded

Using a dedicated host is the easiest way to upload your podcast to the internet

via the site's interface. For example, if you are using Libsyn, you have to sign into your account, select the Media Files tab and click Upload. Then, click on Browse and find the podcast file you want to upload. Click on OK and the file will be uploaded to your account.

If you choose to use an FTP client to upload your files, you should first select one to do the job. FTP (File Transfer Protocol) is an efficient means of transferring files to the web, and very easy to use. There are several free FTP clients to choose from, with many sporting a simple drag and drop interface to

transfer files from a PC onto the web. It's worth trying a few to see what suits you, although the free trial of CuteFTP is worth checking out at *www.cuteftp.com*.

Once an FTP client has been decided upon, you should install it and then log in (typically this will require an FTP address, username and password, which should all be supplied by the podcast host). Then, when connected, set up a new directory to store all of your podcasts in. This will make it easy to search for and upload files, and with most software will be akin to setting up a new folder in Windows.

Uploading files to that directory is easy, as most FTP interfaces will list the your own hard drive files in one column and the FTP directory in another. Simply click on the desired file to upload and move them over to the FTP directory. And that's pretty much all there is to it. ■

PERMISSIONS

When uploading files to a podcast, you should ensure that the correct permissions have been set up on the FTP directory, ensuring not only that those who are uploading files can access and alter them, but that visitors have read only access to them. This can be done on most FTP clients via the client's interface.

Create your own website

Claim your corner of the internet. It won't cost you a penny

IF YOU'VE EVER FANCIED creating your own website, it may not be as difficult as you think. It's a little-known fact that most internet access accounts include a certain amount of web space that you're free to use at no additional cost.

Many ISPs even provide complementary online software such as SiteBuilder. These let you compose pages without having to learn HTML, CSS or JavaScript, the coding that provides the text, and manages images and interaction on websites. Some programs also offer a number of other services, including hit counters, calendars, guest books and forms. It's the ideal way to get familiar with creating and maintaining a site without the expense of paying for a domain name and web hosting.

If you're unsure what's included in your package, check your ISP's website, and phone or email it for specifics if you can't find the information online. The important details to determine include the amount of web space available and the access settings (home page address, FTP upload address, username and password).

Currently, popular broadband companies provide anywhere from 15MB of free space (TalkTalk) up to 100MB (Tiscali). Others offer a mid-range of about 50MB of personal web space with your account (Tesco and Virgin). Even 15MB should be sufficient to put up plenty of pages. You can modify images to be web-friendly by using higher JPG compression settings and can display many pictures on your site with space to spare.

There are also free hosting sites available, but these usually place advertisements on your pages and you have no control over what will sit beside your family photo album. Investigate the ISP option first, as it's more likely to be around long term, and ISPs don't force any

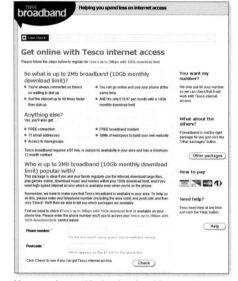

You may be entitled to loads of free web space through your broadband or dial-up account

advertising banners onto your site. You're free to display whatever you like as long as it doesn't break the rules and complies with what your ISP allows. Most have some restrictions about the content of a site.

Even if you have a small home business, this method may be the best way to test the waters with little or no expense. And you can always move to a fully-fledged site, with your own domain name, if the free site proves successful or becomes limiting. You can easily redirect any established traffic to the newer, larger site through your existing home page.

The foundations of a website can be created in a plain text editing program, such as Windows' own Notepad. However, you'd need to type in the tags and codes of HyperText Mark-up Language (HTML) that dictate how your pages look and behave. Most people prefer to use a WYSIWYG (What You See Is

Locate and note down the website access and upload details provided by your ISP

What You Get) HTML editing program that lets you drag and drop images into position, and set the font face, colour, size and styles (italics, bold, and underlined) of text on your pages. An added advantage of using such an application is included instruction, which offers you an extended way to learn about web pages and sites and helps you advance beyond the beginner stage.

HTML editing programs, like most PC applications, come in a variety of packages ranging from free shareware to more expensive suites for more experienced users. If you're just starting out in website creation, or need to get a page or site created quickly, a program that includes templates (or accepts free templates you can download online) will make it much easier.

Templates typically offer an assortment of styles appropriate to personal or professional sites, and you can choose one you like and adapt it to your needs. These programs usually include wizards that step you through the process of creating pages and help with proper linking and naming of files.

The first page, or homepage, of any site is called index.htm or index.html. Simply naming this file properly tells the file server to load the site you've created rather than show the directory of your web space and all of its contents. An FTP (File Transfer Protocol)

PLANNING FOR SUCCESSFUL SITE CREATION

Start as you mean to go on by getting organised. If you have a number of photos, PDF or text files, Flash, video or music files that you want to use on your site, arrange them into folders. Properly organised files will avoid many of the headaches of first-time website building.

Every file that becomes a part of your site needs to be referenced in your HTML and then uploaded to your web space. Arranging their location in advance will keep link errors at bay. Moving a file later requires modifying the link and can become complicated as your site grows.

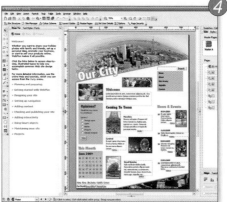
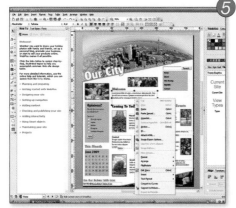

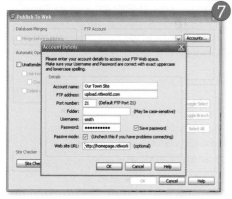

program is used to transfer files you create on your computer to the server space of your site. Some site creation programs include built-in FTP functionality that helps you design and upload your pages, all from the same application screen.

In this example, we're using Serif WebPlus X2, which includes both templates and an FTP facility. Follow our step-by-step instructions, or use similar steps in the application of your choice.

STEP-BY-STEP GUIDE

If the Startup Wizard isn't shown when the program is launched, go to File, Startup Wizard and choose Use Design Template.

1 Scroll through the available templates and choose one that has a layout closest to what you'd like. We've chosen Our City under Entertainment. You can click and drag a corner of this window to enlarge it.

2 When selected, all the template pages for that style – your homepage and other linked pages – fill the right-hand column. Tick the pages you'd like to include in your site.

3 In the Scheme drop-down box at the top of the Template window, choose a colour set that you like. As you select colours, the page thumbnails change to reflect your choice. Click Open when you've decided on a scheme.

4 The homepage is displayed and its name is highlighted in the Pages section to the right. You can switch between your site pages in this way, or collapse sections if you prefer, to give yourself more working space.

In the left pane, there's How To help available for designing and maintaining your site. Tabs alongside let you change the font styles of the text areas of your page.

5 Within the centre pane is your page layout. Right-click a text box and choose Edit Story to replace the template text. Enter your own words in the WritePlus window. A built-in spellchecker ensures that you get things letter perfect.

6 Double-click any picture and browse to and choose your own image. Save often and preview your page in a browser by going to File, Preview Site, Preview Page in and choose your browser from those listed.

Now you need to get your new page to your web space so that others will be able to see it at your web address. You'll need the FTP information you gathered earlier handy, and then head to File, Publish Site, Publish to Web.

7 Click Accounts and enter your details in the new window. Then hit Upload in the next window. Your new page should then be installed in your space. Now you need to repeat the process with the remaining pages so that all of your links will work, and pages will connect to each other, creating your unique website. ■

STEER CLEAR OF COMMON MISTAKES

Any good website is in a perpetual state of evolution, whether simply adding a few photos through the year or updating news entries frequently. If a planned page isn't ready for viewing, avoid linking to it until it's ready. It's disappointing to visitors to click links that lead only to a Coming

Soon page, especially if soon stretches to weeks and months.

Don't cram all your content on to one screen. Long pages that require lots of scrolling may make visitors lose their place. Break long pages into shorter parts and link them to each other.

INTERNET

PROJECT
015

DIFFICULTY LEVEL
HARD
INTERMEDIATE
EASY

TIME REQUIRED

30
MINUTES

Upload videos to YouTube

Capture, convert and upload video clips to YouTube using free software

IT'S EASY TO add digital video to your YouTube account using the site's dedicated upload page, but our tips will help you get the best possible quality.

First of all, capture some footage from the source you want to use. If this is a digital camcorder, follow the manufacturer's instructions for connecting it to your computer. For other video sources – such as a VCR or older camcorder – you may need an analogue to digital converter. Pinnacle's Video Creator Platinum (*www.pinnaclesys. com/publicsite/uk/home*) is ideal for the job and costs around £50.

Windows Movie Maker, which is bundled free with XP and Vista, is an ideal tool for capturing video. Start the program, then go to File, Capture Video and follow the onscreen instructions. We recommend you select the highest quality possible – which means selecting Digital Device Format DV-AVI.

Why choose the highest quality? It's advisable to start with the absolute best source material you can. Before you upload the video, you'll need to convert it to a suitable format, which means adding some compression to make the file smaller. This reduces the picture quality. The higher quality of the source, the better your result will be.

When you've captured a video clip (which should be less than 10 minutes for use on YouTube), you'll need to convert it.

YouTube accepts several video file formats, but through trial and error, we've discovered that MPEG4 is the best format to use. Download the software Free Video to iPod Converter from *www.pazera-software.com*. Despite the name, this tool is ideal for converting clips for YouTube and has a highly customisable interface, as you'll see from our screenshots below.

The final stage is to upload a finished clip to YouTube itself. Go to *www.youtube.com* and create a new user account if you don't already have one. Sign in and click the big yellow Upload button. Fill in the title, description and video category on the first page, but leave the broadcast, date and sharing options at their defaults for now. Tags are keywords you can add to your video listing to make it easier to find. Separate each of these with a space.

When you're ready to add videos to your account, click Upload a video. On the next page, you'll be prompted to browse for a prepared file on your hard drive. When you've located it, click Upload Video to begin the process. You'll see a meter monitoring the progress of your upload.

When that's finished, it may still take another 15 or 20 minutes before the clip actually goes live – as YouTube's software then converts the file for its servers. When that's done, you'll be able to view the clip online and send your friends its web address by email. ▪

CHANGING DETAILS

Once you've uploaded a video, you'll find it listed and available for editing at *www.youtube.com/myvideos*. It's here you can change your clip's description and listing properties by clicking on the Edit button.

In fact, the range of properties available to edit is quite a bit wider than what's available when you first upload your video. You can easily enable or disable comments, ratings and the ability others have to embed your video in your own site. While you're there, it's worth visiting the Insights section.

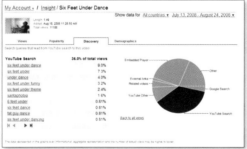

This gives you detailed viewing statistics, complete with an embedded map giving a geographical breakdown.

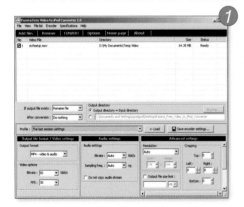

Free Video to iPod Converter looks technical, but is easy to use. Open the clip you want to convert from the file by clicking the Add file button, searching for a clip in AVI, MOV, Flash video or any of the other supported formats.

In the Output file format section, make sure MP4 – video & audio is selected. Choose 700Kbit/s as the bit rate and set FPS to 30. These settings are quite high, but the MP4 codec will take care of compression.

Next, set the video resolution to 320x240 – QVGA in the Advanced Settings section. Finally, click the Convert button to output the video in MP4 format, and it'll make your YouTube-ready video.

Set up an online forum

Add interest to your website with an interactive area for your users

FORUMS ARE A brilliant way for people from all over the world to share their thoughts, using notes (posts) to be displayed for other forum members to read. An active forum can carry on lengthy conversations when members actively participate in the threads, or topics, being discussed.

A forum is most often used in support of a website. If you don't own a site, a group service, such as those available through Yahoo! or MSN, may be better suited to your needs. If you own a site, and pay a provider to host your pages and files, you almost always have access to forums for free, as a part of your hosting package.

The most commonly used method of directly accessing your site account and details is through an application called cPanel. It's a tool that many web providers offer as part of their packages. It's usually reached through an addition to your domain address, such as *www.mydomain.co.uk/cpanel*. You'll need to make sure that you have your account name and password at hand to access this private area.

In cPanel you'll see many options for your hosting plan. Fantastico Deluxe is a collection of scripts and services to add features and functionality to your website. These include forums, called Discussion Boards. It's worth reading up on them before making your choice, because there has been some criticism of Fantastico Deluxe's vulnerabilities online. We use it here strictlly for tutorial purposes, and alternatives are available.

The advantage of installing a forum through your web hosting provider is significant. You won't need to download and then upload any files to your account. Installing and configuring the files needed to set up a forum can be difficult. The hosting service option does it automatically for you, getting your forum up and running in a fraction of the self-install time.

Select phpBB from the choices of Discussion Boards in the Fantastico Deluxe list in cPanel.

Next, click New Installation and you're presented with a form of drop-down boxes and blank areas. Your domain name should be listed in Install on domain. If you have more than one domain, click the drop-down arrow to choose the domain the forum will reside in.

Automatically create a directory for your domain by entering a name in the Install in directory box.

In the Admin access data box, enter an administrator username and password of your choosing. Make a note of both in a safe place, as you'll need them often when working with your forum.

Under Base configuration set other details of your site by entering a site name, short description, email signature (which will serve as your name on all emails to forum members), an email address, such as forum@mydomain.co.uk, and choose your language. Check your entries and click Install phpBB.

Another screen advises you that a MySQL database and user will be created for your forum. This is also a part of your paid hosting service. Check the details are correct, make of a note of the forum address and click Finish installation.

Within a few seconds, the forum has been configured and all the details are set out for you, including the special address of the admin area where you'll set rules and features of the forum. There's also a reminder to bookmark the forum admin address so that you can access it easily, and you can enter an email address to have these details sent to you as an additional precaution.

Help with your forum is available at the phpBB website (*www.phpbb.com*) where a community of users are happy to answer your questions. ■

USING YOUR FORUM

Log on to the admin page with the username and password you created. Click on 'Administration Control Panel' at the bottom, re-enter your password, and you reach the forum management centre.

Take time to explore each tab from General through System to learn the features of your forum. Each screen has **intuitive introductory text that details the various functions.**

Remember to link to your new forum from your site, with an invitation for visitors to register and join. If your forum becomes popular, watch for responsible members who may help with administration duties by assigning them moderator permissions.

To create a forum, you need to indicate where it will live, its name and who's in charge

The start of your forum is where you will add your subject categories

Your forum's Administration Control Panel is the place to set rules and permissions

Set up parental controls

Filter websites to block content that's unsuitable for children

LOGGING ON TO the internet is like stepping into the world's biggest library, and once inside you have access to every conceivable kind of content. It's an amazing learning resource for children, too, but as every responsible parent or guardian knows, it also contains content that's unsuitable for minors.

Software publishers know this, too, and there are many applications you can use to block or filter adult material. But before you consider paying for such software, or seeking out a free alternative from the many on offer, bear in mind that Internet Explorer comes with a built-in Content Advisor tool. By default it's disabled, which is probably why a lot of PC users don't even know it exists. However, it's easy to switch it on.

To configure Content Advisor, you use a series of sliders to specify the types of content users on your PC are allowed to see. So for example, you could specify that sites showing nudity are okay, but sites showing sexual material are not. Rather than trying to automatically identify and block unsuitable sites, the software makes use of a globally recognised rating system developed by the Family Online Safety Institute (FOSI, *www. fosi.org*). This system places the onus on website authors to rate their own sites and provide details of any adult content by filling in a brief questionnaire. The results are integrated into the coding of the site which the Content Advisor then checks against your chosen settings and blocks if necessary.

For the system to work perfectly requires each and every website author to diligently complete the FOSI questionnaire, but as this is obviously wishful thinking, the Content Advisor automatically blocks any site that doesn't have a rating.

If you're certain that a site without a rating is acceptable, you can enter your supervisor password and the site will be added to a list of trusted URLs. You can manually enter the URLs of sites that you want to block, too. ■

Getting started with Content Advisor

The Content Advisor has been part of Internet Explorer since version 3, and the way it works has remained roughly the same. However, to ensure the ratings are up to date, we recommend you upgrade to latest version of Internet Explorer before beginning.

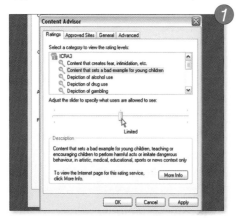

Open Internet Explorer and select Options from the Tools menu, then click on the Content tab. Select Settings and adjust the sliders to suit (by moving the slider to the right you will reduce the levels of restriction). When you have finished, click the General Tab and select Create Password.

The only way a user can turn off the Content Advisor once it has been enabled or allow a blocked site is to enter the supervisor's password. Enter a password that others are unlikely to guess, then enter a hint that will help you remember it. When done, click Apply and OK.

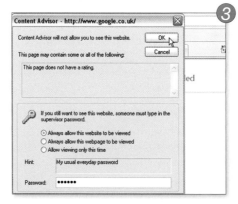

Click Enable and enter your password. The Content Advisor will now be activated. To test it out, go to www.google.com and the site should be blocked because it doesn't have a rating. Choose the Always Allow this Website option and click OK to unblock the site.

By allowing Google it will be added to the list of approved sites. You can add other sites manually be opening the Content Advisor settings and clicking the Approved Sites tab. Enter the URL and then either select whether the site can be viewed Always or Never.

VISTA'S BUILT-IN PROTECTION

Windows Vista includes proper parental controls built in. By going to the Control Panel and selecting User Accounts, you can set up controls on a child's account. In addition to selecting what websites can be viewed, you can also specify which games and programs can be run, and you can limit when your child is allowed online, and for how long.

Promote your website

Get more hits with these tips for giving your website a push

BUILDING A FLASHY website is one thing, but attracting visitors is quite another. The internet is so massive that it's possible to have a great website without anybody knowing about it, and as the whole point of having a site is to get noticed, it's vital to have a plan of action to market it. The good news is that there are some simple ways of doing this that won't break the bank, and you won't need the help of a specialist company either.

Let's start with some ways that are inherent to the way that the page is built. For starters, it's very important that the pages all have titles. As easy as it sounds, there are professional webmasters who forget to name all their pages, leading to problems with bad search engine results and strange-looking lists of favourites. After all, which result is someone more likely to click on from Google? The one that reads Ways to promote your website, or the one below called Page 1? It looks scrappy and points towards a lack of attention to detail, which in itself will cost you visitors.

Search engines will also operate better if keywords are included in meta tags (see the boxout below). All search engines use them and taking advantage of this should move your site up the rankings. It's important to remember that a large number of website hits come from people using search tools, especially now that they are built into web browsers and are becoming more advanced.

When a searcher gets a page of results, they will see the introductions of lots of pages. It's therefore important that the initial text on a page really is the introduction to the site and sums up what can be found there. Frames, JavaScript and Flash all make a site look impressive, but can completely

obliterate its search value. And, of course, none of this can happen without submitting the site to the search engine in the first place – this can be done manually by looking for the relevant link, such as Yahoo!'s How to submit a site at the bottom of the page.

Next up is some more basic advertising. Using a URL at the bottom of a personal or business email will draw attention to the site to every recipient. It's quick and easy to do and simply requires some basic manipulation of a signature file.

The same applies to forums – if they allow it, it's possible to include a link to the site in every single post, which could potentially yield massive traffic. One tiny piece of text in the correct places has the benefit of being incredibly quick to do while having a big impact, particularly on more specialist, personal sites where a forum could provide a captive audience.

Last of all there's the link exchange. This is a great way of getting the site promoted on other sites within the same topic area, thereby bringing in targeted traffic. Submitting the URL to an exchange program will place it into a web ring of other sites seeking to advertise, and everyone displays everyone else's address on their site. Sometimes these will be small banners which, if done well, can look like professional ads.

All it takes is a little effort to attract new visitors, and one line of text could transform an ailing site or kick-start a new one. ■

They may look unfriendly, but meta tags are actually simple and very effective

USING A META TAG

The meta tag should be in the <head> section of the HTML, and look like this:

<META NAME="DESCRIPTION" CONTENT="Good website design, getting more hits to your site, banner advertisements, using tags, making lots of money">

There used to be a similar tag called keywords, although it's no longer used by Google. It's worth leaving it in, though, as other search engines still look for it. Also be honest about the content. Putting 'sex' and 'cash' as keywords when the site is about knitting will be counter-productive.

A link exchange can increase targeted traffic

INTERNET PROJECT
019 DIFFICULTY LEVEL
HARD
INTERMEDIATE
EASY
TIME REQUIRED
15
MINUTES

Test your broadband speed

How fast is your internet connection? Here's how to find out

MANY INTERNET SERVICE providers (ISPs) boast very fast internet speeds , but many of us don't know the actual speed of the broadband we use. And despite what our package literature might suggest, we rarely get to see speeds anywhere near the advertised 2, 4, 8 or 10Mbit/s. But how do you go about checking the speed of your connection? It is, in fact, a fairly simple procedure that takes only a few minutes, using one of many websites built for the task.

1 There are several websites you can choose from to test your internet speed, but for this test, we're going to start with *www.speedtest.net*. Speedtest.net is a site provided by Ookla Net Metrics and, unlike many other speed testing sites, it enables you to not only test the upload and download speeds of your own connection, but also to compare it to others users in your area and across the world.

On the homepage we just select the recommended London server on the European map provided (Speedtest.net detects your location through your IP address), and the test begins.

2 Once started, the test will check both your upload and download speeds by sending data to your PC over HTTP, replicating the way your connection handles data when surfing the internet. Here we see that our test connection is running at speeds of 3.7Mbit/s for downloads and 0.4Mbit/s for uploads. This is from a package that claims to offer "up to speeds of 24Mb", but how near you get to that speed depends on how close you live to the telephone exchange your ISP uses, as well as what other competing internet traffic there is in your neighbourhood. Having lots of users on your home network will slow things down, too!

3 Having supplied your results – and detected your ISP, too – Speedtest.net offers other insights into just how fast your connection is, and how it compares to others. At the top of the screen, we see three tabs: 'My Results', 'My Summary' and 'My Global Stats'. The My Results tab shows a breakdown of your speeds, ISP, IP address, the server you used and a rough estimate of your distance from that server, while the other two tabs offer more options.

My Summary displays not only your latest tests, but your average results, allowing you to check the quality of your service at different times of the day. It also uses your IP address and results to provide the 'How Your Download Speed Compares' boxout on this page, so you can see where your internet connection ranks in your area, along with your global and local rank. For example, our test connection is faster than 71% of connections globally and 83% of connections nationally.

Finally, by clicking 'Global Stats', you can check the speeds of internet providers globally, seeing how your own fares with those on other continents. ■

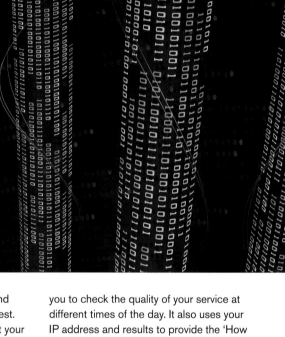

ALTERNATIVE SITES

Speedtest.net isn't the only site out there to test your broadband speed, and it may be worth having a look at other resources, such as *www.broadbandspeedchecker.co.uk* or *www.mybroadbandspeed.co.uk* – to get a fairer idea and average of your own results. Stick to the same test, though, to compare results over a period of time.

030

Organise your bookmarks

Take control of your favourites in Internet Explorer and Mozilla Firefox

SORTING OUT YOUR favourite websites or bookmarks is the kind of task we all put off for as long as possible. But like leaving the dishes to pile up in the sink, it's a job that gets worse the longer you leave it.

That's why we suggest having a thorough spring clean of your Favorites right now. The first thing that you should do is impose some structure. In Internet Explorer, the tools for arranging Favorites are meagre – but they'll do for the moment. Go to Favorites, Organise Favorites to begin. Our first tip, go through the list and delete everything you don't need. Be ruthless. If there are sites bookmarked that you simply never use, bin them.

The next stage of the clean up is to start to categorise your sites. First off, create folders for different types of site and if you've got a lot in your list, you can create subfolders. Simply select an existing folder and hit the New Folder button, providing a name when prompted. So, you might have a main folder for news sites with subfolders for computer, celebrity and sports news. It'll make finding your Favorites much easier in future.

If this sounds like a potentially laborious task – it is! You can make things a little easier on yourself by switching to Mozilla Firefox as your main browser (*www.getfirefox.com*). It has superior bookmark handling features and you can even import your Internet Explorer favourites into the program.

With Firefox 3, bookmark handling improved ten-fold. Go to Bookmarks, Organise Bookmarks and you'll see a window with three panes. The folder list on the left makes it much easier to scroll through and see the contents of existing bookmarks. You can do all the same things as you can in Internet Explorer – delete old bookmarks, create or rename folders – but you can also add comments to folders and tag individual entries. Adding tags gives you a way to track the sites that you save more effectively by making your bookmarks easy to search. You can even add a long description to each bookmark by clicking on the More button to reveal a large text box.

If you prefer not to change your browser, there's another alternative. Move your Favorites to a third-party program. Power Favorites is a piece of budget software from *www.deskware.com*, and offers very similar functionality to Firefox. In fact, it should be possible to manage both Firefox bookmarks and Internet Explorer Favorites using this tool. It costs $24.95, which is about £16. ▬

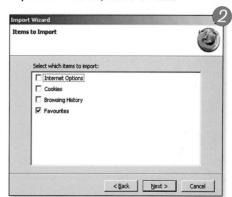

If you switch to Mozilla Firefox, you don't need to abandon the bookmarks you've already created in Internet Explorer. Just open Firefox and go to File, Import. In the Import Wizard make sure Microsoft Internet Explorer is checked, then click Next.

It's really not necessary to import anything but your favourites, so in the next section untick Internet Options, Cookies and Browsing History, then click Next again. It may take a couple of minute for the import to complete.

When the Wizard has done its job, click Finish. Your Internet Explorer Favorites are combined alongside your existing bookmarks. You can now use Firefox's tools to keep them all in an orderly state.

ONLINE BOOKMARKS

These days many people are increasingly accessing the internet away from their PCs. Wouldn't it be handy, then, to keep your bookmarks online, so that you can access them from whatever machine you happen to be using?

Well, Firefox users can give Foxmarks (*www. foxmarks.com*) a try. This service lets you upload your bookmarks, then access them through a password-protected web page. There are organisation tools, too.

Alternatively, you could try Delicious (*www.delicious.com*). This site is part

bookmarking tool, part recommendation engine. It lets you save favourite addresses on publicly accessible pages.

DIFFICULTY LEVEL: HARD / INTERMEDIATE / **EASY**

TIME REQUIRED: A LIFETIME?

Find the love of your life

You, too, could find your ideal partner in cyberspace

INTERNET DATING EXPLODED a few years ago, and although the hype has died down, it's still a viable way of meeting people and potentially finding a date, if not a life partner. The virtual equivalent of the lonely hearts ads in local papers, it gives users the chance to include far more information about themselves and get in touch with people from a much wider geographical area than the traditional method.

Signing up for a site is easy and doesn't always have to cost you anything. Freedating. co.uk does exactly what it says on the tin. It's easy to join (and leave), requires a minimum amount of initial data and doesn't need any credit card details. Here's how you get started:

1 The first page gives you the chance to see some of the site's members. All of the profiles of these people can be seen without signing up or feeling tied into anything. But that's as far as you'll generally get. Try to use the search facility, and you'll need to sign up for membership

2 Registration is a simple process here and much like joining an internet forum. It's important to read any terms and conditions carefully before you sign up, and make sure that nothing seems untoward. If you feel that something isn't quite right, or the site is requesting information that seems unnecessary, then don't sign up. Some dating sites have been known to be fraudulent. Standard information can include current relationship status, appearance, political views, religion, interests, job, financial situation and a short personal introduction. Most of these fields, however, will not be compulsory.

You can then expect to find a lengthy questionnaire, which ideally needs to be filled in. And as you're signed up, the site now shows lots of profiles, and the search function becomes available. Users who are online are flagged for instant contact.

3 Other options are available for those who are prepared to get their credit cards out. A pound will put a picture on the main pages as a featured profile, and also send someone a gift – these are picture-based and work in the same way as sending a virtual greetings card.

After registering, the profile will be manually approved and then it becomes possible to send messages and winks to other

members of the site. What happens after that is the subject of many a self-help book.

Internet dating is very easy to get into, it doesn't need to cost any money, and has the potential to produce the love of your life, providing it's all done properly and not in some dodgy chatroom.

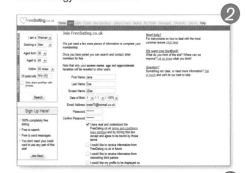

WHAT DOES THE DATA PROTECTION ACT MEAN?

The Data Protection Act 1998 is a piece of legislation that tells companies how they can process, or use, personal information given to them by individuals.

The first principle, which underpins the Act, states that companies should be clear about why data is being collected and what might happen to it. If a dating site is based in the UK and legitimate, it will tell you exactly

where and how it will be stored, as well as giving users the option to opt out of third-party sites and advertising.

The law also has certain things to say about the removal of profiles, the behaviour of company staff and what to do if something goes wrong. Check the site complies with this legislation to ensure maximum safety of any submitted personal information.

Set up an online petition

If you're unhappy with government policy, why not protest online?

LODGING A PETITION of complaint with Downing Street is a great British tradition. It's democracy in action. In the past, though, you would have had to drum up signatures yourself and then deliver a big bundle of papers to Number 10. You can, of course, still do that, but you can now also do the whole thing online. Welcome to the world of the e-petition.

To create one, go to http://*petitions.number10.gov.uk* and then follow the workshop below. There are a handful of rules – see http://*petitions.number10.gov.uk/terms* – but you'll probably be fine so long as you avoid libel, advertising and humour (humorous petitions do slip through, but usually only if they're subtle). Also avoid ranting about things clearly beyond the government's control.

Before being put online, your petition has to be approved. If it gets rejected, you'll be given a second chance. You can edit it, observing the reason for rejection and then resubmit. If it's rejected again, it's game over, and your protest is, for now, over.

Once your petition goes live, it's up to you to publicise it and circulate its web address. People can then sign it. Serious petitions receiving 200 or more signatures usually get a reply from a minister and sometimes even the prime minister.

1 On the homepage, use the Search petitions box. Enter some keywords relevant to the petition you want to create. This will tell you whether someone else is campaigning for the same thing: duplicate petitions usually get rejected. If you're happy, click the Create petition button.

2 Enter your petition's heading. To do that, complete the sentence beginning We the undersigned petition the Prime Minister to… We've gone for 'Include plate smashing in the 2012 Olympics'. Below that, you have up to 1,000 words to explain in detail the reasoning behind the petition.

3 Next, enter a duration. The maximum is a year, which is what we've chosen. You also need to enter a name of six to 16 characters to be used in the petition's web address Additionally, select the most relevant category. When you're ready, click Next.

4 Fill in your name, home address, telephone number and email address. Don't worry, none of these will be published. Your email address won't be spammed, either – it's only used to verify your identity and to keep you informed (sparingly) of petitions you've either signed or created. Click Next.

5 Now there's a summary. Here, if necessary, you can edit your petition's wording and change your contact details – use the Change petition text and Change my contact details buttons. The terms and conditions are listed too, in case you've not read them already. Once you're done, click Create.

6 Within a few minutes you'll receive an email. In it will be a web link. Once you click that, the e-petitions site will pop up and confirm that your petition has been submitted. Now you just need to wait for a second mail, which usually arrives within a fortnight, to see if the petition has been approved or rejected.

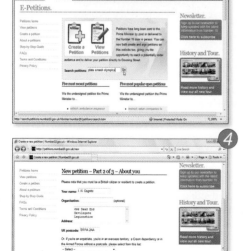

INTERNET

PROJECT 023

DIFFICULTY LEVEL
HARD
INTERMEDIATE
EASY

TIME REQUIRED
1 HOUR

Publish your own book

Want to see your name in print? Let the internet help

WRITING A BOOK is a time-consuming process, but getting your work published and bound doesn't have to be these days, particularly if you're not interested in enlisting the help of agents in breaking into the bestseller charts. Self-publishing is becoming more and more popular, particularly as it's now relatively easy to achieve. What's more, it's certainly preferable to using the services of so-called 'vanity publishers' who deal only in large volumes, which is expensive and could potentially leave you with piles of unwanted copies sitting in the garage. Avoiding such services is easy, however. All you need to begin the publishing process is your completed work (sadly, we can't help you with that bit) and an internet connection.

There are many self-publishing sites on the internet, including Booksjustbooks and Authorhouse, but by far the most popular and well-known site is Lulu (*www.lulu.com*). Lulu calls itself a 'digital marketplace' for user-generated content, but publishing your book through Lulu can enable it to be listed for sale on both the Amazon and Barnes and Noble websites, exposing it to a potentially huge audience.

Publishing written work is Lulu's primary concern, but the site also provides services for those who wish to produce books of photograpy, calendars, posters and portfolios, as well as some digital media (CDs/DVDs and eBooks). What's more, support for the service is huge – Lulu has around 500,000 unique visitors every day and an active community of forum members who regularly answer questions and share their experiences.

The most important aspect of Lulu's service, however, is that it makes the process of getting your book on its way to publication straightforward. Even so, it's a good idea to

watch the brief demo before you start, which you can access by clicking a blue button on the main Lulu homepage. Once you have seen how easy the process is, and you have your book at the ready, you can begin self-publishing with the click of your mouse.

When you select Publish from the tabs on the homepage, Lulu immediately asks you what you want to create. We clearly want the books option, but even here you have a choice of which type of book you want to create. Paperbacks, hardbacks, comic books, dissertations, cookbooks, product manuals, sales proposals and travel guides are all available, and choosing paperbacks (the most popular item on Lulu) takes you to the introductory page for that section.

This page provides an overview of the options you will shortly be asked to choose from, including the size of your book, colour options and how you want it to be bound. In this section, select Self-publish a

Paperback. Lulu will then ask you to enter the title of the book and your name.

You then have three choices. First, you can make your work a private project. You should select this option if you're not ready for your creation to be viewed publicly. This also means that others won't be able to buy your work on the Lulu Marketplace. This option might be best for your first work, as you can always make the project public later when you're happy with it.

The second and third options are 'I want to sell this in the Lulu Marketplace', and 'I want to sell this in online bookstores'. Both options enable you to share your work with other Lulu users and sell your title on through its site, although the third option also helps facilitate distribution of your work to sites such as Amazon, Barnes and Noble and WH Smith when there is a demand. Clearly this is the option for you if you want your title to reach the largest possible audience.

Having made your choice and clicked Save and Continue, you come to the binding and size options. For our paperback project, we're offered the choice of perfect-bound (like the binding of this book), coil-bound and saddle stitched ('staples down the middle of the book fold').

You also have a choice of popular sizes and colour options, including black and white printing (with colour covers) and full colour printing. These choices will affect the cost of

DO I NEED AN ISBN?

Books published on Lulu don't need an ISBN to be sold through the site's own Marketplace, but you can choose to add one to a title when you put it on sale (or even at a later date). Lulu offers 'Published by You' and 'Published by Lulu' distribution packages. The former

costs £59.95 and adds an ISBN to the title, making you the publisher. The latter makes Lulu the publisher and doesn't cost you anything. In both cases, you retain the copyright to your work, and can make your title available to bookstores worldwide.

producing your book, but unless your work includes illustrations, black and white is the obvious preference. For the purposes of our example, we'll combine black and white printing with perfect-bound binding and the standard US trade size of 6x9in (15.24x22.86cm). There are a few additional size options under the 'Tall', 'Square' and 'All' tabs if you decide to investigate further.

Finally, you'll need to specify how many pages your work will be – 32 is the minimum number for the US trade size. Such a size would be perfect for a collection of poetry or a short story, but you'll inevitably need many more pages if you're looking to publish a novel, for instance.

Click Save and Continue again, and you will be asked to upload your chosen file for the title. Once you've done this, you go to the next stage where the print-ready file is produced.

When the process is complete, you may receive notification that your source files have had to be re-sized. This is fairly normal, and simply means that the A4-sized source file we used has been shrunk to fit to our chosen book size. If you have any concerns over how this might affect the print, you can select Download and Review to look at your print-ready file. It's probably a good idea to

do this anyway, as it allows you to see how your work has been laid out. Once you are happy with it, click on Save and Continue again and you can then move on to putting together your book's front cover.

Here again the options are clear, and choosing the right one is easy. You can select your preferred fonts, cover themes and colours, and even upload your own images for the front and back covers, so if you have a personal photo or an image for which you own the copyright, you can completely modify your title's appearance. It's obviously worth taking some time over designing the cover, as even if you're selling your book exclusively online, shoppers like to see a picture of what they're thinking of buying.

Once you've finished designing your cover, click Make Print-Ready Cover, then

Save and Continue and move on to your product description.

Much of the information here is optional and you can return to edit it later, but you can input keywords, description, edition, publisher and ISBN details if you wish (there's more on this in the box opposite).

The only field that is essential here is the category. Once you have chosen this, you can move on to the pricing screen and decide how much revenue you will make from each copy of your book sold. You can also decide how much to charge for downloadable copies of your title if you want to make it available in this form. After you have reviewed your project, you can save it and your work will be published digitally and made ready for order. In short, you will have just published your very own book. ■

PDF FILES

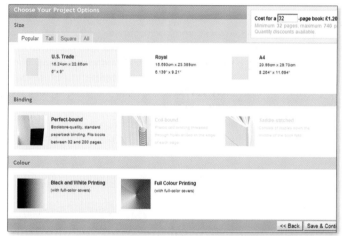

Choose your preferred book size, bindings and colour options

You can customise your cover with your own picture file

Lulu gives you the chance to review your project before you publish

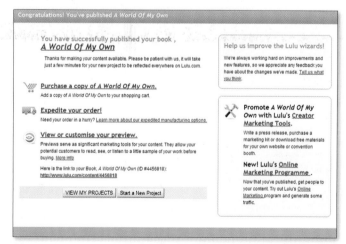

After a short process, your book is published and ready to sell

INTERNET

PROJECT
024

DIFFICULTY LEVEL
HARD
INTERMEDIATE
EASY

TIME REQUIRED
30
MINUTES

Get started with Skype

Chat long-distance on the phone with friends and family for free

VOICE-OVER IP (VoIP) is a method of using your broadband internet connection to make telephone calls to practically anywhere in the world. There are a few criteria that have to be met first, including subscribing to a VoIP service such as Skype.

Unlike some VoIP services, Skype is completely free, provided that the person you're speaking to is also a Skype user, with a comparable broadband connection. In fact, you can speak to someone without a PC or internet connection at all, but that's part of the Skype Out facility, and isn't free. However, let's start by looking at setting up a Skype account and how to make free phone calls.

In order to use Skype, your computer will need a sound card, a microphone or VoIP phone, and if you want to see the person

you're talking to, a webcam as well. Naturally, you'll also need a broadband connection which needs to be at least 384Kbit/s if you intend to use video calling.

Most modern computers will already have the necessary internal hardware. So it's just a matter of deciding between the different types of handheld units and headsets that you prefer. Some of the recent VoIP phones are also dual function, which means they can handle both traditional PSTN (Public Switched Telephone Network) and VoIP calls. In some cases, with this type of equipment, you don't even need to have your computer switched on to make or receive Skype calls.

Setting up Skype is relatively straightforward using the free download from

www.skype.com. You need the largest button on the main page, so it's difficult to miss.

You can either select run or save – choosing the second option downloads the software to your computer. That's a useful facility if you need to install Skype on more than one machine, because you don't have to repeat the download.

During the installation, you'll need to choose a Skype name and decide on the initial settings for your Skype account. These are fairly self-explanatory and can be managed later if you change your mind. For example, you can decide whether to let anyone contact you, or just those in your contact list. In this context, Skype is far more secure than email, because after a user is blocked, they can't ever call you.

Once Skype is running, you need to add your friends to your contact list. You can use either their Skype name or their normal email address. You can also add your contacts from Outlook to your Skype contacts, and use the system to invite anyone you know to join the Skype service.

Making a call is simply a matter of highlighting a name in your contact list and then clicking on the green telephone icon to the right. Your contact's online status is clearly indicated by the symbol alongside their name.

If you purchase SkypeOut credits, you can telephone contacts just about anywhere in the world, at a fraction of the normal price. You can even send SMS text messages from your computer using the same facility. ■

Launch Skype, and then add your existing contacts

Skype Out lets you make cheap calls to any normal landline

WHO'S ONLINE?

The symbol to the left of each name signifies the current availability of the person it relates to. This not only shows who's currently online, it also allows you to change your own availability status. So, if you're busy, you can set your status to 'Away', 'Do not disturb' or 'Invisible'.

Online
SkypeMe!™
Away
Not Available
Do Not Disturb
Invisible
Offline

Set up your own domain name

Stake your claim on the web with your own personalised address

DOMAIN NAMES ARE unique addresses, such as microsoft.com and windows.co.uk, that are associated with a particular person's or organisation's presence on the internet. As the owner of a specific domain name, you can use it for websites, email addresses and other internet protocols. Registering a domain name is relatively simple – you go to a domain registration service website such as *www.supanames.co.uk* or *www.1and1.co.uk* and use the forms online to buy the use of a domain for a fixed period of time.

Thinking up a domain name for a new website is the hard part, as many of the best domain names have already been taken. It's not impossible, though. When you think of a name, try typing it into your browser first. If it takes you to a website or holding page, move on. Alternatively, use the name search facility at a domain name broker. Yahoo!'s service (at *http://smallbusiness.yahoo.com/domains*) is a good bet as it tells you which permutations of a domain name are available. The .com version might be taken, but .net or .me could still be available, for example. You should be aware, though, that if you're running a business, most people will expect your domain name to end in .com or .co.uk.

Rule number one when thinking of a domain name is to keep it short. Just about every single word name you can think of will already have been taken, many of them by cyber-squatters looking for a big pay day. Try unique word combinations, plurals, rhymes and puns instead. For example greenapples. com is taken, but word combinations such as 'flatapples' and 'zappedapples' are still available (at the time of writing).

Your name doesn't necessarily have to be descriptive of your site – there are plenty of successful brands that aren't. Domain names that try too hard to pack in keywords and be descriptive run the risk of sounding cheap. Which site are you more likely to return to: discountdvdsupercentre.com or dvdnow.com?

Above all, the name should be consistent. If your URL is www.zappedapples.com – then your site should be called 'Zapped Apples'. That's the first thing anyone will try in a browser when looking for you. Hyphenated names are fine if you also own the non-hyphenated version of a name, but they're

difficult to type, a pest to remember and a pain to describe verbally.

Lots of web space packages come bundled with 'free' domains. For example, Supanames (*www.supanames.co.uk*) has a series of web hosting deals that feature a 'free' domain name. Before you choose such a deal, though, there are several things you'll need to check out. First and foremost, make sure the domain is registered in your name. It's exceedingly rare that this wouldn't be the case, but it does pay to check. It won't be a problem with any reputable domain name registration company, including Supanames.

If you'd like to check registration details for domains you've already acquired, use Nominet's WHOIS tool (*www.nominet.org.uk*) for .co.uk domains and InterNIC (*www. internic.net/whois.html*) for other top level domains such as .com, .net or .org. Both offer a simple search service that allows you to check in a matter of seconds.

In truth, you never actually own a domain – you merely license its use from the respective registrar – but your name's presence on the registration is your sole proof of that. Registration of a domain name doesn't always give you the right to use it either. In cases where a domain infringes the trading marks of other established businesses, you may be asked to hand over your domain. The process shouldn't usually have to go to court; both ICANN (the US domain name registrar) and Nominet in the UK have dispute resolution procedures in place to arbitrate these issues, although clearly it's best to try to avoid this.

Previous ownership of a domain name doesn't entitle a business to use that name in the future. You should bear this in mind when it comes time to re-register a domain, and keep a close eye out to make sure you do so in good time. A good registration company will warn you in advance. That said, some domain providers offer 'domain catching' services designed to snap up names that lapse. Yours could be on someone else's list.

One word of warning: don't forget to read carefully before sending off cheques in response to invoices that come through the post. An enduring scam targets domain owners with 'marketing' circulars that look like bills. Don't be its next victim.

With all that in mind, let's get your domain name set up and running. The easiest way to use a domain name is to buy a hosting package alongside the domain name, which provides you with web space and email services. These are automatically linked to the domain so you can start using it as soon as your provider has set up the service.

Some services, such as Yahoo! and 123-Reg, provide you with free Domain Name System (DNS) management. This enables you to set up a hosting account with any hosting provider and point your domain name at it. You must enter the addresses of your web space provider's DNS servers into your domain control panel to do this. Check your host's documentation for help.

A cheap and cheerful alternative is domain name redirection. This method – provided by domain name brokers such as uk2.net and others – allows you to specify another web address at which to point your new domain. It uses HTML and frames to hide the real address of the site, displaying your domain name in the location bar of the web browser. ▪

Some firms provide free DNS management

A redirection service is simple to set up

HARD
INTERMEDIATE
EASY

15 MINUTES

Set up an email mailing list

Send multiple emails in one go with mailing lists and groups

EMAILING FRIENDS, FAMILY, colleagues and clients is one of the main functions of many PCs both at home and in the workplace. So anything that keeps emailing from becoming a chore is welcome help for many computer users.

When you need to send the same email to a lot of contacts, or even just a few, it's tedious to open and type in an email address, or paste identical information into each. Happily, you don't have to. All fully featured email clients, whether locally on your PC, or web-based and accessed through a browser, have a facility to create mailing lists.

Using the popular Google Mail (Gmail) browser-based email service, you can create groups that act as mailing lists for whatever contacts you choose to include. With an online service, your mailing list is available from any computer with internet access.

1 To build a mailing list, you first need to log in to your Google Mail account (*http://mail.google.com*) and click Contacts. Next click the New Group symbol. It's the small icon of two heads, with a plus sign by the Search contacts box. Enter a name for your mailing list that reflects the contact types you'll include. You can create more than one, so you can have friends, family and work associates groups, and an additional group that includes everyone. Click OK and your new group shows in your contacts column. Now you can add addresses.

2 If you've already stored contacts in your account, click on My Contacts to see existing email addresses and tick those you want to include (or use Select: All). Then click the Groups drop-down arrow and select your new group name under Add to. These contacts enter your newly created group.

3 To add more new names to the group, highlight the group name, click the New Contact icon of a single head and plus sign, and fill in the information in the blank boxes and click Save. A convenient way to transfer lots of contact details and addresses from other email accounts is to use the Import function. You can import addresses from local mail clients like Outlook and

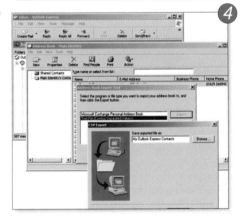

Outlook Express, and other online email accounts, such as Hotmail and Yahoo! Mail.

To create an importable list in Outlook Express, you export a .csv file from your Address Book. Go to Tools, Address Book, File, Export, Other Address Book and choose Text File (Comma Separated Values). Click Export, type in a name for the group of addresses, and browse to where you'll store the file: the desktop is fine for now. Click Save and then Next, and tick the fields you'd like to include for each contact. Click Finish and Close the Export Tool.

4 To import contact lists from one account return to Google Mail, click Contacts, Import and browse to where your .csv file was stored. Be sure to tick the box by Also add these imported contacts to, and use the drop-down arrow to select your new mailing list. When you want to send an email to everyone on the mailing list, open Contacts, click on your mailing list title, click on Select: All (or tick individual names) and click on Email in the right column. A blank email will open with all the addresses you chose already in the To field. ∎

LOCAL LISTINGS

To build an Outlook Express mailing list, go to Tools, Address Book, click New and select New Group. Name your collection of contacts and click Select Members. Simply double-click on addresses to add them to the Members of your group on the right.

Click OK and you'll see your group entries gathered together. Click OK again and close the Address Book. Click Create Mail and then click the drop-down arrow of the To: field. Find and select your mailing list's name. Identical versions of your email go out to each list contact.

Share files using BitTorrent

The faster, more efficient way to download files

THE CONCEPT OF torrent files is one that has emerged only since the advent of broadband connections, where the PC has become permanently connected to the internet. The expression 'torrent' relates to how a downpour of rain is made of tiny droplets or water. When said droplets are combined, they become a torrent. In its computing context, the droplets are packets of data coming from many computers, each connected via the internet to many others, all downloading the same file.

When the torrent is initialised or 'seeded' by the original owner, other computers can connect to that seed and start downloading parts of the file. The clever part is that it doesn't give the same pieces to all those downloading. Instead, it chooses to distribute different bits of data intelligently to each in turn. BitTorrent technology then allows each of the recipients to offer the data they hold to others in the chain, speeding up the distribution dramatically.

The result is an exponential data explosion, where the overall performance of the download is enhanced by the number of people attempting to get the file, instead of

IS USING BITTORRENT LEGAL?

While the technology is often associated with the distribution of copyrighted material by pirates, there isn't anything inherently illegal about BitTorrent or the applications associated with it. BitTorrent is just a very efficient sharing mechanism for files which there are many entirely legal and justified uses. It's been suggested that internet service providers (ISPs) might either block BitTorrent activity or record your activities if they see you using this system, but as many universities and scientific establishments also use BitTorrent then this isn't actually feasible. What it might do is attract those hackers on the Internet looking for copyrighted material, but using a BitTorrent application doesn't innately expose you any more than using a browser, email or chat tools.

creating a log-jammed queue. Once a torrent client has all the data, it becomes a full 'seed', further accelerating the process for those in the chain. In short, your downloads get faster.

For people arriving after this point, they might find hundreds of people seeding, and a download performance that entirely maxes out their connection speed.

The only caveat is that for the system to work effectively it relies on people seeding the system after they've got the file. As such, it doesn't reward the selfish.

In our example, a Linux distribution has been made available via BitTorrent, but how do you actually get it to download?

The system is driven by files with the extension .torrent. This isn't a standard file type, so you'll need to also locate a BitTorrent client application, of which there are many. Ones you might want to consider include BitComet, Deluge and BitTorrent (the official client). Whatever your OS, you should be able to find one for your computer. The official client is located at *www.bittorrent.com*, and takes only seconds to download on broadband.

Installation is just like any other Windows application; it asks you to confirm that you wish to proceed, and then explains the licensing and allows you to decide where on the computer you wish to put the software.

The last question it asks is whether you wish to make BitTorrent the default application for .torrent files, which you do. Once you've installed it your system will automatically direct .torrent files to this tool.

http://linuxtracker.org is a website dedicated to helping Linux users locate the torrents for all the different versions of this operating system available in this way. From here you can download the .torrent – usually this file is only 10-25KB in size. Clicking on the file link will prompt you to open or save the file. Select 'Open' unless you wish to download it later. Downloading the file will cause BitTorrent to run and open the file.

The download is underway. BitTorrent keeps you informed of how long it's likely to take, and where the data you're getting is coming from, among other things. This disc image is 4.5GB, so it's likely to take a while. You can configure BitTorrent to turn the PC off once it's complete. ■

It's worth choosing a default BitTorrent program

Here, we're about to download a Linux torrent

Check out torrent details before downloading

This is the status of our download

COPPER COOLED QUALITY

GIGABYTE™

GIGABYTE Ultra Durable™ 3 Motherboards

DDR2 1366+

Unique Technology from GIGABYTE

Ultra Durable 3

- **2 oz** Copper PCB
- 50,000hrs. **Japanese** Solid capacitor
- **Lower RDS(on)** MOSFET
- **Ferrite Core** Choke

Ultra Durable 3 vs Traditional Motherboard Temp. **Cooler**
50°C

Ultra Cool **2 oz** Copper PCB

PCB

New Design
2 oz
Copper Inner layer

Old Design
1 oz
Copper Inner layer

PCB layer cross-section image, magnified 200x

2 oz Copper Inner Layer

Ultra Cool	Ultra Performance	Ultra Durable	Ultra Power Efficient

DYNAMIC ENERGY SAVER
GIGABYTE Advanced

Supports (intel) Core 2 Quad inside

(intel) P45 EXPRESS CHIPSET

● GA-EP45-UD3P

● GA-EP45-UD3R

● GA-EP45-UD3

Quality Components Makes Quality Motherboards www.gigabyte.com.tw

G.B.T. TECH CO. LTD.(UK) http://www.gbt-tech.co.uk

* Temperature measurements under system setup with water-cooler block and CPU running at 100% loading

Play computer games online

Take your gaming to the next level by playing over the internet

PLAYING ONLINE IS a fun way to stretch out the life span of your favourite gaming title for months, even years after the single-player element of it has been tossed aside. Even so, actually getting online with your favourite title isn't usually the simple, one-click procedure most games seem to suggest. In this guide, we'll explain the problems you might face when trying to play online, and the terminology you might be expected to understand too.

While not always essential, it's worth finding out your IP address when playing online. Note that if you're not directly connected to the internet, you should ensure that you find your WAN (internet) IP address, rather than your LAN (local) IP address.

If you're connected to a router, you'll need to log in to the router's admin page to find the correct IP address, because this is the exact address by which your computer is identified online. If, on the other hand, you are directly connected to the internet, you can find the relevant IP address in the status tab of the connection properties dialog.

One of the main obstacles to gaming online is the problem of correctly assigned port forwarding. If the virtual TCP ports used by a game are not open and/or unblocked, you may have trouble connecting to game servers or other players. If this appears to be the problem, you should find out what ports you need to open (TCP ports are numbered between 1 and 65535) by looking in the game documentation or an online support forum for the title in question. It's always a fair bet, after all, that somebody else has experienced the same problem as you.

To open or unblock the relevant port, log into it and ensure that the correct TCP ports are forwarded to your local IP address (which will usually take the format 192.168.xxx.xxx). If you're not using a router, or you have Windows' in-built Firewall enabled, you should ensure that the firewall is not blocking these ports. This is done by adding them to the exceptions list in your Windows Firewall settings, which can be found in the appropriate LAN connection properties dialog box.

As a last resort, you can test connectivity by assigning your computer's LAN IP address as the DMZ in your router's settings. This will forward all ports to your computer by default, making the router effectively transparent. If this causes connection problems to disappear, then it is likely that the ports are forwarded incorrectly. Check again which ports you must have forwarded, that those ports are forwarded to the correct IP address, and that your firewall is not blocking them.

Be aware too that setting your PC as the DMZ will leave it vulnerable to hacking attempts that would normally be blocked by your router, so it should not be used as a permanent solution.

The last major element of online gaming is your 'ping'. This specifies (in milliseconds) the time it takes for data from your PC to reach the server you are connected to. A high ping will mean an online game can feel unresponsive, and in such cases you will visibly see your actions online lag behind your key presses. A high ping can make an online game virtually unplayable.

To reduce ping, use the game servers that are as geographically close as possible to your PC, and try to ensure that your internet connection is not being used for any data-intensive tasks (eg: downloading files or streaming audio) while you're playing. ▪

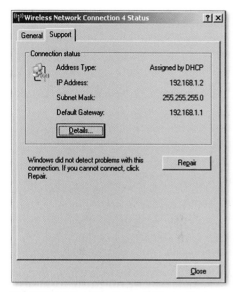

The Status tab of the Network Properties dialog shows either your LAN IP address (if you use a router) or your WAN IP address (if you have a direct connection to the internet)

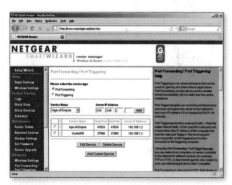

A typical router's port-forwarding configuration page, showing ports forwarded to the correct LAN IP address

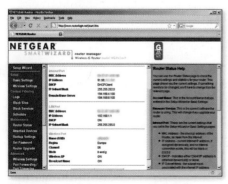

A typical router's status page. It's here that you can find your computer's internet IP address

MORE ON PORTS

Ports aren't just used for gaming – they're used for all incoming and outgoing internet connections. If you want to host other services through your router or firewall, you may find that you need to open and forward ports in a similar manner to when playing a game online.

FTP servers, for example, usually run on port 21, while a web server will run on port 80 by default. Only with the correct ports forwarded will you be able make servers of this kind accessible to other computers on the internet (but check that your ISP terms allow this first!).

INTERNET	PROJECT 029	DIFFICULTY LEVEL	TIME REQUIRED
		HARD / **INTERMEDIATE** / EASY	**30** MINUTES

Back up your data online

Use online data storage to make your files secure

BACKING UP IMPORTANT files is a necessity because computers can fall prey to failure, theft, fire, flood and a host of other less potent disasters.

The best method for ensuring that your important documents are safe from harm is to store them in a safe location a long way from the computer – the further the better. Transferring your files to another location over the internet is an increasingly popular strategy. It has a few drawbacks, but there are plenty of advantages for those who are willing to give it a try.

The first question most people ask is where their data goes. To perform an online backup, you need to sign up with a company that offers such a service. You then send your data to this company over the internet where it is stored on its computers. These companies use security systems to ensure that only you can access the data repository in which your backup is stored. In the event of disaster, you can restore your files to any computer by using the appropriate login and password.

In this project we'll show you an online backup application in action. We've chosen Carbonite for this demonstration.

BACKING UP WITH CARBONITE

This online backup service offers unlimited storage for £49.95 per year, with a reduction for subscriptions of two and three years. If you wish to try it out for 15 days, go to the Carbonite website (*www.carbonite.com*), provide a valid email address and a password, and the application will download.

Installing the tool takes just a few minutes, during which you're provided with a useful overview of how Carbonite works on your computer.

Once installation is complete, it's time to start your first backup. By default, Carbonite offers you the option to save all your Windows settings and any documents that are in the My Documents folder.

If you accept the defaults, Carbonite will start to secure those files to a remote server. Depending on how much data you're backing up, this could take minutes, hours or even days.

You can add files and folders to the list or remove them at any point. Carbonite uses a simple coloured marker on its icons to show their status. A green marker shows that the file has been secured, while a yellow icon means the file is marked for backup. Items that aren't designated have no coloured markers.

Restoring files is easy. An icon on the desktop called Carbonite Backup Drive opens a File Explorer, allowing you to browse the secured files. Simply find the file or folder you want to back up, right-click it and select Restore. Carbonite will then download and restore the data.

If there's a catch to backing up your data online, it's the sheer amount of data that a modern PC can hold and the speed at which it can be secured online. A typical broadband connection may have only a 256Kbit/s upload speed, and with that it can take some time to back up all your data. Luckily, the software usually uploads only those files that have

Applications such as Carbonite can be set to update a backup automatically

changed since the last backup, so once the first backup has been completed, subsequent backups will take much less time.

If you create lots of data, you might need - or indeed prefer - to leave your PC running overnight to give the system an opportunity to secure all your files. As with most of these tools, Carbonite allows you to schedule when the backup occurs so that it doesn't interfere with other uses you might have for your internet connection. It's easy therefore to set it for an 'off-peak' time. Remember, however, that online backup services are not designed to secure the entire contents of your PC – just your data.

If you decide you don't want to use the service any longer, then after a grace period following the end of your licensing period, the data is automatically deleted from the online storage repository. ■

ONLINE BACKUP SOFTWARE

We've mentioned Carbonite, but it's not the only service available that offers this facility. Other services worth considering are HP Upline, SOS Online Backup, Mozy and IDrive. These work in a generally similar fashion to Carbonite, but you may find differences not only in price but in the amounts of data they're prepared to handle. For example, HP Upline allows you to back up 1GB of data for free, but the £59-per-year account removes that limit. Whichever service you choose, it's absolutely essential that you don't forget your login and password, because that might leave your data safe but inaccessible in the event of a PC failure.

The HP Upline site (*www.upline.com*) is an online backup system for home and small business use

You can get a free trial of Carbonite, so you can give the service a try with no risk

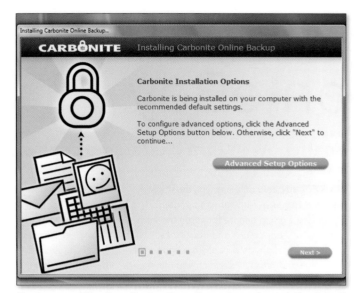

Most users will be fine allowing the software to go through the default installation routine

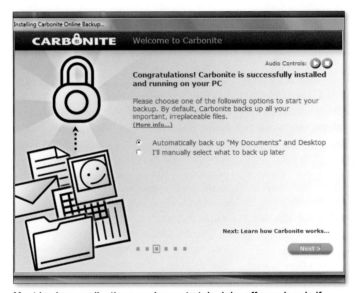

Most backup applications are happy to take jobs off your hands if you're willing to let them

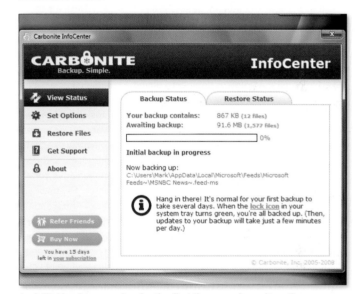

An initial backup, running for the first time, can be quite a time-consuming job

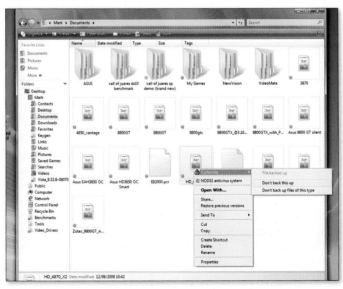

You can select which individual files you want a backup program to exclude from its regular backups. You can also exclude them by file type if you wish

Backup software is the kind of program that most users will ignore until the moment they come to need it. It's therefore worth checking your backups, though, to make sure they're OK

Sell your stuff on eBay

Learn how to turn clutter into cash with an online auction

TO SELL AN item on eBay, you must first ensure that you've registered an account. The link to sign up can be found on the front page (*www.ebay.co.uk*), and the site itself will guide you through the process of choosing a username and password, which you can then use to log in. Once logged in, you'll notice a link in the top right that says Sell. Clicking this link begins the process of listing an item.

If this is your first attempt at selling on eBay, you'll now need to upgrade your eBay membership to a seller's account, which is done by clicking the Create a seller's account button on this page. Be aware that you'll be asked to register a credit or debit card during this process, although you won't be required to pay any money yet – this step is purely to verify your identity.

Once you have a Seller's account, the Sell page will present you with two options: Quick Sell and Advanced Sell.

The Quick Sell option chooses the most popular options for listing a product, while Advanced Sell will give you greater control over the listing options. Until you're familiar with eBay's service, it's best to start with Quick Sell.

To begin the process, you have to enter a few keywords about your item, and then click Start Selling. You will now find yourself on the Quick Sell page. The text in the first box will be used to show your listing in search results, so make sure it's clear what you're offering. Include information that you think would appeal to buyers; for example, if the product is in pristine condition, don't be afraid to mention that by adding 'as new' to the item title. You generally have once chance to catch the eye of a potential buyer, so taking some time on getting your title just right is advisable.

Once you've settled on a title, you need to choose a category for the listing. By default, eBay will try to match your title to similar products and display a list of Suggested Categories. Usually this will contain the best choice, but if not, click on Browse Categories and you'll be able to explore the full range of categories available on eBay.

Next, it's time to add an image to your listing. Including an image of the product greatly improves the chance that an item will sell, because the buyer is able to see exactly what they're getting. Ideally, you should attach a clear digital photograph of your item to the listing, but if you don't have one, a stock image of the product from another website will reassure buyers (though be sure to emphasise that the image is for illustration purposes, and do make sure you're not breaching anyone's copyright). Click 'Add a photo' to attach your image. The first image is free, although in the case of large items you may want to add more pictures, at the cost of 12p per additional image.

Now comes the hard part – writing a full description of your item. Try to be succinct, but include any information that the buyer might want to know. Be aware that if you give misleading information about the product or omit any major details, the buyer may be eligible to dispute the sale, so be comprehensive and truthful. You can use basic formatting in this listing to organise the text if you've written a lot.

The next step is the fun part – choosing a price. Remember to price your auction competitively. The lower you set the starting price, the lower the cost of the eventual sale fee (eBay takes a small percentage of the final sale price as a fee, based on the amount

the item was initially listed at). A low starting cost will encourage interest, but don't price your item for less than you want to sell it, unless you're willing to risk disappointment. A Buy It Now price costs a little extra, but may encourage a quick sale from those idly browsing eBay's listings, who don't want to hang around until the end of an auction to buy your item.

You should now also choose an auction Start Time and Duration. Remember that the start time also affects the finish time, and conventional wisdom says that items fetch the highest price if the auction finishes during work hours on a weekday, when most people are sitting at their computers.

You will now need to enter postage costs, which buyers will be required to pay on top of the final item price. Be fair and transparent in all postage costs; high postage will discourage buyers, so feel free to elaborate in the item description if the postage is expensive because an item is fragile or heavy.

Finally, choose the payment method so that a buyer knows what to do when they win your item. An online payment through PayPal is the most popular method of completing a transaction, but you can also accept a personal cheque, postal order, or even a bank transfer at your discretion. The use of cash is discouraged, as it leaves buyers and sellers unprotected against fraud.

Once you're happy with your item details, click Save and Preview. This will give you one final chance to see how your auction looks and preview how it will appear in the search listings before you put it on eBay.

You can select a variety of optional extras to promote your listing, and you'll be shown the fee you'll be paying to advertise your item on eBay. The cheapest listings can be made for 5p each (and it's worth keeping an eye out for occasional fixed listing price offer days). If you want to alter any aspect of the listing, you can still return to the previous page by clicking Edit listing. If you're happy with it, click List your item and the product will then be put up for sale. Then sit back and watch the bids come in!

Once someone has won your auction, contact the buyer to arrange payment. Be

SUPPLY AND DEMAND

Before selling an item on eBay, you should first ensure that there's a market for it. Try searching for similar products to see how they're performing. This should give you an idea of what the true resale value of your item is. Be sure to play with search terms, and try checking

the 'Include completed items' box – something similar might have just been sold. Remember, listing an item comes with no guarantee that someone will buy it, so you should try to list only products that will sell to prevent fruitless listing fees from mounting up.

The eBay front page

Here's where you choose between Quick Sell or Advanced Sell

Choosing a title and category is done here

Adding a picture and description. Both are vital to a good listing

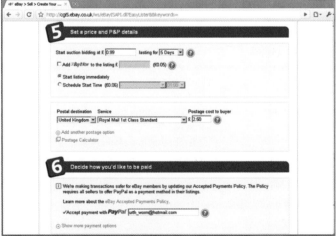
Price and payment details go here

Finally, you click to complete your listing

sure to post the item as quickly as possible once you've been paid, and keep in touch with the buyer during the process. Always use eBay's messaging system to ensure a record of your conversation, should anything go wrong. Be careful if someone approaches you to buy an item directly from you, because sales completed outside of eBay's system are not protected by the service.

FEEDBACK

Building up good feedback is essential on eBay. As a new seller, you may have a zero-feedback rating, which could make people wary of buying from you. Certainly you'll struggle to sell a high value item with a very low feedback score. After **making sales and purchases on eBay, you'll be invited to leave feedback for the people you deal with. If you've had no trouble with them, you should leave positive feedback to increase their rating, and they should reciprocate.**

INTERNET

PROJECT
031

DIFFICULTY LEVEL
HARD
INTERMEDIATE
EASY

TIME REQUIRED
15
MINUTES

Improve your web searching

Get the right results every time by fine-tuning your internet searches

THE INTERNET IS such a gigantic repository of information that it can be very difficult to find specific websites containing the information you need. Search engines such as Google, no matter how accurate in finding matches for your search criteria, can often reveal a large collection of spurious results. This, inevitably, can make some searches a chore.

This situation can, however, be improved by using some tried and tested methods, as well as some of the available advanced search engine options. Let's take a look at a few ideas to help make your searching that bit more efficient.

First, it may be tempting to enter search criteria that include all manner of punctuation and symbols, but this often negatively affects your results. You can simply end up with an unmanageable number of results, and rarely find what you're looking for quickly.

Most search engines don't recognise characters such as exclamations, question marks, @ signs and so on, as these are so commonly used that the results would be almost endless. Even though these are usually ignored, this can still have a detrimental impact on your results, so it's best to leave such characters out of your searches if possible.

It's also worth noting that most search engines are not case sensitive and will recognise names and titles even if typed entirely in lower case. They're programmed to ignore common words and characters, such as the aforementioned symbols. They're also built to usually ignore specific words, such as 'the', 'where' and 'how'. These words won't usually affect your search results, but in some cases, the inclusion of these is needed, or at

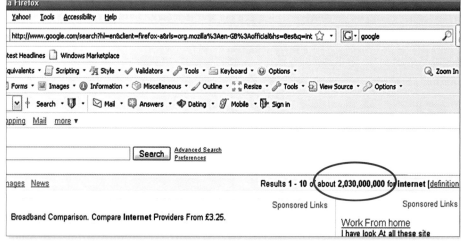

These handy tips may mean you avoid result numbers like this

the very least will improve your search results and make them more accurate.

To ensure common words are included, include a plus sign before the word you're searching for. For example, instead of searching for 'Friday The 13th Part 1', enter 'Friday The 13th Part +1'. This will make sure that the number 1 is included in the search criteria, and will also help limit results to the first film.

If you wish to specifically ignore a word, and trim out any similar search results, you can also use a minus sign in front of the word. Searching for 'Friday The 13th Part -3' for example, would exclude all references to the third film, only returning results for others in the series.

Sometimes, you may wish to search for a specific phrase or music lyric – for example, to find the name of a song. However, simply typing in the actual phrase can cause a

glut of results that match only part of the phrase. To ensure you search for results that only match the entire phrase, all you need to do is include quotation marks around the phrase. So instead of typing 'it was the best of times', you'd type "it was the best of times", with the quotation marks.

Let's look at another example. Simply entering Scotland into an engine such as Google will certainly reveal plenty of results about the country. But if you're looking for something more specific, such as a good place to stop for the night, you'll still have a lot of snooping to do, and at best will probably need to wade through page after page of search results.

It's better, in instances such as these, to try to be more specific. Entering 'Scotland +Hotels' would yield a greater level of accuracy with your results, making things much easier. In fact, a search engine like

Opera can search the internet for any highlighted word

TEXT SEARCHES

As well as searching for actual websites and pages, most users will also need to hunt through text on actual pages as well. All browsers feature this option, but some perform this task better than others.

Firefox, for instance, can look through pages using its built-in search box. Click Edit, Find, and the search box will appear at the bottom of the page. As soon as you

enter text, any results will be highlighted on the page.

The Opera web browser's search is a little more interesting. As well as standard in-page searches, any words on a page can also be highlighted with the mouse, and with a right-click you can then choose to look for the highlighted words using a variety of different search engines.

Be as specific as possible with search criteria for the best results

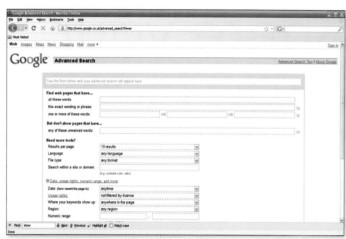

Google's advanced search can greatly refine your results

Google will almost always reveal a useful list of specific hotel results, and a map, too, which is likely to come in useful!

As well as refining your own search criteria, you can use your chosen search engine's advanced search tools. These can can greatly help filter out unwanted pages of results, and allow you to undertake more targeted searches.

Google's advanced search is easy to use and powerful. To access it, go to Google's main page and click Advanced Search to the right of the main search box. You'll see the advanced search form appear. Here, you can enter a range of information. Search words to be included or excluded can be entered in the first two sections. You can then further refine the search by limiting or increasing the results per page that you're presented with (from 10 to 100).

Of particular interest is the language option. Most searches will reveal results in a variety of different tongues, which isn't useful if you can't speak the respective languages. Thus, you can choose to be presented with results in English only. File type is also an often overlooked filter that can be very useful. So, if you need to find a file online in a particular format – for example, PDF – you can set this here.

A powerful option is to take advantage of the site or domain search. Using this, you can limit searches to specific websites or domains.

You can set a permanent language and other preferences in Google via the Preferences page

Results shown will only be from the specified criteria. So you could search *www.bbc.co.uk* solely for results about your favourite football team, for instance.

Under the Date, usage rights, numeric range and more section, you'll find very useful filters such as the page date feature. This can limit search results to pages that are as recent as you specify – for example, up to a year old at most. You can limit results to pages with specific user rights, including those that contain information and media that can be publicly shared.

Other advanced features than can help target your desired results include the ability to choose where on the page your search terms appear (anywhere, in the title, main text and so on), limit the pages by region and the ability to enter a numeric range, which can be useful for searching for prices.

Other sites, such as Yahoo! also feature advanced search options that include many of the same features as Google, and these can also be found in an advanced search section. It's certainly worth exploring your search engine of choice to see what it offers. ▪

YAHOO!'S SEARCH ASSIST

Auto complete is nothing new, and most browsers can fill in text boxes by using your previously entered criteria. However, Yahoo!'s Search Assist offers far better functionality.

When activated, it will analyse the text you type into the search box, and will then suggest a range of possible search terms. For example, typing 'Batman' will result in a

list of Batman movies, games and comics, which can then be clicked on.

Search Assist should be activated by default, but if you don't have it, click the Options' link to the right of the Yahoo! search box (on any results page) and select Preferences. Next, click Edit in the Search Assist section and then change the setting to the value you wish to use.

Yahoo!'s Search Assist makes it easy to narrow down results and find accurate criteria

HARD
INTERMEDIATE
EASY

15 MINUTES

Share your large files

How do you get that large file from A to B? Here are several handy solutions

SENDING SMALL FILES to your friends or colleagues is easy. Just Zip them up, using a program such as WinZip, and email the archive. But what do you do with a folder full of holiday snaps that's way too large to email? And what about that 1GB project you're working on that your manager needs right now? How do you get such a large amount of data from one place to another? There are several ways, all of which have their own advantages and disadvantages.

Porting your data around has been made much easier by USB memory sticks. Flash drives, thumb drives, pocket drives, USB drives; they're all different terms for exactly the same thing, and they're the easiest and cheapest way of transferring large files between computers that aren't too far apart.

Using a flash drive is really easy. First of all, plug it into a spare USB port. Many PC cases have a port at the front specifically for this. Then open My Computer (or Computer, if using Windows Vista), found under the Start menu. Your flash drive appears as a removable storage drive, and is assigned its own letter. Click on the flash drive's icon to open a window showing everything currently stored on it.

If you get a message saying the drive has not yet been formatted, the computer can't read it until you format it by following the on-screen instructions. This erases all data on the drive – not a problem if you've just bought it and are using it for the first time, but if it's someone else's drive and there's already data there, it best to consult the owner before you format it.

To transfer files to the flash drive, drag them onto the open drive window or the flash drive's icon in My Computer. The files are then copied to the flash drive – this may take some time if they're large, and especially so if your computer only uses the slower USB 1.1 standard, rather than the more modern, faster USB 2.0 technology.

When you've finished copying the files, you can remove the storage drive, but it's important to do this safely. See the icons at the bottom-right of the screen? Hover over the one that looks like a computer drive with a green arrow over it. You're offered a list of removable drives. Click on the one you want

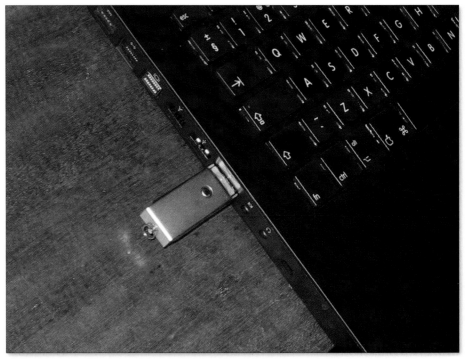

A USB flash drive is one of the easiest ways to move large files around

to remove, which in our case is drive 'E:', and you're told it's now safe to remove the hardware – then you can just pull it out. With the files safely on your flash drive, you can transfer them to another computer simply by plugging it into a spare USB port and dragging the files on to the desktop. It's as easy as that.

The advantage of sharing large files with a USB flash drive is it's cheap – you only have to buy the drive once, and then you can use it over and over again. As you can save documents and projects stored on a flash

drive without transferring them to a computer first, it's also great for carrying data you need to work on using different computers. The disadvantage, of course, is that you need to physically transfer the flash drive from one computer to another, which isn't much use if you're in Brighton and you want to pass a file to your uncle in Edinburgh. Flash drives are also notoriously easy to lose – just ask an assortment of government officials if you don't believe us!

There are plenty of other options, though. These days, blank CDs and DVDs

FLASH DRIVES

You can now get all sorts of flash drives at all sorts of prices. Sizes of up to 16GB are common, with a 32GB drive also now available. Large sizes can be expensive, but you can get flash drives with an 8GB capacity for under £20. Shop around before buying – it's amazing what bargains you can get. It's best to buy as big a drive as possible. However much you think you'll never fill it, time will prove you wrong.

There's a huge choice of flash drives

The flash drive shows up as a removable storage drive in the My Computer window, with its own drive letter

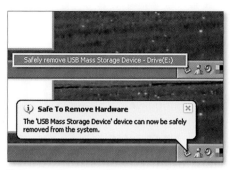

Before unplugging a flash drive, select it in the taskbar (top). You're then told it's safe to remove it (bottom)

The Jon's Games folder has been copied to the CD drive window, ready to be burned

Upload your files to RapidShare, and they can be downloaded by any computer with an internet connection

are phenomenally cheap. When bought in reasonable quantities, and without the possibly unnecessary casings, blank discs cost just a few pence each. This makes them ideal for sharing large files by post. You can simply burn your files to a disc, then put it in the postbox.

To copy files onto a blank disc, your optical drive must be a CD/DVD writer as well as a reader. Most computers today come with a writer already fitted, but if yours lacks this function, you can easily upgrade by replacing the drive. If you don't fancy taking your computer apart (although this is one of the very easiest upgrades to perform), buy an external DVD writer and plug it into your computer's USB port – it will work in the same way, just a little slower.

To copy files to an optical disc, first insert a blank CD or DVD into your computer's optical drive. A CD can store up to 700MB, with a DVD offering 4.7GB of space, so choose accordingly.

You're then offered the opportunity to automatically open a writable disc folder, select media to copy using Windows Media Player or take no action. Take your pick, depending on what it is you want to copy to the disc. Of course, even if you take no action at this stage, you can still open a window by going into My Computer and clicking on the Disc Drive icon.

To copy files to the CD or DVD, open the disc's window and simply drag the files you want to copy into it. They're copied there as

temporary files until you burn the disc, and can be deleted using the options in the left-hand window. When you're satisfied with your disc's content, you're ready to burn it. Click on the option 'Write these files to CD/DVD' in the left-hand window and choose a name for your disc when instructed. The disc is then written and ejected.

The main advantage of using optical media is that the discs are cheap enough to be disposable, so you can post it to someone without worrying about it being returned. The disadvantages are they can't be reused unless you go for rewritable media, which is more expensive, and they're more susceptible to damage than flash drives.

If there's no time to post a disc, and distances prevent your using a flash drive, the internet is your only option. Email's out, because the file is too large, so why not try a hosting service? We'll look at RapidShare here, but there are others to choose from.

RapidShare (*www.rapidshare.com*) enables you to upload files over the internet, which can then be downloaded by anyone who has the correct link. Files are uploaded one at a time, so if you want to share, for example, a folder full of photos, Zip them up first (again, using a program such as WinZip, available from *www.winzip.com*).

You access the RapidShare site through your web browser and then follow the onscreen instructions. It's easy – just press the Browse button and navigate to the file you want to upload. Then click on the Upload

button, and your file is copied to the RapidShare server.

When a file has been successfully uploaded, you're offered two internet links. The first is the one you share with others – simply email them the link, and they can click on it to download the file you uploaded. Either copy and paste it onto an email, or send it through the form under the links. The second link deletes the file from the RapidShare server, should you so wish. The file is automatically deleted if no one's downloaded it for 90 days. Files uploaded to RapidShare are limited to 200MB in size, though you can split larger files into several pieces and upload them one by one.

The RapidShare database is not searchable; the only people who can download your file are the ones to whom you've given the web link. Thus it's a completely private way of sharing files – you're only sharing them with your contacts, not with the internet at large.

The advantage of RapidShare and other file hosting sites is that you can pass on relatively large files without waiting for the post, and also that you can pass the same file to as many people as you like simply by emailing them all the link. The main disadvantage is slow transfer speeds, though most sites offer a faster, better premium service for paying users. ▪

The SendSpace file-hosting site

HOSTING SITES

RapidShare isn't the only website that allows you to upload files to share with other internet users. Other hosting sites include:
- Box.net (*www.box.net*)
- FileFront (*www.filefront.com*)
- MediaFire (*www.mediafire.com*)
- Megaupload (*www.megaupload.com*)
- Sendspace (*www.sendspace.com*)
- Steek (*www.steek.com*)
- YouSendIt (*www.yousendit.com*)

HARDWARE PROJECTS

Here you'll find everything from different ways to upgrade your computer, through to PC maintenance, watching TV, setting up a wireless network and syncing your mobile phone.

PROJECT
033

DIFFICULTY LEVEL
HARD
INTERMEDIATE
EASY

TIME REQUIRED
1
HOUR

Upgrade your graphics card

Get more from your games with a simple upgrade

AN OLD OR underpowered graphics card won't be able to run modern games at the high resolutions for which they are designed. Game worlds that seem astonishing in the publicity pictures will look blocky and basic on your monitor. Here, we'll show you how to install a graphics card and get maximum power from it.

1 Uninstall the drivers for your current graphics card by going to Start, Settings, Control Panel. Double-click on Add/Remove programs, then look for an entry that has ATI or Nvidia in the name. Click Change/Remove. Make sure you uninstall all relevant programs, then reboot your computer.

2 Shut down your PC, switch it off at the mains, unplug the power cable and press the on/off switch to clear any charge remaining in the power supply or circuitry. Touch an exposed part of a radiator to ground yourself. Now remove the cover from your PC case and take out your old graphics card, first unscrewing its backplate. There may be a catch at the back of the slot holding it in place. Treat the card carefully: you may need it later if there's a problem with your new card.

If your motherboard has integrated graphics, you can't remove it. When you install a new card, the integrated graphics will either be disabled automatically or continue to function as a secondary display adaptor.

3 Check all the cables and other cards in your system. Make sure nothing will get in the way of your new card. If it needs a lead from the power supply, make sure there's a large drive connector free that will reach all the way to the card's power connector. If not, rearrange your power connectors.

When everything's ready, place your graphics card on the graphics slot. Make sure it's properly aligned, then apply gentle, even pressure along its length. You should feel the card click into place. Screw in the card's backplate using the screw you removed in the previous step. Plug your monitor into the monitor output of your new graphics card.

If your monitor has only an analogue D-sub input, you may need a DVI-to-D-sub adaptor. These are quite cheap, but the card maker may have provided one in the box.

4 Plug in your computer and reboot it. It may start up at a low resolution. You must now install the driver for the graphics card. If you have a broadband internet connection, download the latest drivers from the Nvidia or ATI website before you start installing the card. Follow the driver wizard to get the right driver, otherwise you could have problems. Alternatively, use the driver disc that came with the card.

Wherever your driver file is located, run the install routine by double-clicking it. If Windows XP or Vista warns you that the driver isn't certified, don't worry; click on the button that tells Windows to install the driver anyway. If you're installing an ATI card and choose the Custom Install option, remember to install the ATI Control Panel, as it adds crucial settings.

5 Next, optimise your driver to get the best results from your card. Right-click on your desktop, choose Properties and go to the Settings tab. Click on Advanced. A new window will appear. If you have an ATI card, you need the 3D tab; for Nvidia cards, click on the tab named after your graphics card.

The two settings that make the most difference to games quality are anti-aliasing and anisotropic filtering (in the ATI driver, tick 'Use custom settings' to access these). Using trial and error, turn them up as far as they'll go without slowing down your favourite game.

6 Some cards have built-in overclocking modes. Check your manual to see if yours can be boosted in this way. If it does have options for this, you'll be able to increase the speed of your graphics card for free. The options usually let you increase the speed of your graphics card's memory, which lets it shift data around quicker. You can also usually change the graphics chip's speed, so that it displays graphics at a faster rate.

You should be careful when using any overclocking options, as they can damage your graphics card. You may also invalidate your warranty, so overclock only if you know what you're doing and you're confident that you won't cause problems. If you do overclock and your PC starts crashing a lot, particularly when you're playing games, reset the options to the manufacturer's default settings.

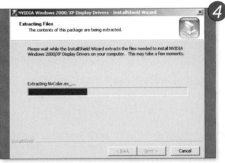

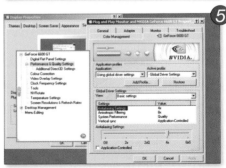

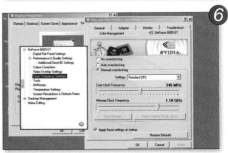

Install extra memory

Boost your PC's performance by adding more RAM

FEW UPGRADES ARE as effective as adding RAM to your PC. When there's not enough memory to go round, your computer uses the hard disk as a substitute and performance drops rapidly. Adding more RAM should make it faster. For the best performance in Windows XP, we recommend a minimum of 512MB of RAM, and for Vista at least 1GB of memory, though 2GB is better.

Good-quality RAM is now remarkably cheap. You can buy 1GB for just £15, but first you need to be sure that it will work in your PC. If you're fitting additional memory, you'll need to fit exactly the same type as that already installed. The free utility CPU-Z (available from *www.cpuid.com/cpuz.php*) can tell you what's currently installed.

If you're not sure what RAM to buy, try entering your system or motherboard model into the online configuration tools provided by major memory manufacturers. The System Scanner at *www.crucial.com/uk* tells you your computer's current frontside bus (FSB) speed, which can help you choose the right upgrade if your motherboard supports a range of different bus speeds.

Finally, look in your motherboard's manual to see whether it supports a dual-channel mode. Such boards typically have memory slots arranged in coloured pairs, and will run slightly faster if each pair of slots contains identical sticks of memory.

1 Disconnect your computer's power and peripherals, and open the case. Lie your PC down so that the motherboard is parallel with the surface on which you're working. Locate the board's memory sockets, which are usually near the processor.

For easy access, you may need to remove any system components that are in the way, or cables that run across the top of the memory modules. On many motherboards, it's hard to release the memory socket clips without first removing items that are in the way, but make a note of anything you move so you can put it back later.

If you're replacing your existing memory, remove it from the motherboard by pressing down on the plastic retaining catches at each end of the memory slot. It's best to release both ends at once, checking for obstructions if the catches seem too stubborn.

Each slot will have one or two plastic ridges along its length, as shown in the picture on the right, which stop you inserting the wrong kind of memory. Examine the slots carefully to find the position of the ridges, as you'll need to match them with the notches on your new RAM.

2 First, you must decide which slots to use. On motherboards with dual-channel support, each channel's slots are usually the same colour and should contain identical memory sticks for optimum performance. Other boards may have two, three or four slots. You should usually fill these from the lowest-numbered slot upwards, but your motherboard's manual will tell you what to do.

Once you know which slots you are using, press down on the plastic catches at each end so that they pivot open. Carefully open the anti-static packaging of the first memory stick, and find the notch or notches on its connecting edge. Be careful to handle it by the other three edges only and line it up with the memory slot, making sure that the notches are in the right place.

Insert the memory stick by pressing it down at both ends. The two catches should clip over the ends of the module as it moves down into the slot. If you encounter a lot of resistance, check the notches are in the right place and make sure the memory is lined up

properly. When it is, it should slide gently into place and the catches will lock.

3 Use the same method to add any other modules. Check the catches are properly engaged in each occupied memory slot and replace any components you removed before closing the PC's case.

When you first switch on your PC, look at the information the system BIOS displays and check that the amount of memory it shows matches the total you expect. If it doesn't, check that the memory is seated properly. ■

INSTALLATION TIPS

Memory is easy to install, but it's very sensitive to static electricity and should be handled with care. Before you start, and at regular intervals as you work, touch the unpainted part of a radiator to discharge any static electricity that you may have built up. Always handle memory sticks by the edges of their circuit board and avoid touching the chips or any exposed pins.

HARDWARE

PROJECT
035

DIFFICULTY LEVEL
HARD
INTERMEDIATE
EASY

TIME REQUIRED
2
HOURS

Change your processor

Boost your PC's speed by upgrading this crucial core component

MORE THAN ANY other component in your computer, the processor determines how quickly your system can run your applications. Replacing an old processor can give your computer a new lease of life, enabling you to tackle intensive tasks such as video editing that would otherwise be impossible, no matter how extensively you upgraded your other components.

We'll assume you're attempting to add a new processor to an existing motherboard. However, we'll also explain how you can tell whether your existing components will make a simple processor swap difficult or ineffective. In these cases, you may also want to consider buying a new motherboard (see page 56). This increases the cost of your upgrade, but lets you choose any processor you want.

 REMOVE AN AMD COOLER AND PROCESSOR
AMD coolers are held in place by two metal catches that connect to plastic clips on the motherboard, one of which has a plastic lever. Raise the plastic lever to loosen the cooler, then unclip both sides and lift it out. The cooler may be stuck in place with thermal paste. If it's not easy to remove, gently slide it from side to side to free it from the processor. Put the cooler to one side, placing it upside down so you don't get thermal paste on anything.

The processor will now be exposed. Next to the processor socket is a lever. Lift this into a vertical position to free the processor's pins. Holding the processor by its edges, lift it out of the socket. It should come out easily. If there is any resistance, make sure the lever is completely upright. Now skip to Step 4.

2 **REMOVE A SOCKET 478 COOLER AND PROCESSOR**
Intel Socket 478 coolers have two retaining levers opposite each other. To release the cooler, push down on the levers simultaneously to release them, and lift the cooler straight off the processor. The chip

MOTHERBOARD COMPATIBILITY

It's often possible to fit a faster processor into your existing motherboard, but you must be sure that the new chip is compatible. This demands careful research.

First, check your board's processor socket. The two main processor manufacturers, Intel and AMD, use different sockets and regularly bring out new ones. Only processors designed for the socket standard your motherboard uses will fit in your board.

The current Intel socket standard is LGA775, but for AMD it's slightly more complicated. The newest socket is Socket AM2+, which is backwards-compatible with Socket AM2. The Phenom processors

will also work in some AM2 boards (check your motherboard manufacturer's website for details), but you'll get the best performance by using an AM2+ board. If you have an older socket, you may still be able to upgrade. Your choice will, however, be limited to Intel's Socket 478 and AMD's Socket 754, so you may need to replace your motherboard.

A limited selection of Athlon 64 X2 dual-core processors are available for AMD Socket 939 motherboards, so an upgrade could be worthwhile.

Another compatibility issue that only affects Intel processors is the frontside bus (FSB) speed. The FSB is the interface that

connects the processor to the board's memory controller, and different Intel processors require different FSB speeds. Your motherboard will support only certain FSB speeds, and you can't enhance the range allowed with a BIOS update. Before you buy a processor, make sure that your board's bus can run fast enough.

The bus speed quoted for the processor will be four times the bus speed of the motherboard. For example, a 1.86GHz Core 2 Duo E6300 has a 1,066MHz FSB, so your board's bus will have to run at 266MHz, while a 3GHz Core 2 Duo E8400 has an 1,333MHz FSB, so needs a motherboard with a 333MHz bus.

will sometimes come out with the cooler, but this shouldn't do any damage as long as you lift the cooler off straight.

To remove a Socket 478 processor, look for a lever next to the processor. Lift this into a vertical position to free the processor, then grip its edges and lift it straight out of the socket. If it doesn't come away easily, check that the lever is fully upright. Now go to Step 4.

 REMOVE AN LGA775 COOLER AND PROCESSOR

Socket LGA775 coolers are not held in place with clips. They have four feet that clip into holes in the motherboard. On each foot is a slot and an arrow. Insert a flathead screwdriver into the slot and turn each foot 90° clockwise towards the arrow. One at a time, grip each foot and pull it straight up. It should click up and come free. When all four feet are free, lift the cooler straight up from the processor. If a foot appears to be stuck, give it another tug to make sure that it's free.

Socket LGA775 processors are held in place by a cage in two halves. There is a lever next to the cage. Push the lever down slightly and then across to clear the catch. Lift the lever into an upright position and open both halves of the cage. The processor doesn't have any pins, so you can pick it straight up.

4 Intel Socket 478 and AMD Socket 754, 939 and AM2 processors have hundreds of pins on the bottom of the processor that fit into holes in the socket. To fit the processor, first make sure the lever is upright. There is an arrow in one corner of the processor, and a similar arrow in the socket's plastic surround. Align these and place the chip on the socket.

The processor should drop into place without requiring any force. If it doesn't go in, or some pins drop in and others don't, you

may have some bent pins. AMD's Socket 939 and AM2 chips look very similar, but won't fit in each other's boards.

Remove the processor and look sideways at the pins. If any look out of place, slide a credit card between the rows of pins and very gently straighten them. Once the processor is in place, lower the lever to lock it down.

To fit an LGA775 processor, make sure the cage is open. These chips have small indentations on the edge of the plastic surround. Match these to the notches in the socket and lay the chip on the pins. If you've inserted it correctly, it will sit level. Close the cage and lock the lever in place.

5 Some processor coolers already have thermal paste on their underside, but if not you need to apply some. If your cooler already has paste on it, you can skip this step. Thermal paste smoothes over the microscopic imperfections in the cooler to ensure that the maximum amount of heat is

transferred between them. Make sure that the processor is clean, then squeeze a dollop of thermal paste on to it and spread evenly with a piece of card.

6 Next, place the cooler on top of the processor. To fit a Socket 478 cooler, make sure the levers are in the open position, then place the cooler on the processor and attach all four clips to the socket's notches. Apply pressure to both levers at once to lock the cooler in place. To fit a Socket 754, 939 or AM2 cooler, attach the clip on the opposite side to the lever, then attach the other clip and lower the lever to lock the cooler in place.

For Socket LGA775 heatsinks, use a flat-bladed screwdriver to turn each foot anti-clockwise away from the arrow. Put the cooler on the processor with each foot in one of the holes on the motherboard. Now press each foot down with your thumb until it clicks into place. Finally, plug the fan back into the header on the motherboard. ■

PROJECT
036

DIFFICULTY LEVEL
HARD
INTERMEDIATE
EASY

TIME REQUIRED
2
HOURS

Change your motherboard

Find out how to transform your PC and improve its upgrade potential

COMBINED WITH A processor upgrade, a new motherboard can speed up your computer enormously, allowing you to do things your system previously couldn't manage, such as video and audio editing.

Buy the right motherboard and you'll get lots of useful extras, including good surround sound, an integrated network adaptor and even built-in anti-virus and firewall capabilities. What's more, upgrading your motherboard is a great way to become a PC expert: once you've done it, you'll literally know your PC inside out.

In this step-by-step guide we'll show you how to choose the right motherboard, how to install it and how to deal with any potential problems you might encounter.

Most people combine a motherboard upgrade with a processor upgrade, because keeping your existing processor will limit the performance benefits and severely restrict your choice of motherboard. It's best to decide which processor you want first, then find a compatible motherboard that offers the features you want.

Once you've chosen a processor (see page 54), you can focus on choosing a

motherboard that has the appropriate socket. For Intel processors we'd recommend a motherboard that supports 1,333MHz FSB models. Motherboards with Intel P35 and P45 chipsets are a good choice. For AMD, a Socket AM2+ motherboard will give you the best future upgrade potential. AMD 790 and Nvidia nForce 700 chipsets are good choices.

1 Unplug your PC, then press the power switch to ensure any remaining charge is drained. Lay your PC on its side and remove the side panel. Touch a central heating radiator or cold mains tap to ground yourself.

Take the new motherboard out of its anti-static bag, lay the bag on top of the box, put the supplied sheet of foam on the bag and the motherboard on top. You should build your system outside the case first so you can make sure it works before you fit the board inside.

2 All processors have markings to indicate which way they fit into their socket. These usually include a gold triangle in one corner, which you line up with a triangle on the socket. Be careful not to fit the processor the wrong way round.

Next, smear thermal paste over the top of the processor. This ensures a good fit between the chip and the heatsink, which stops the processor overheating. An even covering is fine. The paste is toxic, so it's wise to use surgical gloves.

Once you've applied the thermal paste, gently but firmly fit the heatsink and fan. When these are in place, connect the fan on top of the heatsink to the CPU fan connector on the motherboard.

3 If you're reusing memory from your existing motherboard, remove it by pushing apart the clips at both ends of the sockets. Slot your memory modules into the new motherboard's sockets, lining up the notch on the memory with the ridge in the slot. You'll need to apply some pressure, but if you have to push hard then something's wrong.

If your motherboard has a dual-channel memory controller, make sure you install the memory modules so that each controller has a module. The sockets are usually colour-coded to help you: fill two sockets of the same colour using identical modules (two 256MB DIMMs, for instance).

SATA CONNECTORS Get a board with plenty of fast new SATA connectors to make adding extra storage easy.

IDE CONNECTORS All motherboards have IDE connectors. Make sure there are enough to plug in all your hard disks and optical drives.

MEMORY The fact that your existing memory fits your new board is no guarantee it will work. It also needs to be the correct speed for the processor.

PROCESSOR SOCKET This needs to match the processor you plan to fit. Select your processor before you choose a motherboard.

FORMAT The size of the board and the position of its screw holes will adhere to one of several standards, the most common being ATX and microATX. Your case needs to support the same standard as your motherboard.

GRAPHICS CARD SLOT You won't be able to buy a new motherboard with an AGP slot, so get a board with a PCI Express x16 slot.

POWER Most motherboards have an extra 12V connector. If yours does, make sure that your PC's power supply unit has a matching plug; not all do.

PORTS Check that the motherboard provides all the ports you need for external devices. FireWire is useful for old DV camcorders. You'll also want plenty of USB ports for peripherals.

Remove the drives from your old case and attach them to the new board with the appropriate connectors. If you have a single IDE hard disk, make sure it's connected to the primary IDE controller; if you have more than one, check the master/slave setup on the back of the hard disk. Don't force any connections.

Be careful if you're fitting a floppy drive: some drive cables have one pin-hole filled in, but your drive or motherboard connector may have a pin in this position, in which case you'll need a cable that has all its holes open. SATA drives are much easier to connect and don't require configuring as master or slave.

4 Slot in your graphics card. Remove the power supply from the case in which you'll be fitting the motherboard, and plug its connectors into your motherboard, drives and any other power sockets. Make sure you plug in the extra four-pin connector and any power your graphics card needs. Attach a keyboard and mouse, and connect a monitor to the graphics output.

Check your motherboard manual to find out which pins on the board connect to the PC's on/off switch. Very gently touch both pins (and only these) at the same time with a screwdriver. Your system should boot up.

If you need to install Windows XP or Vista to support your new motherboard, put your

Windows installation disc in the optical drive now and restart your PC. If it doesn't boot from the disc, you'll need to enter the BIOS and configure it. After running the Windows installation, reboot your PC.

Once you have installed Windows, install the drivers that came with the motherboard. This will get all the important devices working, such as the PCI bus and USB ports. You'll also need to install drivers for any other hardware you have upgraded, such as the graphics card. You should download these from the relevant website before you start.

Once your graphics card is installed, reboot your PC and resize the screen. Having done this, reboot the PC again. If everything is working, you can shut down.

5 Disconnect everything from the motherboard except the processor and memory. Your case should be almost empty apart from the old motherboard and the expansion cards. Remove anything that will get in the way of removing the motherboard from the case, including any expansion cards, drives, cables or parts of the chassis. Note exactly where each item went and how it fitted. Then remove your old motherboard and put it somewhere safe.

Screw the studs or spacers into the holes in your case that correspond with the holes in

your motherboard. The board will come with a port panel, which is a thin sheet of metal with cutouts for all the ports. Snap this into the back of the case, replacing the old one.

Next, gently place the new motherboard on top of the studs and screw it into place. Refit all the components you installed when the board was outside the case. Be very gentle and don't touch the contacts on any cards or chips. Fit your expansion cards and any other components you want, and screw your drives and PSU back into place.

6 Connect your case's power, reset and other switches according to the motherboard's manual. Add any ports that came with your motherboard but aren't integrated, such as USB, FireWire and audio ports on blanking plates. You'll need to plug these into the appropriate headers (groups of pins) on the motherboard, as well as screwing them into your case.

Reconnect your PSU, keyboard and mouse, then start the system. Windows should boot. Install the drivers for any remaining devices, then check Device Manager; there should be no yellow question marks, exclamation marks or red crosses. If there are, download the manufacturer's latest drivers. Make sure everything is firmly screwed down, then replace the side of your PC case. ■

PROJECT	DIFFICULTY LEVEL	TIME REQUIRED
037	HARD / INTERMEDIATE / EASY	2 HOURS

Change your PC's case

With a new case, you can ensure you have room for the best peripherals

YOU CAN ADD a host of wonderful things to a computer to improve its performance, but only if there's room inside the case. You may find that your existing case has no spare bays for adding disk drives, or that its design doesn't provide enough room for a large processor cooler.

There's more to choosing a new PC case than buying one you like the look of, though. Motherboards come in standard sizes and layouts, known as form factors, and you will need a case that is compatible with yours. If you have a normal desktop computer, its motherboard's form factor will be ATX or microATX. Small microATX cases have room only for microATX boards, but most larger ATX cases can hold ATX or microATX boards.

Your new case must be able to accommodate your existing drives and any that you plan to add later. Drive bays come in two sizes: 3½in bays suitable for hard disks and floppy drives, and 5¼in bays for CD and DVD drives. Some bays open out to the front of the PC. These external bays can be used for floppy or optical drives. Internal bays are suitable only for hard disks.

Make sure that your new case is at least as well ventilated as your old one, and better cooled if you plan to perform further upgrades in future. Most cases have fans that are 80mm or 120mm in diameter. Larger fans are generally quieter and more efficient. Check that there are places to mount any additional fans you need to keep powerful devices cool. See page 74 for more on cooling your PC.

1 Remove any expansion cards from the motherboard, making sure that you first remove any power or data cables plugged into them. Sound cards or modems may have audio cables connecting them to the motherboard or to an optical drive. Unscrew or unclip each card from the case and pull it vertically out of the socket. Grip the edges of the card's circuit board, not its components or connectors.

Most graphics cards are held in with an additional clip at the back of the AGP or PCI Express slot, which you must release before you remove them. Place each extracted card on a dry, dust-free surface or an anti-static mat. Unplug the 20- or 24-pin ATX

motherboard power connector and any other four-pin, eight-pin or Molex power connections attached to the motherboard.

Before removing your floppy drive's ribbon cable, note at each end the orientation of the wire marked in red. Also note the hard disks and optical drives connected to each IDE ribbon cable. Unplug any SATA data cables. Remove the SATA, Molex and floppy drive power plugs from all your drives and disks. Wobble stiff Molex plugs gently from side to side to free them – never up and down.

2 Depending on the case, all or some of the drives may be screwed into a drive bay or a removable caddy. Optical drives are often mounted on runners that slide into place from the front. These are normally released by pinching in catches on the runners.

If a disk is screwed to the drive bay, you may need to remove both sides of your case to get at all the screws. All 5¼in drives should slide out of the front of the case. Depending on the case design, the floppy drive may slide forwards or backwards.

3 Before you remove your motherboard, make a note of the remaining connections. Pay particular attention to the position and orientation of the front-panel connections. Most motherboards mark the pins for the reset and power switches, and the hard disk and power LEDs, but not always particularly clearly. The motherboard manual should contain a diagram with detailed connection information.

With the motherboard safely placed to one side, remove the board's backing plate from the back of your old case by gently pushing its corners towards the inside of the case until it pops out. If you are transferring your power supply between cases, remove the screws fixing it to the back of your case, then slide it forwards and out.

4 Use an air duster to remove the dust from your old components. Fit the motherboard backing plate into your new case, pressing it into place from the inside. Make sure it is oriented to match the ports on your motherboard. If necessary, insert the

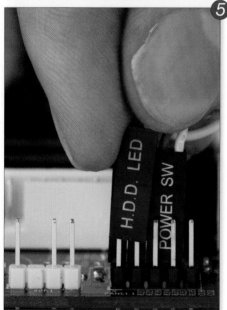

power supply and screw it into place, tucking its cables out of the way.

The inside of your new case will have many holes to which you attach the mounts for your motherboard. Put your board into the case and line up its ports with the backing plate. Use a pencil to mark the holes in your case that line up with screw holes on your motherboard, remove the board and fit a mount into each marked hole. Remove any mounts that aren't under a hole in your motherboard.

Lower your motherboard back into the case and align its ports with the backing plate. Many backing plates have springy metal tabs that rest against the side of your board's ports. Make sure that none of these is caught in the ports as you move the motherboard into place. The ports should end up flush with, or slightly inside, the backing plate, and the motherboard should also be aligned with the mounts beneath it. Don't worry if the alignment isn't exact, but make sure there is a mount under each of the board's screw holes before screwing it into place. At each mount point, fit a screw of the correct size and turn it until it is engaged in the mount point's thread.

Don't tighten any screws fully until you have fitted one to each mount point and are happy that the motherboard is seated correctly. Once it is, tighten each screw until you meet resistance, being careful not to overtighten any of them.

5 Locate free bays for your hard disk, floppy disk and optical drives, and follow the case manufacturer's instructions to fit them. Add runners to disks where necessary. Before you insert external-facing drives, you may have to remove blanking plates from the front of the case. These can usually be unscrewed or popped out, but any internal plates behind them may need to be

broken free with repeated wobbling. Once you have cleared a drive bay, slide the drive in from the front and secure it with screws or clips.

Attach the connectors for your case's front-panel buttons, status lights and speaker to your motherboard's headers. The case's header plugs may not be exactly the same as those in your old case, but they will be labelled. Be careful to connect the power and hard disk LEDs the right way round; switches work either way.

Any front-mounted FireWire ports should have a 10-pin connector labelled 1394, which fits into the corresponding header on your motherboard. USB ports have only four pins. On a modern case, two ports usually share a 10-pin connector or have a pair of four-pin plugs. Rarely, each USB port may have four individual connectors. The 10-pin plug usually has a blocked pin to ensure the correct orientation, but be sure to fit four-pin connectors the right way round.

Your manual should guide you if you need to connect front-mounted headphone and microphone sockets to the correct pin headers. If your case has many small audio connectors, observe their correct polarity.

6 Remove blanking plates from any slots you need for your graphics card, sound card or other expansion cards. Holding each card by its edges, line it up with the slot and push it into place. Connect any auxiliary power your graphics card requires and any cables you removed from other cards. Plug the motherboard power connectors in. These will fit only one way, so don't force them in.

Reconnect the floppy and hard disk data cables according to the notes you made earlier. Hard disk cables go in only one way, but align the floppy cable carefully. Plug a power cable into each drive. Most boards have headers for case fans, but if you have lots of fans you may need a Molex adaptor cable. ◼

HARDWARE

PROJECT
038

DIFFICULTY LEVEL
HARD
INTERMEDIATE
EASY

TIME REQUIRED
45
MINUTES

Spring-clean your computer

Wipe away the dirt from inside your PC and improve its cooling

THE DIRT YOU can't see inside your computer may not seem like much of a problem, but it is. Dust builds up and clogs your fans, so they're less efficient at cooling. It also acts as an insulator, so your computer will run hotter and may crash sporadically. Here we'll show you how to spring-clean your keyboard and the inside of your computer.

1 Cleaning the surface of your keyboard is quite easy; cleaning the muck from under the keys is the hard part. You need foam cleaner, a dry cloth, plastic safe wipes and a can of air duster, which is available from shops such as Maplin for around £10. Don't spray the foam cleaner directly on to the keys, as this may interfere with the switches underneath. Spray the foam on a dry cloth and then apply it to the keyboard's flat surfaces. Leave it for 15 minutes or so, then remove with the dry cloth.

It isn't possible to clean the sides of the keys or underneath them without removing them from the keyboard. Using a flat-bladed screwdriver, gently lever off each key. Some large keys may have extra springs or bits of metal attached to them, so don't lose these.

2 Use the air duster to blow the dust and dirt out of the upturned keyboard. You may want to use the plastic safe wipes to get rid of any dried-on dirt. Soak the keys for around 15 minutes in a bowl with some washing-up liquid. This should get rid of most of the muck, but rub a cloth over each one to remove any residue. Any moisture left in the keys could damage the keyboard, so leave the keys to dry before pressing each one back into position on the keyboard.

3 To clean inside your case, take off the side of your PC and remove the expansion cards from the motherboard. If your computer is particularly dirty, you may have to remove the motherboard, hard disk and optical drives, too.

Starting at the top, spray the air duster down over the motherboard, so that the dust collects in the base of the case, or into a bin if you've removed the motherboard from the case. Use a vacuum cleaner to remove the worst of the dust from the bottom of the case

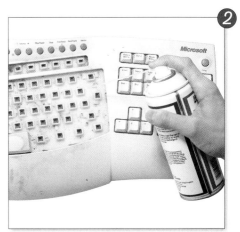

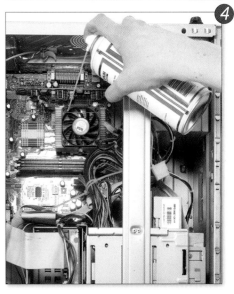

and from the processor's heatsink, fan and case fans. Next, use a plastic safe wipe to remove dust from the cables inside your case.

4 The dust on your expansion cards can also be removed with the air duster.

Make sure you've removed all the dust wedged underneath components such as capacitors, and check that the heatsink and fan on your graphics card are free from dust. Also, blow the air duster into your expansion cards' ports and sockets. ■

CLEANING THE OUTSIDE OF YOUR CASE

Cleaning the outside of the case is quite simple, but don't spray the foam directly on to the front or rear of your PC as it could get into your drives, power supply and ports. Spray the foam on a cloth and apply it to the front of the case, including the optical and floppy drives. If there are any indentations around the power button or power and hard disk LEDs, you may need a cotton bud to remove dirt.

The rear of the case will be mainly metal, but rub a foam-covered cloth over the parts of the case that wrap around the rear of your computer. Use a separate cloth to wipe the case clean after you've left the foam for 15 minutes.

Calibrate your monitor

Adjust the settings on your screen to display colours more accurately

MOST MONITORS LEAVE the factory with high brightness and contrast settings, and a brilliant blue-white tone. However, this setup doesn't reproduce colours accurately, so colours in a printout may not be the same hue as the colours you see onscreen. To correct this, you need to calibrate your monitor.

To check how images look on your screen, you can use a monitor test program, such as the free Monitors Matter CheckScreen application from *http://tinyurl.com/monitorsmatter*. Once you've installed the software, click on the CRT monitor or LCD display tab, depending on the type of monitor you use, and then on the Colour button. For the best results, perform the test in a dimly lit room.

The test cycles through the standard Windows colours when you click the mouse. Look at each colour and check that it looks okay. Pay particular attention to the black and white tests. If your monitor is not set up correctly, blacks and whites will both appear grey, and your screen will need calibrating.

1 Windows Vista has colour calibration built in, but if you use XP and have Photoshop Elements or another Adobe product installed on your computer, you can calibrate your monitor for free using Adobe Gamma. You'll find this in either the Control Panel or on the Start menu.

Start with the Wizard mode. In the first step, choose a new profile name. Then set the monitor contrast to maximum and reduce the brightness so that the central dark-grey square in the window is just visible.

2 Ignore the next step prompting you to identify your monitor's phosphors. However, the gamma correction step is important. If the View Single Gamma Only box is ticked, you'll see a single square with a slider. Move the slider to make the brightness of the centre box the same as the striped surround. You'll find it helps if you squint. However, it's better to untick the box, so you can adjust the red, green and blue gammas individually.

3 In the next step, you're asked to pick a hardware white point. You can choose a value from the drop-down menu. Alternatively, click the Measure button to judge the white point manually. You should train your eye to recognise the colour shifts. Keep your eye on the centre square and click repeatedly on the left-hand square. The centre square will get more and more blue until the left-hand square disappears. Click repeatedly on the right-hand square until it disappears, and the centre square will get warmer.

Once you've trained your eye using this method, use the left and right-hand squares to adjust the middle square until it is a neutral grey, neither too warm nor too blue. To set this as your white point, click the middle square. To cancel the whole procedure, press Escape.

4 Go to the final screen. This has Before and After buttons, so you can see what difference the calibration process has made. Usually, you can expect to see the screen go a little darker and less blue. ■

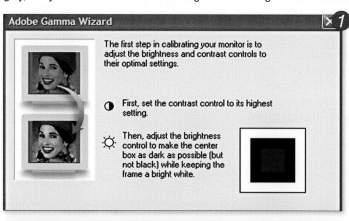

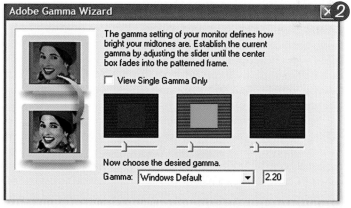

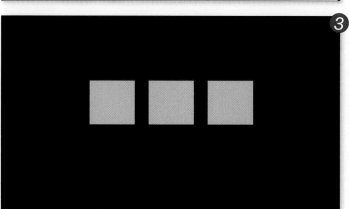

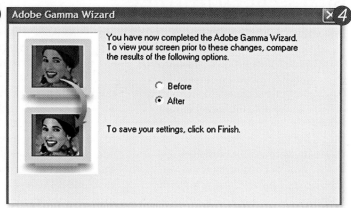

HARDWARE

PROJECT
040

DIFFICULTY LEVEL
HARD
INTERMEDIATE
EASY

TIME REQUIRED
30
MINUTES

Set up a dual-screen system

Make more room for your applications by setting up an extra display

IF YOU'VE UPGRADED your PC recently, you may have an old monitor lying around that isn't worth selling. Alternatively, you may find that you're constantly running out of space on your desktop and need more room for your applications. Setting up an extra monitor on your computer is easier than it sounds and in most cases won't cost a lot, either.

If you have an old monitor, the chances are it uses a VGA (DE15HD D-sub) connector rather than the newer DVI standard. This being the case, you may need to buy a small VGA-to-DVI adaptor. If you don't already have an old monitor and need to buy a second one, or you're thinking of upgrading your current monitor and want to set up the old one as a secondary display, you may find it uses an HDMI connector. Again, there are adaptors to convert from HDMI to DVI, although some new graphics cards will also support HDMI.

The second consideration is your graphics card. Older graphics cards and PCs with integrated graphics may have only a single VGA output. The simplest solution in this case is to buy a new graphics card with two outputs. This way, you will avoid any possible driver conflicts associated with having two graphics systems, and also save space in your PC. A graphics card capable of handling two displays will cost as little as £15. See page 52 for the project on upgrading your graphics card.

You'll need to check what connector your PC uses for graphics cards. Computers that are over 10 years old will support only PCI cards, but luckily these are still available. A decent PCI card that supports two monitors

will cost at least £30. Computers over five years old will probably have an AGP slot but, again, AGP cards are still widely available, and cheaper than PCI cards. The current standard is PCI Express (PCI-E), and a dual monitor card will cost as little as £15.

Once you've bought your new card, don't start installing it without removing your old video drivers and utilities. This can be a bit tricky, so check the website of your current card's manufacturer for instructions. If you own a PC with an integrated graphics chip, you may need to reboot and then go into your BIOS setup to disable the internal graphics.

To install your new card, follow the manufacturer's instructions carefully. This will involve delving into your PC's case, so make sure you follow safety guidelines with regards to static discharge. With the new card installed, you should be able to plug in both your monitors, using adaptors if necessary. When you restart your PC, the new monitor will be detected. To get the best out of your monitors, it's best to find specific drivers from the manufacturer's website, rather than use Windows' default Plug and Play monitor driver.

To tweak the way your desktop is displayed across the two screens, go into Windows Control Panel and open Display properties (Windows XP) or Personalisation (Windows Vista). Choose the option to extend your Windows desktop across both displays. Your graphics card manufacturer will provide Control Panel software that may offer extra features, such as the ability to display the taskbar on both monitors. ■

Older monitors may need a VGA-to-DVI adaptor to connect to a new graphics card

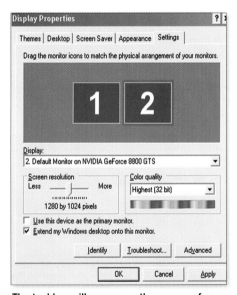

The taskbar will appear on the screen of your primary monitor

Windows Vista should detect your new display automatically. If it doesn't, the options can be found in the Control Panel

DUAL-SCREEN UTILITIES

Driver Sweeper
www.guru3d.com/category/driversweeper
This little utility hunts down and erases all traces of old driver software on your PC. Make sure you choose the right options, or you might delete the wrong drivers.

DisplayFusion
www.binaryfortress.com/displayfusion
The free version of this utility lets you choose a separate wallpaper for each

of your monitors. It will even let you set wallpapers to cycle on a timer, and download them from *www.flickr.com*.

UltraMon
www.realtimesoft.com/ultramon
This simple utility allows you to extend your taskbar across both screens, among other things. You can also choose to show in each screen's taskbar only those applications running on that screen.

TIME REQUIRED   DIFFICULTY LEVEL   PROJECT   **HARDWARE**

1 HOUR

HARD
INTERMEDIATE
EASY

041

Upgrade your optical drive

Burn your own movies by fitting a DVD writer to your PC

IF YOU'RE INTERESTED in movie making, a DVD writer is an essential upgrade. You'll be able to burn your productions to DVD, so that you can watch your work on either a set-top DVD player or your PC.

With the latest dual-layer writers, you can even create feature-length discs without compromising video quality. A DVD writer is also ideal for backing up files. The latest drives are quick, filling a disc in under six minutes, and with 4.7GB or 8.5GB capacities available, you'll be able to burn huge amounts of data to a single disc.

Blu-ray has won the format war, so there's no point buying a standalone HD DVD writer. However, if you want to watch movies, a combination HD DVD/Blu-ray drive is a good choice, as HD DVD movies are so cheap. To get smooth playback, you'll need a modern ATI or Nvidia graphics card.

The software bundled with DVD writers varies widely. Windows XP can write to CD-R, CD-RW and DVD-RAM without any help, but to write to any other media, you'll need disc-burning software. Vista provides full DVD support, too. Some original equipment manufacturer (OEM) drives, designed for PC system builders, are sold without any software, while some retail packages include full software suites worth almost as much as the drive itself.

1 First, open the drive tray and unclip the front panel from the tray. Use a flathead screwdriver to push the clips that hold the rest of the front fascia, and slide it off. Clip the two parts of the fascia you want into place, in reverse order, and shut the tray.

Take both side panels off your computer; they're usually held in place by screws at the back. If you're replacing an old drive, unscrew it on each side, remove its power and data cables and slide it out. If you're using an empty slot, first remove the blanking plate.

2 Each IDE channel on the motherboard can be cabled to two drives, but you need to set one as master and the other as slave. This is done using jumpers – clips that slide on to pins found on the back of all IDE devices. It's easiest to do this before you slide the drive in, as it will have a guide to its jumper settings printed on top. Try to keep your primary IDE channel for your hard disk(s), and make sure a hard disk isn't sharing a channel with an optical drive. For HD optical drives, you'll need a spare SATA port. Connect an IDE cable with three ports if you're connecting two optical drives to one IDE channel: one for each drive, and one to connect to the motherboard.

3 Find a spare power plug from your PC's internal power supply and untie cables so that it reaches the drive, then push in firmly. Your optical drive probably has audio output sockets; you can ignore these, but connecting an audio output to the CD audio input on your sound card or motherboard means you'll be able to play the few music CDs that have copy protection.

Use the screws provided with your drive to fix it into the case. Replace the panels and start your PC. You should see your drive listed on the POST screen that appears first, and in Windows it should appear in My Computer. You don't need any drivers. Finally, insert the CD that came with your drive and follow the instructions to install the software. ■

UNDERSTANDING DVD FORMATS

There are currently seven writable DVD formats in use. Fortunately, modern drives support most of the available kinds of DVD media. They all support the write-once DVD+R and DVD-R formats and their rewritable DVD+RW and DVD-RW counterparts. A more recent development is dual-layer media. Two-layer writable discs are available in two variants – DVD+R DL and DVD-R DL – and can hold 8.5GB of data, which is nearly twice as much as the 4.7GB of the original formats.

The final DVD format is DVD-RAM. This is rarely used, though, so we'd recommend that you avoid this format unless you specifically need it.

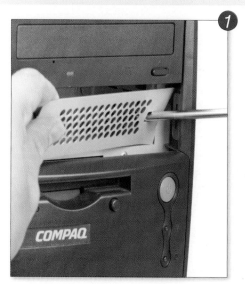

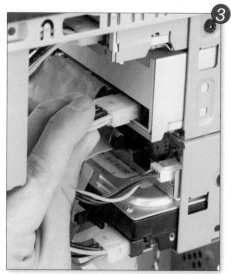

HARD
INTERMEDIATE
EASY

15 MINUTES

Mount an external hard disk

Boost your storage space with an external drive

PERMANENTLY MOUNTING AN external drive isn't too difficult, but a little know-how will help you to understand the many benefits of performing the task. Here we'll explain how to do it.

1 Getting a PC to recognise an external drive is as straightforward as booting up your PC and connecting the USB, eSATA or FireWire cable to one of the ports on your system. This works well for the simple copying of data to and from the drive, and allows you to unplug the drive and use it elsewhere.

However, if you want to create a permanent directory and give the external drive a more lasting presence while still allowing it to be portable, a little modification of Windows' Disk Management is necessary.

To access Disk Management, you need to right-click on the My Computer icon on the desktop and select Manage. This opens up Windows' Computer Management (in Vista, just type 'Computer Management' in the search bar from the Start menu).

Once open, select Disk Management – the penultimate option in the list in the right-hand pane – and a list of drives will show up on the right.

2 We currently have three drives attached to the system: one internal (C:), a flash drive (F:) and our external drive (E:). The internal drive is the only permanent drive here, but you could use the E: drive for all your backups, internet downloads or even files that you want available on any PC you work on, for example. This not only saves remembering that the drive is E: at home and drive F: at work, it also allows you to tell your browser or backup software to download or work to a set directory.

To make that directory, right-click on the E: drive and select Change drive letter and path. Next, click Add and select the option called 'Mount in the following empty NTFS folder', then choose Browse. Open the C: drive and choose New Folder, then rename the external drive. Here we've chosen to call it External Drive Downloads.

3 You now have a permanent path and mounting place for the external hard disk. You can check that the drive is listed correctly by opening the C: drive in My Computer and making sure that it's listed there. Now, whenever your external drive is connected, you can use its permanent directory as a place to store files or configure it as the default location for backups.

When you've finished, you can disconnect the drive and set it up and use it in the same way on another system. ■

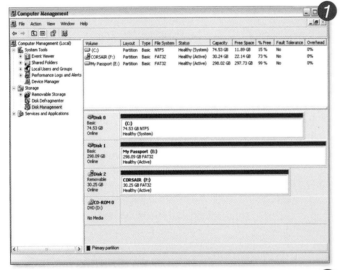

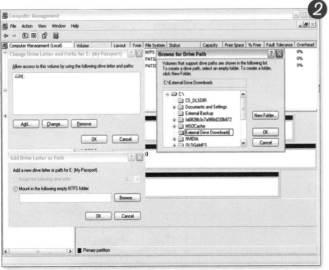

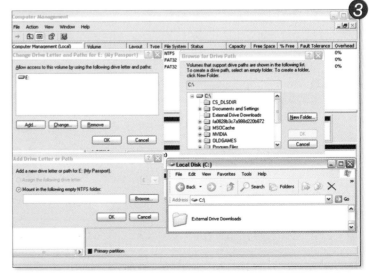

Transfer a hard disk to a new computer

Boost your storage space and increase security by reusing your old drive

WHEN YOU BUY a new PC to replace your ageing relic, you'll probably want to transfer all your documents, music, photos and videos from the old system to the new one. However, there are several advantages to transferring the physical drive itself.

First of all, you gain extra storage space, especially if you delete all the unnecessary files such as the operating system and contents of the Program Files folder (which is where all your old applications were stored). There's also the benefit that all your precious files are immediately available, and there's no need to use Windows' Files and Settings Transfer Wizard, which could take hours.

Furthermore, there's the security that comes from having two hard disks. You can use a simple file synchronisation utility such as Microsoft's free SyncToy (available to download from *http://tinyurl.com/mssynctoy2*) to mirror the contents of two folders, allowing you to have identical copies of your My Documents folder on both disks. If one disk fails, you've always got an up-to-date backup of your files on the other.

You need to bear in mind that you may invalidate the warranty of your new PC when you open the case, so check with the manufacturer before proceeding.

1 Remove the side panel or entire case from your old PC. Usually there will be two or three cross-head screws holding it in place. Locate the hard disk, which is usually mounted at the front of the case. Remove the power cable with a firm tug, but leave the data cable attached as you'll need it. Simply detach the other end of the data cable from the motherboard.

Identify how the disk is secured to the case – usually there will be two screws on each side, but there could be a quick-release mechanism that allows the drive to slide forwards or backwards. Once the disk is out, remove any tray or side runners from a quick-release system.

2 Take the side panel off your new PC and locate a free hard disk bay at the front of the case. Unless there's a quick-release mechanism, use the screws from the old PC to secure the disk into the bay.

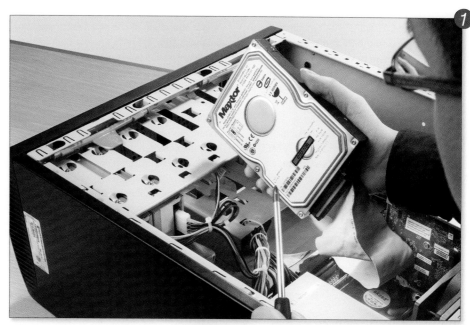

Position the data cable so it's out of the way and doesn't obstruct airflow inside the case. Assuming that the disk isn't the newer SATA type, find a free EIDE connector on the PC's motherboard and plug in the disk's data cable. If it's a SATA disk, find a free SATA port and plug the cable into that.

Locate a spare power connector on the PC's power supply and, if necessary, cut any cable ties that prevent it reaching the hard disk's power socket, and then plug it in.

3 Boot up your PC and check that the disk is correctly detected by watching the information that appears onscreen (you may have to press Tab to remove a full-screen logo). If it isn't listed, reboot the PC and press Delete, F1 or F2 to enter the BIOS. In the first menu, usually labelled Standard Features or similar, check each EIDE or SATA port to make sure it's enabled. Reboot again, and the disk should be detected.

Once Windows has loaded, click on My Computer, and your disk should be visible next to the existing disk or disks. ■

HARDWARE

PROJECT
044

DIFFICULTY LEVEL
HARD
INTERMEDIATE
EASY

TIME REQUIRED
1
HOUR

Upgrade your laptop's hard disk

Prolong the life of your laptop by boosting its storage space

ALTHOUGH LAPTOPS ARE much harder to upgrade than desktop PCs, there's still plenty you can do to them to keep them up to date. Most laptops have easy-access panels that let you upgrade and change the memory and hard disk. Here we'll show you how.

Laptop hard disks tend to have considerably smaller capacities than their desktop PC counterparts. However, a hard disk upgrade is a cost-effective way of prolonging your laptop's life.

Upgrading the hard disk also provides you with a golden opportunity to update your

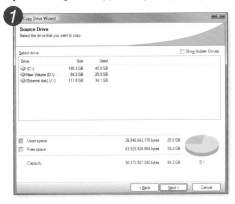

operating system or create a fresh installation, but make sure you back up your documents and files first. If you're creating a new installation, make sure you have your laptop's restore disc or Windows CD, or buy a new operating system. If you're planning to use a restore CD, check with your laptop's manufacturer that it doesn't rely on information stored on your original hard disk.

If you want to keep your existing operating system, use a disk-imaging program such as Norton Ghost – which we've used here – to clone your entire hard disk to the new drive. To do this, you'll need an external 2½in disk enclosure, or caddy. These cost around £15 and are available for both IDE and SATA laptop drives, so make sure you get one that fits your computer. You'll also need a spare USB port on your laptop to plug it in.

1 Run Norton Ghost 14 and select the Copy My Hard Drive option from the Tools menu. Click Next on the first Copy Drive Wizard window, then select your current disk on the Source Drive page and click Next again. In the Select Destination list, choose

your new hard disk and click Next. In the Options screen that appears, select the 'Resize drive to fill unallocated space' and 'Set drive active' options. Click Next and then click Finish to begin the operation. This may take several hours.

2 Most laptops have removable panels underneath that provide easy access to the hard disk. You can usually remove these by undoing a few screws and unclipping them from the main case. Read your laptop's manual to see if it tells you how to access the hard disk.

In most caddies, the drive is held in place by four screws. Others clip together to form a box, and it may not be obvious how to open them. Check for screws first, then look for a place at either end to insert the blade of a blunt knife or screwdriver and gently work the caddy open, as shown. You'll need to re-use the caddy, so be careful not to damage it.

The old disk should now be free. Remove your new disk from the external enclosure if you used one, and fit it into your laptop's drive caddy, remembering to transfer any adaptor. Carefully replace the caddy in your laptop.

3 If you cloned your old disk, your computer should now boot from the new drive as before. If everything works, you can fit your old hard disk in your external drive enclosure, format it and use it as a spare portable drive.

If you're creating a brand new installation, you need to prepare your new disk by booting from your manufacturer's restore CD or installing an operating system. Once your new installation is up and running, restore any data you need from your old hard disk. ■

Upgrade your laptop's memory

Adding extra memory can make your laptop faster and more responsive

AS SPACE IS limited inside laptops, many of the components they use are physically smaller than those found in desktop PCs. This includes memory modules: whereas desktop computers contain DIMM modules, notebooks use the far more compact SODIMMs.

There are three main types of memory, but they're not compatible, so it's essential that you understand which type your computer uses before you buy. Laptops built in 2002 or earlier are likely to use SDRAM memory running at 66MHz, 100MHz or 133MHz. Most recent laptops, and a few systems that date back to 2002, use DDR memory. Such laptops require either PC2100 or PC2700 DDR memory, although some particularly powerful laptops may use faster PC3200 modules. Finally, Intel-based laptops built after 2004 may use DDR2 memory, available in PC2-3200, PC2-4200, PC2-5300 or PC2-6400 speeds. Only very recent AMD-based notebooks with Turion 64 X2 processors use DDR2 memory.

To be absolutely sure you buy the correct type of memory for your laptop, we recommend that you use the configuration tools available on the websites of memory manufacturers, such as *www.crucial.com*.

1 Switch off your laptop and disconnect the power adaptor. Then turn it upside down, laying it on a soft surface to avoid scratching the lid. If your laptop's memory slots are on its underside, locate the panel that covers them. This is sometimes labelled with text or a memory icon, but it's often unmarked. Remove the screws that hold the panel in place and pull it open.

If your laptop's memory is installed under the keyboard, you'll need to remove this first. If you have the manual, check it for instructions on how to do this without damaging your laptop. Otherwise, you'll have to work out how your keyboard is secured. First look for any screws that are fixing the keyboard to the computer's base. These may be covered with a trim panel that simply clips into position. Once you have removed any necessary trim panel, extract any screws that hold the keyboard in place.

Often the keyboard is also held down by catches or lugs along its base and perhaps its

sides. You need to prise these open before you can lift the keyboard away. The keyboard's fragile ribbon cable will remain connected to your laptop. Take care not to twist, stretch or tear this as you lay the keyboard down on the wrist rest. In many laptops, the memory slots are covered by an additional plastic or metal sheet, which you need to lift out of the way.

If you're replacing one or more memory modules that are already fitted in your computer, release them one at a time by pressing outwards on the catches at either end of the memory slot. Each SODIMM should spring up, enabling you to grip it by the edges and pull it away from the slot.

2 With the memory slots exposed, open the anti-static packaging of the first memory module. Note the position of the module's notch so that you can align it correctly with the ridge in the memory slot. If you're fitting two modules and your slots are stacked on top of each other, fill the bottom slot first. Place the module's connecting edge into the memory slot as shown, checking that the notch is aligned correctly. Without using force, make sure the SODIMM's connecting edge is located snugly before pushing on the opposite edge. The module should pivot until it lies parallel with the slot and the catches engage.

3 Once you have installed the first memory module, use the same method to add any others. Check that the catches have engaged properly in every memory slot you have filled and refit any internal covers you removed. If you're working on the base of your laptop, replace the external panel by engaging any lugs. Press around the panel's edges to make sure any clips are in place and replace any screws.

If you removed your keyboard, take care not to twist or trap its ribbon cable as you replace it. Engage any lugs or catches as you lower the keyboard into place. Replace any screws and trim panels you had to remove to gain access.

Lock the battery in place before plugging in the AC adaptor and turning on your laptop. Enter the BIOS utility and check that it shows the correct amount of memory. ▬

Enhance your laptop's capabilities

Give your laptop a boost by adding extra storage, a sound card or a TV tuner

IT'S EASIER TO upgrade your laptop than you might think. You can easily add extra storage or a DVD writer, improve audio quality or even boost performance without getting out a screwdriver and poking around inside the computer. Thanks to the ubiquity of USB peripherals, you can simply plug in an external hard disk or sound card.

STORAGE OPTIONS

If you're running out of space on your hard disk, or you want to back up precious files, the easiest upgrade is a portable USB hard disk. Iomega's 250GB eGo, which costs around £60 including VAT, even includes the necessary software to automate your backups. Most portable disks take power from the USB cable, so there's no need to plug in a separate power supply.

If you need more than 500GB, you'll have to buy a physically larger external disk, which will need plugging into the mains. These disks tend to be better value, though; you can buy Western Digital's 1TB MyBook II for under

£100. Desktop drives are usually a little faster than portable versions, especially when you're copying files to them.

For those who don't need this much storage, a USB flash drive is a useful extra. Capacities range from 512MB to 64GB, but an 8GB or 16GB drive is the best value at around £15 and £30 respectively. Flash drives are generally slower than hard disks, but if your laptop runs Windows Vista you should look for a flash drive that supports ReadyBoost. When you plug it in, Vista will ask if you want to enable this feature, which speeds up the laptop by using the free space on the drive as an extension of the laptop's main memory. The performance increase may be small, but it's worth having.

A slimline USB DVD writer such as LG's GSA-E50L, which costs around £50 including VAT, allows you to burn all sorts of data as well as video DVDs. If your laptop doesn't already have a DVD-ROM drive, this will give you the additional benefit of being able to watch DVD movies. DVD writers usually come with all the software you need. As with hard disks, there are also desktop versions available, which require mains power; these cost around the same as portable models.

SOUND INVESTMENTS

The sound cards in laptops are often basic. However, it's easy and affordable to upgrade

your sound card. Asus's Xonar U1 Audio Station, which costs around £50 including VAT, is a USB peripheral that will give a noticeable improvement in sound quality, and it doubles as a handy volume control.

The speakers in most laptops are also low quality and may not be loud enough for your needs. A decent portable set such as Creative's TravelSound 250 will set you back only around £30, and will be at least twice as loud as your laptop's speakers.

SHOW STOPPERS

Another useful laptop upgrade is a USB TV tuner. As well as enabling you to watch digital Freeview channels on your laptop, the tuner's software will take advantage of your laptop's hard disk to let you pause and rewind live TV as well as record programmes. Dual-tuner models, such as MSI's Digivox Duo (around £30 including VAT), allow you to record two programmes at once or watch one programme while recording another. See page 86 for our project on watching TV on your PC. ■

Iomega's eGo portable hard disk and Corsair's Flash Voyager flash drive provide useful storage boosts for a laptop

Asus's Xonar U1 Audio Station is a USB peripheral that can greatly enhance sound quality, and it doubles as a volume control

MSI's Digivox Duo dual-tuner will let you record two programmes at once or watch one show while recording another

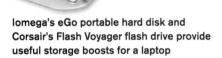

Link your games console to your PC

Connect your PC to your games console to play back media files

IF YOU HAVE a Windows XP PC or are running any version of Vista without Media Center, such as Vista Basic, you can use Windows Media Player 11 to share music, photos and videos with your Xbox 360 or PlayStation 3 (PS3).

If your computer is running Vista Home Premium or Ultimate, you can use the Xbox 360 as an extender for Windows Media Center, thereby giving you all the features of Media Center on your Xbox.

Both games consoles will need to be connected to the same network as your computer for this to work. An 802.11g wireless network is fine for sharing music, but for video or for using a Media Center Extender, you'll need a wired network.

1 Firstly, download and install Windows Media Player 11 from *www.microsoft. com*. Run Media Player, click on the Library button and select Media Sharing from the menu. In the window that appears, tick the Share my Media box and click OK. There will be a pause, and then your console will appear in the box below (the PS3 may be shown as an Unknown Device). Select your console and click Allow, then click OK.

The Windows firewall will be configured to allow media sharing. If you have a third-party firewall such as Norton or ZoneAlarm installed, you may need to configure it manually to allow media sharing. Leave Media Player 11 running.

2 For an Xbox 360, go to the media tab in the dashboard. There are buttons for music, pictures and videos, so select the type of media you want to share from your computer. The browser will default to your

console's hard disk, so press the X button to change source. Your PC should appear in the list. If it doesn't, check the firewall on your computer. Select your PC, and you'll be shown a list of folders containing its media files. Select a file to play and then use your gamepad to control playback. The Xbox 360 can only play files that it supports; we recommend encoding audio to WMA or MP3 format, and your videos to WMV or DivX.

On the PS3, go into the Settings menu, then into Network Settings and enable the Media Server Connection. Next, go to Music, Video or Photo and select Search for a Media Server. The PS3 will find your computer and display a Windows icon with your shared folders next to it, which you can browse for files. Sony's console can play most popular audio and video file types – check the online manual at *http://tinyurl.com/ps3manual* for more details.

3 For a flashier and more powerful interface, you can use your Xbox 360 as an Extender for Vista Media Center, as long as your PC is running Vista Home Premium or Ultimate. Make sure your Xbox 360 and PC are on the same network. Turn on your Xbox. On the computer, an icon will appear in the taskbar saying that a Media Center Extender has been found on your network. Click on the icon and answer Yes to the question about setting up your extender, and follow the steps. You may have to disable or configure any third-party firewall software.

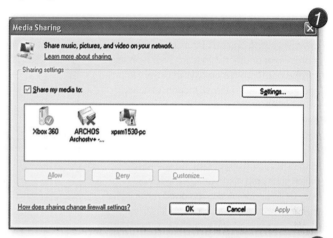

Once you've finished, go to Media in the Xbox's dashboard and click Media Center. You'll now see an interface just like Media Center on your PC. It can still only play files compatible with your Xbox, though, so make sure they're in the right format. ■

TVersity can transcode media files to a format compatible with your games console

TRANSCODING YOUR MEDIA

The biggest problem with sharing media with your games console is that it can only play certain types of audio and video files. Unlike with a PC, you can't install extra software on a console to expand its capabilities. One way around this is to use a transcoding media server on your computer. This will detect the type of console you have and convert your files on the fly to a compatible format.

A good free example is TVersity, from *http://tversity.com*. It can be a bit fiddly to set up, though, so have a look at the support forums before you begin.

PROJECT	DIFFICULTY LEVEL	TIME REQUIRED
048	HARD / INTERMEDIATE / EASY	2 HOURS

Overclock your processor

Increase the speed of your PC without having to spend a penny

OVERCLOCKING IS THE process of manually taking control of the speed at which a processor or other chip (such as a graphics card) runs. There are no physical levers to pull and no switches to throw, though. Instead, overclocking involves tweaking settings in the motherboard's BIOS, which is the basic software that specifies the settings for your PC's core components. By changing settings in the BIOS and increasing the speed at which your processor runs, you will increase your PC's performance. The good news is that this won't cost you a thing.

Before we go any further, we should issue a warning. Following the steps in this tutorial will force your processor to run faster than its manufacturer has specified. This means increased heat and greater wear and tear on the processor, and it may invalidate your warranty. That said, as long as you're not increasing the voltage levels to crazy heights and you monitor the temperatures carefully, basic overclocking need not be considered a dangerous activity.

The results of overclocking will vary depending on several factors. Because the process is exploiting the way that processors are manufactured (see the box below), it stands to reason that different chips will overclock to different levels.

BE PREPARED

First you should do a little research into the way your PC currently runs. This is easy, but you'll need to download two free applications: Core Temp (*www.alcpu.com/CoreTemp*) and Prime95 (*www.mersenne.org*).

Core Temp will tell you the name and model number of your processor, and the temperature at which it's running. If you're not using any other applications, this temperature is known as the idle temperature. More important is the load temperature, which is the temperature you get when the processor is

working. When overclocking, you need to make sure the load temperature doesn't get too high or else the PC could crash or corrupt data, or at the very least suffer excessive wear and tear over time.

To test the processor's temperature under load, run Core Temp and then Prime95.

HOW IS OVERCLOCKING POSSIBLE?

Overclocking takes advantage of the fact that the speed of a computer is not the fixed value that Intel, AMD and other technology firms would have you believe – far from it. These companies offer customers a choice of chips specified to run at various speeds, and they cost more according to the speed at which they run.

This is for both practical and business reasons. The practical reason is that, due to the complex way in which

processors are manufactured and the wide range of heat, power and other technical considerations, fewer processors run successfully at very quick speeds. This scarcity accounts for their higher price. Commercially, of course, companies also need to offer customers products at a range of prices.

Over time, it may be that factories perfect the manufacturing process, or the design proves more robust than the

engineers predicted. However, the companies will have committed to offering a full range, so need to stick to it. This means processors that can actually run quicker may end up being badged as slower chips simply in order to satisfy market demand.

Overclockers can use this to their advantage, especially if they're willing to ignore official power and heat guidelines in their pursuit of free speed.

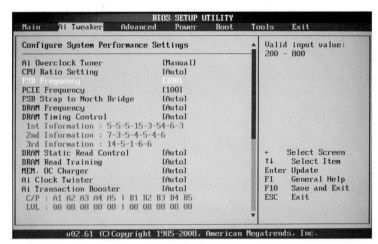

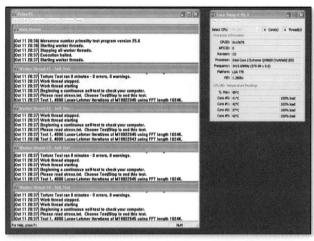

The BIOS looks intimidating, but you don't need to know what everything does – just head straight to the FSB

Prime95 was developed to research prime numbers, but as it's so demanding on a processor, it's ideal for stress testing

Click Just Stress Testing and choose the 'Large, in place FFTs' test, which is the most demanding test for a processor. Then click Advanced, Round off Checking to make sure that Prime95 will halt if it detects an error in its workings; this is the signal that your overclocking is unsustainable. While the test is running, watch how the temperature of the processor rises as it has to work, and make a note of where it peaks. This will give you an idea of how well your PC copes with heat; if the temperature rises dramatically at stock settings, overclocking will be more difficult than if the temperature rises only a little.

GETTING UP TO SPEED
A processor's speed is determined by two factors: the speed of the main system bus – this is the frontside bus (FSB) in Intel systems and the HyperTransport bus (HTT) in AMD systems – and the chip's own clock multiplier. An Intel Core 2 Quad Q6600 runs at 2.4GHz, and uses an FSB of 1,066MHz. This is then divided by four because it's 'quad-pumped' when running; it's actual speed is a quarter of that value, namely 266MHz. This particular processor has a clock multiplier of 9, so its speed is 2.394GHz (266 x 9 = 2394).

A processor's clock multiplier is usually locked on all but the most expensive processors, so when overclocking you'll need to alter the FSB or HTT. For this project, we're going to use an Intel system, but the steps are similar for an AMD PC.

The FSB is controlled by the BIOS. To access the BIOS, you need to press a key (usually Delete) as soon as your computer is switched on. You may need to press this key several times in order for the PC to recognise the input. The BIOS doesn't look very friendly when compared to modern Windows applications; there's no mouse support, and usually only two or three colours. However, don't let this put you off. It's easier than you might think to find the options you need.

CONTROL EXPERIMENT
Once you're in the BIOS, you'll need to find the overclocking controls. This will depend on the type of motherboard your PC has. If your PC is from a big-name manufacturer such as Dell or Sony then it will probably have a minimum of options. However, if your PC uses a high-end motherboard from a large Taiwanese firm such as Asus, Gigabyte or MSI then the chances are it will have plenty of options.

The BIOS usually has multiple 'pages', which you can move between using the left and right arrow keys. Look for a page with an FSB value on it, as this is where the overclocking options can be found. The FSB will probably be set to Auto or to a speed such as 266MHz. It may appear greyed out, but you should be able to use the arrow keys to move the cursor to it and change the option to manual. If you're lucky, you may also see controls for adjusting voltages and memory speed (although some motherboards put these on separate pages). We'll cover these options in our second project on overclocking, which you'll find overleaf.

Once you've found the page with the FSB control, you can start overclocking. A chip such as the Q6600 has a 266MHz FSB as standard and is known to be an excellent overclocker, so 290MHz is a good first step. It's only 24MHz faster than the default, but because the chip has a high multiplier it will add over 200MHz to the processor speed (290 x 9 = 2610, or 2.61GHz). Once you've typed in the value, you'll need to save your settings and then exit, either by going to the right-hand page in the BIOS or, more commonly, by pressing F10.

The PC will now reboot, and one of three things will happen. First, it may not turn on at all, which means that your overclocking experiment has failed. If this is the case, you'll need to reset the BIOS to its default values; this is called 'clearing the CMOS'. If you need

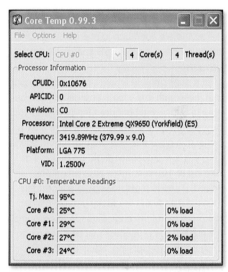

Core Temp is an excellent free application for monitoring your processor's temperature

to do this, check your motherboard's manual for the exact procedure. Usually, it involves turning off the PC and removing the motherboard's battery.

The second thing that might happen is that the PC begins to boot, but freezes during loading or when in Windows. If this is the case, you've overclocked too far and you need to go into the BIOS for more tweaks. Finally, the PC may load Windows as normal, in which case your overclocking has been successful.

CHECKING FOR HEAT
In Windows, you can load Core Temp to check the processor temperature and make sure that the BIOS has applied your settings. If everything looks good, load up Prime95 and run the test to see if the PC is stable. Ideally, you should run the test several times in a row. If the PC behaves as normal, you've just boosted your PC's performance for free.

If it doesn't, you can either return to the BIOS and reset it to the default speeds, or take a look at our advanced overclocking project on the following page. ■

Advanced overclocking

Find out how to wring every last megahertz of speed from your processor

OVERCLOCKING IS QUITE simple, as we saw on page 70. A processor's clock speed is determined by two numbers: its clock multiplier and the speed of the main system bus. The clock multiplier can only be revised downward in most processors – only Intel's expensive Extreme or AMD's Black Edition processors enable you to increase it – so there's not much to overclocking beyond increasing the FSB speed. Modern processors, particularly those made by Intel, offer a considerable amount of headroom such that, even with this simple approach, you'll be able to add several hundred megahertz to your processor easily. It's only when you're after a boost of a gigahertz or more that it gets tricky.

While a processor might be capable of running at 1GHz or more above its stock speed, it needs more voltage to support this. Think of it as fuel – the faster you drive a car, the more petrol the engine needs to consume. It's not just the processor that requires more juice when overclocking. Raising the FSB so far from its stock speed means that it also needs voltage to drive it. The FSB system comprises multiple components, as it links the Northbridge and the memory, so these will need more power, too.

WARNING SIGNS

With more power come several dangers. The first is heat. The higher the voltage, the more waste heat the computer produces, and this will need to be safely dissipated. Second, the

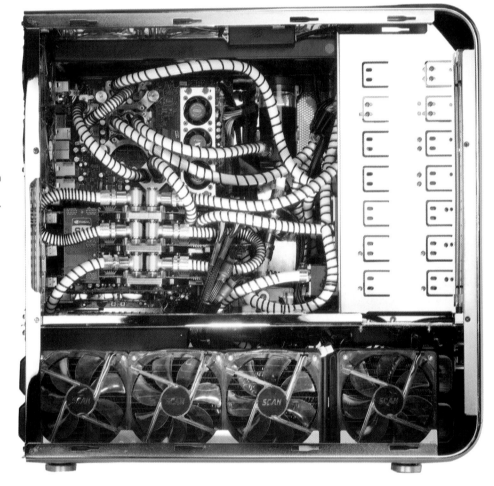

One of the keys to successful overclocking is better cooling, so invest in a new processor cooler if you're after really big speed boosts

components will all have a limit to the amount of voltage they can cope with; go over this limit, and the system will become unstable. The worst-case scenario with extra voltage is that you can permanently damage your components. That said, if you take sensible precautions, gradually increasing speed and voltage, you should find the system's natural limit well before smoke and sparks set in.

Since the key to successful overclocking is higher voltage and better cooling, you'll need to be discerning about your components if you're after really big speed increases. Go into the BIOS of your motherboard and see what sort of voltage controls it has. Ideally, you'll want to be able to overvolt the processor (sometimes called vcore), the memory (vdimm), the FSB and the Northbridge. If you can also increase the voltage to the Southbridge and other components, so much the better. If your

motherboard doesn't have this range of controls, consider investing in a decent overclocking board from a company such as Asus, Gigabyte or Foxconn. It may seem counter-productive to spend money to overclock, given that the point of overclocking is free speed, but you'll pay less of a premium for an overclockers' motherboard than you will for a top-of-the-line processor.

After you've established the voltage controls, you should consider investing in a new processor cooler. In the previous project, we explained how temperatures can rise quickly when a PC is running overclocked. However, it's extra voltage that can really turn up the heat. A decent heat sink fan such as the Arctic Cooling Freezer 7 Pro costs less than £15 and is simple to fit, yet will cope with an overvolted processor far better than the reference Intel heat sink fan. See the

Memory speeds can become a real issue when overclocking

Before overvolting your processor, check to make sure what voltage it currently uses

'Extreme Cooling' box below for more details on cooling.

CORE VALUES

Once you're happy with your hardware, it's a good idea to check how far you can overclock your system without extra voltage, following the steps on the previous page. For this project, we'll be using an Intel Core 2 Quad Q6600, which is one of the best overclocking processors ever made. In our test system, it successfully benchmarked at 2.7GHz with an FSB of 300MHz, with no extra voltage required. However, when we tried to push this to 330MHz (with a processor speed 2.97GHz) the PC froze when loading Windows. The obvious solution was to head back into the BIOS. The two likely culprits for a failed overclock at this stage are memory speed and voltage.

Memory speed becomes an issue when overclocking. Raising the speed of the FSB also increases memory speed, since the FSB is the link between the memory and the processor. This becomes a problem when your memory is forced to deal with FSBs faster than those for which it's rated. PC2-6400 DDR2, for example, is rated to run at

800MHz (a figure that you divide by two to relate to the FSB in the BIOS, as DDR stands for double data rate). This means the memory can run at speeds of up to 400MHz, which is well above the 330MHz overclock.

However, modern PCs don't always run the memory 1:1 with the FSB, so be careful which divider is in operation. Think of the divider as being like the gears in a car; to deploy power optimally, you need to be in the correct gear. Make sure the divider you're using doesn't push your memory too far beyond its rated speeds.

VOLT LINES

Once memory is taken care of, you can get to grips with the voltage. Before overvolting the processor, we need to ascertain what voltage it currently uses. While you can use Windows applications for this, the values are never as accurate as those in the BIOS. When it comes to voltage, small increments make a big difference. Find the section called Hardware Monitor (or similar), where the BIOS will display a range of temperatures and voltages.

By default, the Q6600 in our test PC had a score of 1.288V. We increased this to 1.3V. This may not seem like much, but processors

are incredibly complex and delicate; you can't just whack in loads of voltage and hope for the best. You need to gradually work your way upwards with speed and power. Our PC successfully booted with a 330MHz FSB.

Once your overclocked PC is stable enough to boot into Windows, test it out with Prime95 (free from *www.mersenne.org*) and watch the temperatures using Core Temp. Make sure that there are no errors in the program and that the heat sink fan has the heat under control.

MOVING ON UP

Now you can refine your overlock. Only increase voltage when the system is stable; your aim is to use as little as possible, as this will minimise heat and wear and tear. As you reach high FSB speeds, you'll find you need to add extra voltage to both the FSB itself and the Northbridge.

The amount you need will vary, depending on the processor and motherboard that you're using. Try searching online to see what other enthusiasts have managed with similar hardware. Make sure you test your work at every step, and you'll find you have a PC that's freakishly fast and the envy of many. ▬

EXTREME COOLING

While we've talked about replacing your processor's cooler with a bigger, better heat sink fan, that's only the beginning when dealing with the heat created by overclocking and overvolting.

Water-cooled PCs have a waterblock attached to key components such as the processor. Water is pumped through these metal blocks, where it heats up, transferring heat from the processor. The water is then pumped around the loop to a radiator, where it can be cooled down

before repeating its journey. A variety of all-in-one water-cooling kits can be bought online, but you should research your purchase thoroughly, as many cheap kits don't outperform heat sink fans.

If you want to push your processor to the limit, you'll need to go beyond water-cooling. To cool a processor below ambient room temperature, extreme overclockers use dry ice and liquid nitrogen. This enables them to set record overclocks and benchmark scores; some

overclockers have pushed processors over 6GHz using these methods.

Cooling a processor with liquid nitrogen creates difficulties. It has to be fitted with a copper pot, into which the liquid nitrogen is poured. The processor and motherboard need to be protected from condensation, and the motherboard may also need to be 'volt-modded' to enable it to deliver the ludicrous amounts of voltage necessary to push the processor to its absolute limits.

HARDWARE

PROJECT
050

DIFFICULTY LEVEL
HARD
INTERMEDIATE
EASY

TIME REQUIRED
90
MINUTES

Make your PC cooler

Follow these tips for a cooler and quieter PC

Improve the airflow in your PC's case by tying back any loose cables

A COMPUTER'S CORE components generate heat. As with a car engine, this heat hinders performance, so it needs to be dissipated. PCs often come with a fairly modest quantity of low-quality and often noisy cooling hardware; it's good enough to get the job done, but no more. This is a shame, as a cooler PC not only makes less noise but also runs faster when under load for long periods, which is particularly noticeable with demanding tasks such as games. This project will show you how to make your PC cooler, and therefore more efficient.

Most PCs are cooled by heatsinks and fans. A heatsink is an array of metal fins designed to dissipate heat by providing the maximum surface area. A fan accompanies the heatsink, blowing cool air over its surface and eventually out of the case. In general, having many large heatsinks and many large fans makes for better cooling.

ADDING CASE FANS
Most cases on the market ship with one or more fans installed, but the vast majority have additional fan slots. Fans are relatively cheap, so installing them in any available slots will significantly improve cooling at little extra cost.

Most PCs follow a similar airflow scheme: cool air is pulled in through the front and sides of the case while hot air is pushed out through the back and top. When you install additional fans, make sure you align them in accordance with this pull/push principle. Otherwise, they may work against each other and impede the airflow through your system.

Use larger, 120mm fans wherever possible. Large fans push more air and require fewer revolutions to do so, which means they

make less noise. Smaller fans need to spin much faster to push the same amount of air, which results in more noise.

Once you have aligned the fan so that it moves air in the appropriate direction, simply line it up with the holes in your fan slot and screw it into place.

PROCESSOR COOLERS
Processors usually ship with coolers that are able to reduce heat to an adequate standard. However, investing in a superior model is a sound move.

Different coolers use different methods of installation. The Tuniq Tower 120 is a very effective cooler and easy to install. The most popular socket type is that used by Intel's Core 2 Duo processors, so we'll use that for our example. First, stick the backplate to the underside of the motherboard.

Next, find the metal bracket shaped like a capital H. The manual will confirm which part it is, so check this if you're unsure. Rest the bracket on the base of the cooler as shown in the picture (below left). Align the four holes with those on the motherboard and screw the bracket to the backplate you attached to the underside of the motherboard.

HARD DISK CADDY
A hard disk caddy pulls cool air in over your hard disks in addition to providing better airflow through your case. Most models are also equipped with vibration-dampening rubber stoppers that will reduce the noise levels of your PC.

The hard disk caddy will take up three of your 5¼in drive bays, so make sure your case has enough bays to accommodate it.

You install a hard disk caddy in your PC as you would an optical drive (see page 63). Simply remove three 5¼in bezels, insert the hard disk caddy and screw into position.

CABLE MANAGEMENT
The insides of PCs are often a labyrinth of messy cables, but it doesn't have to be this way. Leaving messy cables everywhere will significantly reduce airflow. Cable management simply means keeping cables out of the way or bunching them together with cable ties.

When managing your cables, whether in a finished PC or while building a new one, the best approach is to work on one 'layer' at a time. For example, disconnect all your fan cables and start with those. Once you've arranged them neatly, turn to the front-panel cables, tidying the power switch and front-panel USB wires before moving on to the next step. With these cables out of the way, you'll find it much easier to work with the cables from your power supply and, finally, the SATA and EIDE cables. This method makes the job easier to digest and a lot less daunting.

MAINTENANCE
Cleaning is one of life's annoyances and, unfortunately, it extends to your computer, too. Over time, heatsinks can get blocked up with dust, which hinders their ability to conduct and dissipate heat.

The most effective way to clear heatsinks of built-up dust is to use a can of compressed air, available from any decent hardware shop. Work the nozzle into all your heatsinks and loosen the dust. Once they're dust-free, carefully vacuum the dislodged dust from the bottom of your case. ■

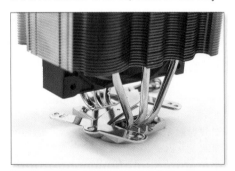

The Tuniq Tower 120 is a very effective processor cooler and is easy to install

WHY USE THERMAL PASTE?

Many coolers ship with pre-applied thermal paste, which fills in microscopic cracks in the surface of the processor and the surface of the cooler, ensuring that there's efficient heat transfer between

the two. However, applying higher-quality paste can help cool your processor even more. Arctic Silver 5 is widely recognised as the best thermal paste on the market, and a small tube costs less than £5.

JOB DONE

OUT

New from Epson. The Epson Stylus Office BX600FW is an ultra fast wireless 4-in-1 business inkjet printer that gives you laser-like text and colour when you need it. Amazingly it only needs a fraction of the power of a laser printer and with high yield individual inks running costs are comparable too. Making your day that much more productive.

To discover more visit us at:
www.epson.co.uk/businessinkjet

EPSON®
EXCEED YOUR VISION

HARDWARE

PROJECT
051

DIFFICULTY LEVEL
HARD
INTERMEDIATE
EASY

TIME REQUIRED
30 MINUTES

Optimise your printer

Keep your inkjet printer in top condition by following these simple guidelines

1 Most printers take you through the process of aligning your print heads when you first install them, but it's important to do this after changing your ink cartridges to ensure sharp, high-quality prints.

Go to Windows' Control Panel and double-click on the Printers and Faxes icon in Windows XP (or Printers in Vista). Right-click on your printer and select Properties, Printing Preferences. Most Canon, Epson and HP printers have a maintenance tab that includes an option marked Align Print Heads or similar. Most Lexmark printers have a menu bar, from which you'll need to open the Options menu and click on Printing Status Options. This will open the Lexmark solution centre, where you can select Maintenance.

The maintenance menus also contain tools to check and clean your print heads. If prints suffer from white horizontal streaks or areas of missing colour, your print heads may be clogged. Cleaning them flushes ink through them to dissolve blockages. Repeated cleaning may be required, but consumes ink. Cleaning is particularly important on printers that have built-in heads, as most Epson printers do.

2 If your documents look like they've been slightly shrunk on the page, your printer could be set to use the wrong paper size. For example, some HP printers default to the American Letter paper size. Fortunately, it's easy to correct.

Go to Windows' Control Panel and open Printers and Faxes (or Printers in Vista). Right-click on the printer's icon and select Properties from the menu. Go to the Device Settings tab. Under the Form To Tray Assignment heading, there should be a pull-down menu labelled Main Tray or Auto. Change the entry in the pull-down menu from Letter to A4. Click Apply.

Go back to the general tab and click on Printing Preferences. If your printer uses preset page and quality configurations, Letter-type paper may also be set here. Your printer's Preferences window may include multiple tabs. Change Letter to A4 anywhere it occurs and then click Apply. Click OK to exit the window and to exit the printer's Properties window.

3 When printing ordinary documents, you can ensure better-looking prints by using 100gsm paper rather than 80gsm copier paper, as heavier paper absorbs ink more effectively. This more expensive paper is ideal for formal letters and invitations.

For optimal photo printing results, it's usually best to use the manufacturer's own paper and ink, as they are designed to work together to create accurate, long-lasting colours. Even when you're using the manufacturer's papers, however, some will prove better than others.

The most obvious example of this that we've seen is from HP's own-brand photo paper; prints made on Premium Plus paper were far more accurately coloured than those on Advanced Glossy paper. Our preferred Epson paper is Premium Glossy Photo Paper, and we've had excellent results from Canon inkjets on both Canon Photo Paper Plus Glossy and Photo Paper Pro.

Lexmark photo prints often suffer from ink that fails to dry completely. We found that this was improved by switching to a high-quality third-party paper such as Ilford's Premium Photo Paper Glossy or Gallerie Classic Gloss Paper, which gave us smoother, dryer prints. The Ilford papers also produced stunning results with Canon printers. ■

EPSON PRINTERS AND COLOUR MANAGEMENT

While Epson's Photo Stylus range of printers can produce stunning photos, the default colour management settings of some drivers can produce prints that come out with a magenta tint.

This made skin tones look unrealistic in photos. To correct it, open Properties before you print. Click on the Advanced tab, select ICM under Colour Management and tick the Off (No Colour Adjustment) option.

Disabling colour management can make low-contrast images look too dark, so it isn't suitable for all photos. If you have the patience, you can use the same settings to create custom colour profiles.

Refill your ink cartridge

Save money on replacement inkjet print cartridges by refilling them yourself

REPLACEMENT INK CARTRIDGES aren't cheap, but you don't have to buy a new one every time you run out. Instead, you can buy a refill kit for around half the price and refill your empty cartridge three times over.

First, you need a refill kit, and you may be surprised at the savings you can make here. Whereas cartridges can cost £15 to £20 in some cases, the black kit we've used here was just £7.15 from a local shop (the colour kit cost £9.99). It's best to check prices and availability online, and different kits will include instructions for different printer makes and models. But with a standard tool set provided in each kit and awareness of the features of your particular cartridge, any kit should be usable with your cartridge.

Apart from the kit, you'll also need paper towels, disposable plastic gloves (if they aren't included in the kit) and a flat work surface that you won't mind getting a little ink on (or a surface that is protected by paper towels or a protective covering).

1 Having read the filling instructions, removed your cartridge from your printer (see the printer manual for details on how to do this) and inspected your cartridge, it should be clear which route you need to

follow. Our Lexmark cartridge isn't covered by the instructions provided, but the HP cartridge instructions are also applicable to our cartridge.

First, locate the fill holes. For this black cartridge there are three, found on the top of the cartridge by peeling back the label. Once located, you will need to widen the holes to enable the syringe included with the kit to fit inside. To do this, hold the cartridge firmly, and use the screw that came with the kit to open the hole slowly until you feel it push into the body of the cartridge and the sponge below. Carefully remove the screw and repeat as necessary. Once done, fill your syringe with ink.

2 Slowly fill each hole with ink (for colour cartridges, each one will be for cyan, magenta and yellow), keeping an eye out for any ink oozing out of any holes, and especially out of the printer head itself. It's easy to get carried away pushing ink into the cartridge and not notice any escaping out of the printer head until it is too late.

Once the cartridge is filled up and ink starts to escape, blot any excess ink from the printer head and wipe away any from the fill-holes. Now you'll need to cover the fill-holes, using the cartridge label if it is still intact and usable, or a piece of Sellotape, securely pressed down and flattened to stop any flow of air entering and drying the ink.

Once that's done, place the print cartridge securely back in your printer, go through any necessary installation procedures and print a test page to ensure your cartridge has been refilled successfully. ■

Set up a family network

Share files, printers and your network connection between family members

IF YOU'VE GOT more than one computer in your home, the chances are that you have important files spread throughout your house on multiple PCs. It doesn't have to be this way, as a family network can let you share files, printers and even your internet connection.

There are many ways to set up a home network, but the easiest way is to buy a broadband router, even if you don't have broadband internet. Routers have extra technology built into them that makes networking easier. For example, all routers have a built-in Dynamic Host Configuration Protocol (DHCP) server. This automatically gives connected computers an IP address (a unique address that's the electronic equivalent of a postal address), which means that you don't have to understand how the underlying network technology works.

If you have broadband internet, a router is essential. It will let you share your internet connection easily, so that everyone in your house can be online at the same time. Choosing a model that matches your needs should be easy. First, buy a router that has the right type of connection for your broadband connection. If you've got a cable internet connection from Virgin Media, you'll need a cable router; if you get your broadband through your telephone line, you'll need an ADSL router.

We recommend that you buy a Draft-N wireless router, as this will give you the best range and performance. Make sure you buy one with the WiFi logo on it, as this ensures compatibility with other wireless devices. Finally, for every computer that doesn't have wireless built in, you'll need a wireless USB adaptor made by the same manufacturer as your router. Computers that you plug in through a wired connection will need a Cat5e Ethernet cable of the correct length.

Look for the WiFi logo on your chosen router. The 'n' on the right is important if you want your router to be interoperable with other 802.11n devices

With a home network, you can share files and your internet connection between several PCs

In this project, we'll show you how to set up a wireless router securely with a shared internet connection, and how to share files and printers in Windows XP and Windows Vista. Check any manuals that came with your router, as modern routers often have setup wizards that take you through configuration. In any case, these steps should serve as a useful guide for modifying settings.

1 Follow the instructions in the router's manual to connect it to your broadband connection (if you have one) and a computer via an Ethernet cable. Turn on the router and computer. When your computer has started, you're ready to connect to your router's web interface. Open your web browser and type http:// followed by the router's IP address. If you don't know this, press the Windows key and R simultaneously, type cmd and press Enter. Type IP Config and

make a note of the default gateway address, as this is your router's IP address.

When your router's web page appears, log on to it using the username and password in the manual. Select the internet settings (often under Basic Settings or similar). Using the information your ISP provided, enter your internet and logon details, plus any additional configuration information.

2 Next, you need to configure your wireless networking settings. First, set up the wireless network's service set identifier (SSID) by typing a name. This can be anything, but don't use anything obvious. Next, set up the wireless channel. In the UK there is a choice of 13 wireless channels, numbered from one to 13. Only channels 1, 6 and 11 should be used, as they don't interfere with each other. If you've got a Draft-N router, you may also have a choice between a 20MHz

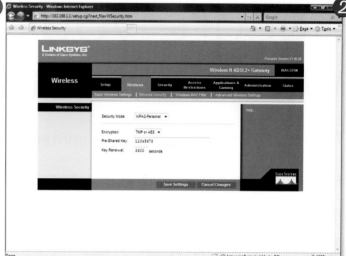

and 40MHz mode (sometimes called 270Mbit/s and 130Mbit/s). If you're having trouble getting a reliable signal, try switching to 20MHz mode and changing the channel.

Next, set up wireless security by clicking on the appropriate link. Select WPA or WPA2 as the security mode, but don't use WEP as it's difficult to configure and is not secure. If you're given the choice, select TKIP or AES as the encryption standard, then enter your pre-shared key (password). This can be anything, but make it something you can remember. Save the settings.

3 You can now plug the rest of your wired computers into your router. To connect the wireless computers you must install the wireless adaptors (if needed) as directed by the manufacturer's instructions.

Once you have installed your wireless adaptors, you can connect to the network. The following instructions assume that you're using Windows' wireless application, which is built into Windows XP and Vista. You may find that your wireless adaptor has installed third-party software; refer to your adaptor's manual to find out how to turn this off.

In the Notification Area (next to the clock) you'll notice a network icon that looks like two computer monitors. In Windows XP, double-click this; in Vista, click it once and select Connect to a network.

From the list that appears, double-click your network, type in your network password and click Connect to continue.

4 To share a folder in XP, use Explorer to find the folder. Right-click it and select Sharing and Security. Click 'If you understand the security risks but want to share files without running the wizard, click here'. Select 'Just enable file sharing' and click OK. Select 'Share this folder on the network' and, if you want users to be able to write files, 'Allow network users to change my files'. Click OK.

To share a printer, open the Printers option from the Control Panel. Right-click the printer you want to share, select Sharing, choose 'Share this printer' and click OK.

5 Open the Network and Sharing Center from the Control Panel. Under Sharing and Discovery, make sure file and printer sharing are switched on, and that Password protected sharing is off. Use Explorer to navigate to the folder you want to share. Right-click it and select Sharing. Choose Everyone from the drop-down menu and click Add. The default permission level, Reader, allows other people to copy files only; change this to Co-owner if you want to let them write files, too. Click Share to continue.

To share a printer, open Printers from the Control Panel. Right-click the printer you want to share and select Sharing. Choose 'Share this printer' and click OK.

6 To access shares, open Explorer from another PC. In Windows Vista, expand Network; in Windows XP, expand My Network Places. Vista lists all the PCs on your network, but in Windows XP you may have to expand the other sections to find them. Double-click the PC with the shared files, and you'll see the shared folders and printers. Double-click folders to copy files, and printer names to install them as local printers on your PC. ■

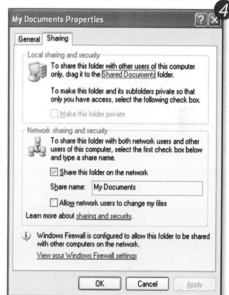

Secure your wireless network

An unsecured network is an invitation to hackers. Here's how to stop them

FAILING TO SECURE your wireless network leaves your system open to attack from bandwidth thieves and hackers. If the hacker uses your network for bandwidth-intensive applications such as file sharing, you may experience a very slow internet connection. A more mischievous intruder can use an unsecured wireless connection to access the computers on your network. Once they have access to your network, it's easy for them to steal your data.

Then there's drive-by pharming. This is where a hacker sets up a web page with some hidden code that makes changes to the configuration of your broadband router or wireless access point without your knowledge. The hacker then has control of your internet connection and can send you to any site they like, regardless of the address

you enter. This type of attack relies on the fact that many people don't change their router's default password.

The first thing you should do when you set up your wireless network, even before you give the network a name, is to change your router's default password. If you don't do this, anyone who logs on to your network can reconfigure your router. You should also give your network a name. In many cases a wireless network's default name, referred to as its service set identifier (SSID), is the router's own model name.

WPA is far easier to set up than the less-secure WEP protocol. To begin, type your router's IP address into your web browser's address bar. This will open the router's presentation page.

encryption and you can't mix different encryption standards on the same network, so we'll use TKIP.

2 Now you must enter your pre-shared key. Pre-shared means that the individuals who configure the network clients must know this key before they can connect to your network, as it will not be generated for them. As you are configuring your own clients, this won't be a problem.

Choose a key that you will be able to remember but that others won't be able to guess. Avoid the name of your partner, pets or children. Try to use both upper- and lower-case letters and numbers. When you've entered the key, press Apply. Your router will restart and use the new setting.

1 Navigate to the wireless security section of your router's presentation page and choose the method of encryption you want to use. Some routers label these plainly as WEP, WPA with TKIP and WPA with AES. The router in our example doesn't mention WPA, but both the TKIP and AES settings refer to WPA encryption. If your hardware supports it, we suggest that you use the stronger AES standard. Unfortunately, not all the adaptors on our network support AES

3 On a PC that you wish to connect to the network, double-click the wireless network icon in the Windows taskbar. If your wireless router broadcasts its SSID, this will appear in the list of networks found. Double-click your network, enter your key and your PC will connect to the wireless network. If your network's SSID is hidden, click on 'Change advanced settings' on the left-hand side. On the Wireless Network tab of the Wireless Network Connection Properties box, click Add and enter the name, encryption type and key for your wireless network. Click OK and your PC should connect to your network. ∎

TIME REQUIRED   DIFFICULTY LEVEL   PROJECT   HARDWARE

1 HOUR

HARD
INTERMEDIATE
EASY

055

Boost your wireless network

Improve your WiFi coverage with a powerful antenna or WiFi repeater

A WIRELESS NETWORK can be liberating, but it can also be a source of frustration. Walls, floors and furniture can all get in the way of the wireless signal, and you may find that you have trouble getting a reliable, fast connection from certain areas.

However, there are two simple and inexpensive ways to improve your wireless network's signal. The cheapest and easiest option is to upgrade the antenna on your router. You may also be able to do the same for your wireless adaptors, as PCI adaptors for desktop PCs and some CardBus adaptors for laptops have antenna sockets. Antennas are available in indoor and outdoor versions. Outdoor antennas are built to withstand the elements and can be wall mounted. If you simply want to add a new antenna to one or more wireless devices, see the box below.

Alternatively, you can extend your network's range by using another wireless device. If your router supports the Wireless Distribution System (WDS), you can extend its range by using it in conjunction with another WDS-compatible router. Unfortunately, WDS isn't a universal standard, so WDS-compatible routers from different manufacturers may not work with each other. We recommend that you choose a WDS router from the same manufacturer as your current router, and preferably the same model.

If your existing router doesn't support WDS, you can use a wireless repeater, also known as a wireless range extender, to expand the range of your network. Some repeaters work only with routers from the same manufacturer, while others claim to work with a wide number of models. As with WDS, we recommend that you choose a repeater from the same manufacturer as your router.

When you connect to your wireless network through a WDS router, your network throughput is reduced, which results in slower file transfers.

Before you install a router, make a note of its unique MAC address, and the MAC address of your existing router. You'll need these to help identify devices during configuration. MAC addresses should be printed on each wireless device and on its box or setup sheet. Some wireless routers may have two MAC addresses, one each for the wired and wireless interfaces.

Some routers can be configured over a wireless connection, but it's better to use a wired Ethernet connection to your computer during the initial setup.

Most routers have a web-based configuration interface. You'll find the address and default login information for this in the router's documentation. WDS is turned off by default, so you have to find the option to enable it on both routers.

For WDS to work, both routers must have the same network name, or service set identifier (SSID), and the same WiFi-protected

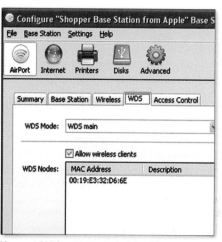

You use MAC addresses to identify your devices when settting up a WiFi repeater

access pre-shared key (WPA-PSK) password. They should also be configured to use the same radio channel. WDS routers identify each other by their MAC addresses. If the setup utility or web interface for your WDS router doesn't automatically detect your other WDS router, you'll have to enter the MAC address on each router yourself.

When making any changes to a wireless router, remember to save them on each separate page of the configuration interface by clicking Save or Apply, which may cause the router to reboot. To verify that your WDS network is set up properly, move your router to its new location and try it out. ∎

CHOOSING AND INSTALLING AN ANTENNA

Before you buy an antenna, check that it's suitable for your wireless equipment. An antenna's specifications tell you the amount (in dBi) by which it boosts your wireless signal. Check your router or repeater's specifications for its output power in dBi. Add the figures together to find a total output. Higher figures give you better coverage, but the total must be below 20dBi to avoid breaking UK law.

If you need to extend the range of your wireless network in a specific direction, such as down a long hallway, choose a unidirectional antenna. These concentrate a powerful signal in a comparatively narrow angle. If you need to improve your coverage in all directions, choose an omni-directional antenna.

Installing a new antenna is as simple as unscrewing the existing antenna and screwing on your new one. However, if you're going to mount an outdoor antenna on a wall or pole, make sure you have the building owner's permission and consider factors such as planning permission and interference. While most routers have an SMA antenna socket, outdoor antennas often use TNC connectors. Many of these come with a suitabsle adaptor; if not, you can buy one for as little as £3.

Set up a HomePlug network

It's easy to extend your network using the electrical wiring in your house

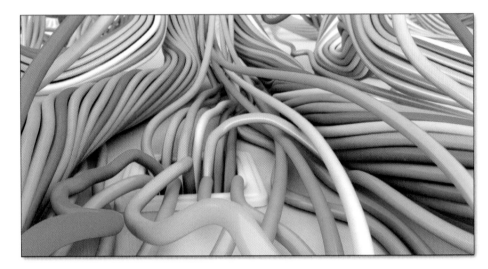

A HOMEPLUG NETWORK, also known as powerline networking, sends data across the electrical wiring in your house. A typical HomePlug adaptor plugs into a wall socket and has a port for an Ethernet lead that allows you to connect it to your PC, router or anything else with a network port.

Just like Ethernet and wireless networking, HomePlug equipment is available in different speeds. There are currently two standards that you're likely to encounter. HomePlug 1.0 is the older standard, capable of transmitting data at a meagre 14Mbit/s, although a non-standardised 85Mbit/s Turbo version is also available. However, you should look for equipment that meets the HomePlug AV standard. This has a theoretical maximum data transfer rate of 200Mbit/s, although the fastest average speed we've seen in our tests has been 59.4Mbit/s.

There's an increasing variety of HomePlug equipment available, including routers that combine powerline networking with wired Ethernet and Draft-N wireless networking. At around £80 for a pair of adaptors, HomePlug kit is still expensive compared to most other networking equipment, but it's ideal if you have poor wireless reception and don't want to run Ethernet cable all over your home.

1 The minimum you'll need to set up a HomePlug network is two adaptors. Each of these will require a dedicated plug socket. Avoid using plug bars or extension leads to connect your HomePlug adaptor, as this can cause a huge drop in performance.

Some adaptors have a built-in power pass-through that you can use to plug in electrical equipment, and continue to use the socket normally as well as for networking, but you can expect to pay around £50 each for these. If you want to access the internet using HomePlug, one adaptor will have to be connected to your router. The other can be plugged into a socket anywhere you want your network to reach, with an Ethernet lead connecting it to, say, a PC in another room.

2 Although HomePlug signals are stopped when they reach the electricity meter, neighbouring houses and flats often have shared wiring, so your neighbours may be able to access your network if they also use HomePlug. To prevent this, HomePlug equipment has built-in encryption.

Older HomePlug adaptors relied on 56-bit DES encryption, but this is relatively easy to crack. Most modern adaptors use either 192-bit 3DES encryption or 128-bit AES encryption, both of which are considerably more secure. Encryption is enabled by default, but this offers limited security, as the standard password will be the same on every unit produced by a manufacturer. Often, you can only change the password using a Windows utility, which presents a problem for Mac and Linux users.

3 Several manufacturers have now produced adaptors that use a push-button system to associate with each other and generate a unique secure password. These are worth buying, as they take the hassle out of setting up a secure network.

Add a network storage device

Keep your movies, music and other files in one place for everyone to share

MORE AND MORE homes now have a network of computers, but a good network needs a file server that acts as a repository for shared files. You could set one of your home PCs to act as a file server for music, photos and other files, but you'd need to leave it switched on to give your other computers access to the data.

A better solution is to buy a dedicated network storage device. These are smaller and use less power than a PC. You can leave them powered up on your network, providing storage for your PCs whenever they need it.

You can buy network-attached storage (NAS) devices with wired or wireless Ethernet interfaces. Wired Ethernet is cheaper and quicker than even the fastest wireless network. If you have a wireless router, it should have some Ethernet ports to which you can connect a wired storage device, making it available wirelessly.

However, we wouldn't recommend spending extra on a wireless storage device unless you lack an up-to-date wireless router or you need to place the file server somewhere you can't reach with cables.

1 The easiest place to put your network storage device is near your router or switch. You can put it in a nearby cupboard if you're worried about noise from its disks or cooling fan, but make sure you can reach it to turn it off, and that it has ample air for cooling.

Plug one end of an Ethernet cable into your network storage device and the other end into a free port on a hub, switch or router. If both your storage device and switch support Gigabit Ethernet, you'll need to use a Cat5e or Cat6 Ethernet cable for the best performance.

2 If your network storage device doesn't support Microsoft's Universal Plug and Play (UPnP) protocol, you should install the necessary drivers or utility software according to the manufacturer's instructions. Make a note of any IP address or Windows File Sharing name assigned to the network storage device during the setup process, as you'll probably need this information later.

If your network storage device supports UPnP, you shouldn't need to install any additional software, but make sure UPnP is

enabled on your PC. In Windows XP, select Add/Remove Windows Components. Choose Network Services in the window that appears and click the Details button. In the next window, make sure the tickbox for UPnP User Interface is checked. In Windows Vista, UPnP is switched on by default.

3 You should now be able to connect to your network storage device. If your device uses UPnP, it should be represented by an icon in My Network Places on your desktop or in the Start menu. You should be able to copy files to and from it.

If your device doesn't use UPnP, right-click on My Network Places and click Explore. In the window that appears, select Entire Network, then Microsoft Windows Network. You should see a list of the workgroups on your network. Your NAS device should have the workgroup name you gave it when running the installation.

Alternatively, you may have to access the device by typing its IP address or Windows File Sharing name into the address bar of Windows Explorer or Internet Explorer. If you didn't write these down when you configured your device, run the manufacturer's configuration utility or installer again. Right-clicking on a network share and selecting Map network drive lets you access your NAS as a normal drive. ■

HARDWARE

PROJECT
058

DIFFICULTY LEVEL
HARD
INTERMEDIATE
EASY

TIME REQUIRED
30
MINUTES

Set up a wireless IP camera

Keep an eye on your home while you're out with a wireless camera

IP CAMERAS ARE much like traditional CCTV cameras and are ideal for home security. They have many uses, the simplest of which is to keep an eye on what the kids are doing in another room. More advanced uses include setting the camera to record still images or a video clip when it detects motion while you're out of the house, and configuring the camera to email the evidence to you.

Generally, IP cameras are for indoor use only. If you need to mount one outdoors, you'll need a waterproof camera. Night vision is also rare, so if you need to monitor an area in the dark, you should look for a camera with infrared LEDs. Most IP cameras use the wireless standard 802.11g, but some have only a wired Ethernet port, which isn't very convenient if you want to mount the camera a long way from your router. Some cameras have built-in microphones that allow you to hear what's going on near it. Cheaper cameras tend not to have a microphone, but our advice is not to skimp on this or else the resulting recorded video will be less useful.

Most basic cameras are fixed models, but if you spend more on a camera that pans and tilts, you can control remotely where it points. Spend even more and you can get a zoom lens, which you can also control remotely.

Although each camera's setup procedure varies slightly, yours shouldn't deviate much from that of the basic Linksys camera that we're using in this walkthrough.

1 First, connect the supplied Ethernet cable to the camera and the other end to a free port on the back of your router. Plug in the power supply and turn it on. LEDs should flash to indicate that the camera is booting up. There should be an installation CD, so insert that into your computer and run the setup wizard or a discovery utility.

2 The wizard or utility should scan your network and locate the IP camera. Next, you need to enter a few details, such as a name for the camera – Driveway Cam, for example – and a username and password to prevent unauthorised access to the camera's video feed and settings.

You should assign the camera a fixed IP address if you want to access it over an

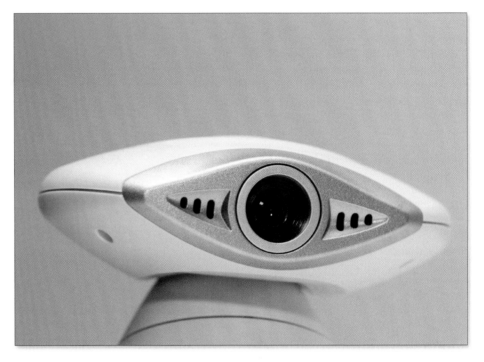

internet connection, as your router is going to need this information to 'find' the camera on your network. Here we've used the wizard's recommended settings, but you need to make sure the address you give the camera matches your router's IP address – except for the last digit, which must be different. The Gateway field is simply your router's IP address. Next, the wizard may let you select a WiFi network to connect to and its passphrase.

3 Once all the settings are applied, you'll need to disconnect the Ethernet cable from the camera and unplug the power cable. Wait around 10 seconds and plug it back in. This forces the camera to switch from using the Ethernet cable to using WiFi to communicate with your router. If you disabled the LEDs, you won't be able to tell whether the camera has managed to establish a wireless connection or not; the only way to check is to try connecting to it.

4 Start your web browser, then either type in the IP address you assigned in Step 2 or type //thenameyougavethecamera. You should see the camera's web interface. The first thing you'll want to do is check that the video feed works. Click on View Video or

similar, and you'll probably be presented with a blank window. Your browser will ask your permission to install an ActiveX control and you should allow it. This is a small program, downloaded from the camera itself, which is essentially a tiny proprietary video player. Once installed, you should see the camera's video feed.

5 Click on Settings and enter the username and password you chose during the setup routine. Most cameras allow you to disable the LEDs to make the camera less conspicuous, so look for this option if this is what you want.

The most useful settings will be found under the Video or Image section. This Linksys camera is typical in that it can stream video in two formats: MPEG4 and MJPEG. The MJPEG format tends to be better quality, but MPEG4 is more efficient, so leads to better frame rates and smaller files. For viewing over a local network you'll want to choose a resolution of 640x480, but 320x240 is better for viewing over the internet.

6 If your camera came with software, you should install it now. However, many cameras allow you to configure motion

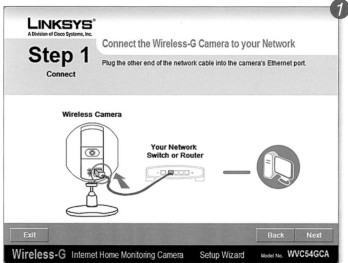

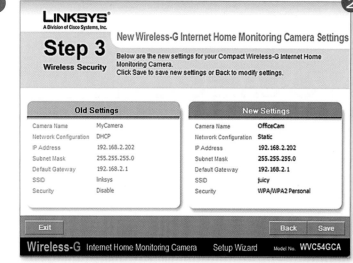

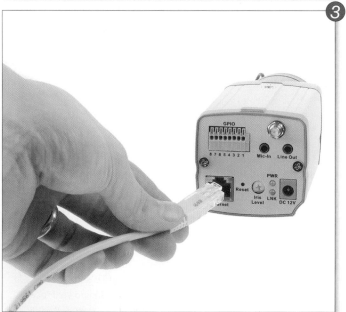

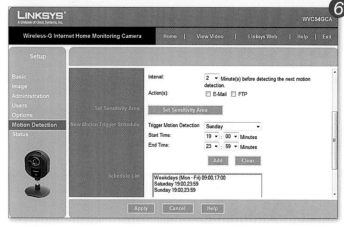

detection and schedules through the web interface. First, you'll need to decide what you want to happen when motion is detected: take a still photo or record a video. For video, you must select the format; usually there will be a choice of MPEG4, 3GP or ASF. You should also set pre- and post-capture times, which let you add a buffer of a few seconds before and after the motion event.

Next, you need to configure what happens to the photo or video. The most common choices are email and file transfer protocol (FTP), which allows you to send large files over the internet. FTP is the best choice for video, as video files will quickly fill up an email inbox.

You must then set the area and sensitivity. You should be able to select up to three areas of the image in which to detect motion. You'll need to set the sensitivity level by trial and error. Set it too low, and nothing will be recorded; set it too high, and leaves blowing in the breeze will trigger it off.

Finally, set a schedule for when you want motion detection to be active. We've set the camera to monitor activity in weekday office hours, and weekends in the evenings. ▄

Add TV to your computer

It's easy to watch TV programmes on your PC's desktop

IF YOU WANT TV functionality on your PC, it's easy to fix up. You just need the following:

● A Windows PC with a 2GHz processor
● A graphics card or integrated graphics with an 'overlay' feature – most do these days
● 512MB of RAM
● A free USB port, PCI or PCI-E slot or, if you're using a laptop, a PCMCIA or Express Card 34 slot
● Access to a working TV aerial antenna

You can add TV viewing capabilities to your system in a number of ways, usually with an external USB or internal PCI card adaptor. Whichever one you choose, the process is the same. Just install the hardware and software and scan for channels, just as you would if you were tuning in a new television.

To install PCI or PCI-E cards in your PC, you'll need to open it up. Make sure the power is turned off before inserting the card into an appropriate slot. Follow the installation instructions that come with your product. In this project, we're going to guide you through a typical USB product installation, as these are the most popular. We've used Terratec's Cinergy XS digital TV receiver, which costs around £75 including VAT.

The Cinergy Hybrid T USB XS FM is a small dongle device that you push into an available USB port. It comes with a small antenna, but we'd recommend that you use the converter provided to connect a traditional roof-mounted TV aerial if you want to ensure a good-quality picture.

Once connected, the system will notice the device and ask for the driver. At this point, you'll need to install the software from the CD provided. It's also a good idea to see if the hardware manufacturer has updated the drivers on its website, in case new ones have been released. Once the drivers have been installed, you'll need to install the TV viewer application. In our example, the software is Terratec's Home Cinema; you'll find this on the installation disc.

Before scanninng for channels, you should make sure that the antenna is connected. The default on the Terratec software is to scan by region. To begin the process, just press the Scan button. It will take several minutes to search the full frequency range, and any channels that are located will be shown in the right-hand panel. If you have a hybrid TV device such as this one, you may need to perform this search twice: once for analogue transmissions, and once more for digital.

You should now be able to view TV on your Windows desktop. Using this software, you can surf the channels and even pause or record live TV, thereby turning your PC into a personal video recorder (PVR). The image can be made full screen or placed in the background, allowing you to work while keeping an eye on the news, sport or whatever else you fancy.

As an alternative software source, if the hardware device is Media Center-compatible, you can use it with the tool in Windows XP Media Center Edition, Vista Home Premium and Vista Ultimate editions. As this replaces Terratec's Home Cinema software, you'll have to scan again using the TV setup controls in Windows Media Center to find your local channels. Once this is done, you can use all the features of Windows Media Center with your TV capture hardware. ■

CHOOSING A TV ADAPTOR

There are three main types of TV adaptor: analogue, DVB-T and hybrid.

In the UK, conventional TV is distributed by ground-based antenna using an analogue signal in a format known as Phase Alternating Line, or PAL for short. However, alongside this is a broadcasting standard known as Digital Video Broadcasting – Terrestrial (DVB-T), which looks set to take over completely in 2012. After this time, there won't be any analogue TV signals in the UK.

Hybrid adaptors can tune into both types of signal. Depending on your location, a hybrid design could offer the best channel choice – at least until DVB-T transmissions are enhanced, once analogue is switched off in your area.

Turn your computer into a powerful recorder with Terratec's Home Cinema application

CyberLink's PowerCinema allows you to schedule, record and watch TV shows

For this project, you'll need an internal PCI card adaptor or external USB device such as Terratec's Cinergy XS (above)

Print on CDs and DVDs

Personalise your discs with your own images and words

BEYOND USING A marker pen, there are three ways to make your mark on the surface of CDs and DVDs. Here we'll show you how to put text and images on to your discs.

USING PRINTED LABELS

This is the cheapest and easiest method, although the results aren't as nice as printing directly on to the discs. Labels for CD or DVD media usually come on A4 or letter-sized adhesive sheets. They are available in a range of paper qualities and finishes, including gloss and metallic. These sheets can be sent through any PC printing system, from a big laser printer to a small inkjet. You just have to make sure you can register the position of the words and images respective to the labels on the sheets (usually two per page).

To apply the label you need an applicator, which usually comes as part of a kit, with some label-designing software. Once the label is printed, it's placed adhesive side up on to the applicator. The CD or DVD is aligned, and the two are pressed together. You might need to push any air bubbles to the edge using your fingers, so it's best to use labels that you've allowed to dry.

PRINTING ON SPECIAL MEDIA

The idea of printing directly on to a CD or DVD might seem crazy, but many inkjet printers come with a special tray designed specifically for this purpose. HP, Canon and Epson all make inkjets that can do this. To use this facility, you also require some blank media that allows you to print on to its surface. A wide range of CD and DVD types are available in matt and gloss finishes.

The process of creating a printed disc starts with burning the data as usual on to the disc. Then use the software that comes supplied with your printer to design the label for the disc. For instance, Epson's printers are packaged with a tool called Epson Print CD.

Once you're happy with your design, place the disc (printable side up) on to the tray and press Print. The tray and disc will then be pulled into the printer, where the design is applied. The results can be more colourful and detailed than with commercial discs, which use a silk-screen method.

WORKING WITH LIGHTSCRIBE

This method requires a special type of CD or DVD writer that bears the LightScribe logo. The technology is very similar to inkjet printing, in that you use a simple graphics application and print the results. The difference is that there's no printer. The images are burned on to the special LightScribe media using the same laser that burned the data on to the disc. Only special LightScribe drives and media can do this, so don't try it with ordinary media.

After the design is created and the data burned to the disc, the media is returned to the tray upside down, so the data surface is face up. The LightScribe application then burns a monochrome image on to the top surface; this process can take anything from 20 minutes to an hour. The results aren't as good as labels or printable media, but at least you don't require a special printer or applicator to achieve this effect. ■■

TRANSCODING YOUR MEDIA

With printable media, there can be variations in the inner and outer diameter where you're allowed to print, because the coating doesn't extend over the entire disc.

You'll need to measure how far from the inside and outside edge of each disc the printable surface extends, and enter these measurements into the design application. If you don't do this, either the graphic won't cover the whole printable area or the printer will attempt to print on a part of the disc that isn't absorbent.

To get this absolutely right, you may also need to calibrate the printer for disc printing using a couple of spare discs. The printer's manual will have more information on this process.

HARDWARE

PROJECT	DIFFICULTY LEVEL	TIME REQUIRED
061	HARD / INTERMEDIATE / EASY	2 HOURS

Stream multimedia around the home

Enjoy photos, music and video off the PC no matter where you are in the home

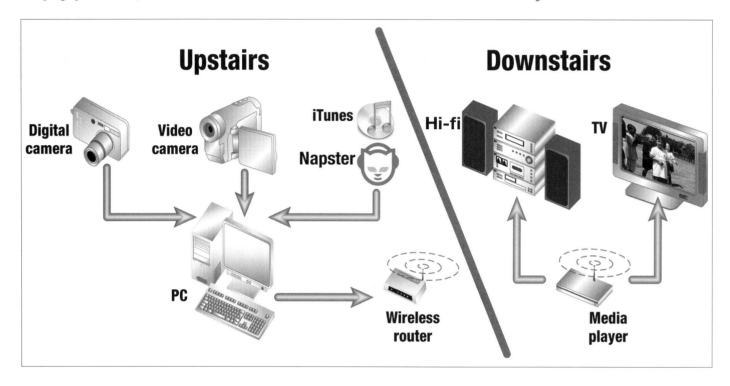

IT'S QUITE LIKELY that you have a wide range of media files, such as music, photos and videos, on your computer. If your PC is tucked away in a spare room, you probably wish that you could enjoy your collection somewhere more comfortable. With the help of this project, you'll be able to do just that.

With the right gadget, you can stream your files to your living room and browse them from the comfort of your sofa. You can listen to your MP3 collection on your hi-fi, show friends and family your photos on your TV, and watch home movies without needing discs or tapes.

If you already have a simple PC home network set up, you're well prepared for this

upgrade. You just have to buy a suitable streaming media player and add some server software to your PC.

STREAMING MUSIC
Before you can set up a system to stream media files to your living room and play them on your hi-fi or TV, you'll need to consider the types of file you'll want to access. This will dictate the kind of software you need to install on your PC and the type of player you'll need in your living room.

Most people will want to stream music. This is generally easy, but if you buy music by downloading, it is probably protected by a digital rights management (DRM) system.

That being the case, you'll have to make sure your player and server software support the specific DRM used.

There are no such problems with music ripped from CDs. Most people copy CDs to MP3 format. All the streaming media players we've seen support MP3, which has no copy protection. This makes it the easiest audio format to stream; however, little commercial music can be bought online as MP3.

AAC is Apple's native format for iTunes and iPod players. Music downloaded from the iTunes Music Store is in AAC format and is copy-protected with the FairPlay system. The only way to stream these files is to use Apple's own Airport Express and Apple TV devices.

WMA is Microsoft's audio format. WMA files ripped from CDs are not copy-protected, unless you choose this option in Windows Media Player's Options. Commercial WMA downloads are always copy-protected and many online music stores, including Napster's subscription service, use this system. To stream this music, you'll need a Microsoft Plays for Sure-compatible device. You can get these from manufacturers such as D-Link, Pinnacle and Philips.

USING AV CONNECTIONS

To stream music, you'll need a spare audio input on your hi-fi. Most players have phono outputs, so a phono lead is all you'll need.

For video and photo files, you'll need to connect your TV. Look for spare SCART or S-video inputs on your TV. Buy a two-way SCART switcher if you need an extra socket. You are going to need HDMI or component outputs for HD video.

STREAMING PHOTOS AND VIDEO

If you want to stream photos and video as well as audio, you'll need a player with video outputs. Photo support is usually limited to JPEG files, although this shouldn't be an issue for most users.

Buying video content online hasn't really taken off yet, so copy protection isn't an issue. Simply consider which video files you use at present and then select a player that supports those formats. You may also want support for high-definition (HD) files, although these can be too large to stream over a wireless network, and you'll need an HD TV to view them properly. We'd recommend that those users who want to stream HD video use a wired network (100Mbit/s is fast enough) or a Draft 802.11n wireless router.

If a wired network or a Draft-N router aren't possibilities – because of thick walls, or because you don't want to run cables all round your home – then consider HomePlug adaptors. These plug into your standard wall sockets and turn your electrical cables into a home network. Devices simply plug into the adaptors via a standard Ethernet connection.

Your choice of streaming video player will largely dictate your choice of server software, and manufacturers generally bundle a compatible server program for you to install. Most devices are compatible with Universal Plug and Play (UPnP), in which case you can use Microsoft's Media Connect, which is built into Windows Media Player 11. If you've got Windows Vista, you'll have this already. Windows XP users can upgrade to it for free by downloading it from *http://tinyurl.com/MediaPlayer11*.

As WMP doesn't support H.264 HD video, there are other UPnP servers available, such as TwonkyMedia, which is available from *www.twonkyvision.de*. ITunes acts as a server using its built-in AirTunes feature. For more details, go to *www.apple.com/airportexpress/features/airtunes.html*.

INSTALLING THE MEDIA SETUP

Installing your new streaming media setup should be straightforward. Follow these steps, but also pay attention to any instructions that came with your device. Make sure that your player supports your chosen audio and video formats before you begin.

1 If your streaming media player came with its own software then follow the instructions provided in order to install it. If you're using an Apple AirPort Express or Apple TV, all the software you need is included in iTunes version 7 or above.

For UPnP players, we strongly recommend that you use Microsoft's straightforward Windows Media Player 11

Install the software and let it find your media. You have to share media by type. Click the icon at the top left and select music. Right-click the Library and select Media Sharing. Then tick the 'Share my media to:' option. Windows will display detected PCs and media streamers, so you can choose to allow or deny media sharing for each one. Click OK, and then repeat the task for photos and videos by selecting them via the top-right icon.

2 Follow the manufacturer's instructions on how to plug in your streaming media player. Make sure that the wireless devices are positioned to receive the best possible signal from your router.

Audio-only players with built-in LCD screens require only power and an audio input. If your player or hi-fi uses a 3.5mm mini-jack audio socket, get an inexpensive phono-to-mini-jack lead.

Streaming media players that also support video playback need to be connected to your TV. Even if you're only using it to play music files, you'll need to have the TV on, as these players tend to lack LCD screens.

3 Once you've plugged in your player and switched it on, you'll need to look at its Settings menu. Check your manual for details on where to find this. You'll need to adjust the network settings for the device to work with your network. The easiest method is to set the device to Dynamic Host Configuration Protocol (DHCP), as this will allow your router to assign it a network address automatically.

With a wireless network, you'll also need to configure WEP or WPA security. Choose the setting that matches your network and enter the correct pass key. Also make sure that your router is set to support the same wireless standard as the player. If you're in any doubt, set the router to b and g mode to be sure. If everything is correct, the router should add the player to your network.

Now return to your computer and bring up Media Connect by double-clicking the icon in the System Tray at the bottom of the screen. The streaming media player should now appear on the Devices page with the word 'Denied' displayed in red text beside it. Select the device and click the Allow button. The

player should now be able to access any compatible files in the previously specified folders on your PC.

Apple's AirPort has no screen, so you must control it entirely from your PC. Connect to it wirelessly by right-clicking on the wireless icon in the System Tray and selecting View Available Wireless Networks. You should see an entry called Apple Network. Double-click on this to connect to it. Open iTunes and follow the instructions provided with the player. ■

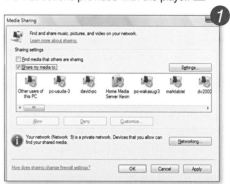

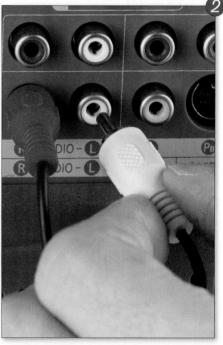

Optimise a surround-sound system

A few speaker adjustments can greatly enhance your listening pleasure

IF YOU HAVE surround-sound speakers attached to your PC, you'll need to position them carefully to get the best sound. We'll assume you have a set of 5.1 speakers attached to a computer using three of your sound card's analogue audio outputs, and that your computer feeds each speaker with its own separate sound. If you have a home-cinema amplifier connected to your computer via a digital S/PDIF cable, you'll need to read the amplifier's manual to find out how to apply these adjustments.

We've used a computer with a Realtek HD Audio sound card for this project, but even if your options are slightly different, the principles are the same.

1 First, place your speakers in the optimal positions. Ideally, you should locate your computer midway between two walls and place the front two speakers at least 1m apart. The centre speaker should be in line with the front speakers horizontally, but if you have to place it higher – say, above your screen – that's acceptable. The rear speakers should be placed behind you, about the same distance and height from you as the front speakers are. If you can't locate them behind you then place them at either side of you at roughly the same height as the front speakers, or at least at ear-level (when seated).

The sound from a subwoofer is non-directional, so it doesn't really matter too much where you put it. However, for maximum bass you should place it in a corner, close to the wall.

2 On your computer, find the audio management program. This may be listed in the Start menu or next to the clock in the System Tray. Check that the speaker configuration is set to 5.1 and not Stereo or Headphones. If there's a test button, press it and check that sound is emitted from the speaker that matches the onscreen graphic; this will let you know that everything is working properly, and alert you to any speakers that aren't working or that are in the wrong place.

3 Look for settings that allow you to set how far the speakers are from you. Setting these figures correctly will determine how realistic the surround-sound effect is. You'll need to measure the distances from your chair to the speaker with a tape measure, but these only need to be accurate to the nearest 10cm.

You may also find gain controls that allow you to increase the volume of individual speakers; experiment with these if certain speakers are too loud or too quiet. It's best to use a game or movie to test whether your settings are correct. You'll probably need to increase the volume of the rear speakers, especially if they're small satellite speakers located several metres behind you.

Finally, look for a bass adjustment control on your subwoofer. Play a section from a movie – preferably the loudest section, such as a series of explosions – so you can set the bass to an appropriate level. ■

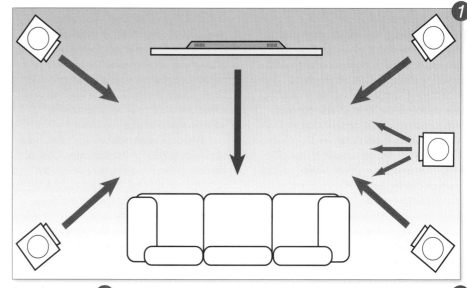

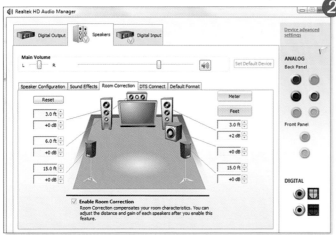

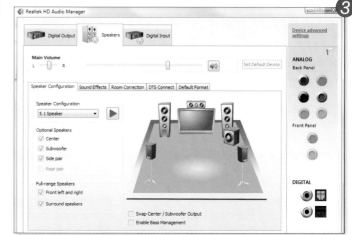

Set up your own webcam

Let your friends see you in real time while chatting online

CHATTING WITH FRIENDS online is a great way to keep in touch, and voice chat is getting more popular as broadband becomes more widespread. To take this to the next level, you can add video to your chat so that your friends can see you while you talk. If they also have a webcam, you can have a real conversation with someone on the other side of the world.

The first thing you need to do is to choose a webcam. You may already have one installed if you've recently bought a laptop computer, as they have become a standard feature. A lot of multimedia PCs also include one as part of the package. If you have an older computer or the quality of the included webcam is poor, however, you should invest in a standalone webcam. These are available for as little as £15 and often include a built-in microphone. Spending a bit more will increase the quality of the camera from 0.3 megapixels to two megapixels. More expensive models will add auto-lighting and autofocus features, and some even include face tracking, so you won't have to worry about moving around while you chat.

Installation of a webcam can vary widely from one manufacturer to another, so it's important to read the instructions that come with your model. Some require you to attach the webcam via USB and then install the drivers, while others will require the driver software to be loaded first. Getting this wrong can cause complications, so you should follow the manual's instructions exactly. It shouldn't take more than a few minutes.

Which IM clients support webcams?	
Skype	www.skype.com
Windows Live Messenger	http://get.live.com/messenger
Yahoo! Messenger	http://messenger.yahoo.com
AIM	http://dashboard.aim.com
ICQ	www.icq.com

Positioning the webcam correctly will ensure that your friends see you at your best. Try to have the camera in front of you and at the same level as your face. Avoid having a light behind you that will put your face in shadow. If you can't avoid this – if there's a window behind you, for example – then put a light behind the webcam, pointing at your face, to compensate for the backlight. More expensive webcams will adjust the picture automatically to compensate for bad lighting.

Once your webcam is installed, you can start using it straightaway in a number of popular instant messaging clients. However, it's worth checking that the picture looks OK and that the permissions are set correctly so that only the people you know can see your video online.

① WINDOWS LIVE MESSENGER
For Live Messenger, click on the Menu icon on the far right of the main toolbar, and then choose Tools, Webcam settings. Here you'll see a preview of your video feed, and you can use the Advanced button to tweak the camera's settings further.

If you want to turn off access to your webcam feed, there's an option in the Personal section of the preferences; however, it doesn't give you the option of just letting friends see you.

② SKYPE
For Skype, click on the Tools menu item and then choose Options. Clicking on Video Settings will show your video preview, and the boxes below let you choose who sees your webcam. Click on the Webcam Settings button to adjust your camera further.

③ YAHOO! MESSENGER
Yahoo! Messenger behaves slightly differently. Once you choose My Webcam from the Messenger menu, your webcam will be permanently broadcasting to whoever wants to tune in. In the My Webcam window, click on File and then select Preferences. Here you can choose whether to vet each person who requests access, or allow a select list of friends to tune in whenever they wish. ∎

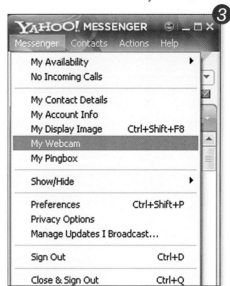

Back up flash media

Backing up your flash drive means you'll always have the right files to hand

IF YOU CARRY work documents, photos or even your personal novel on a flash drive with you when you're on the move, the files you keep on your home PC will quickly become outdated, with backups missing crucial information. Regularly backing up the files on your flash drive to an external hard disk, home system or laptop is the best way to ensure that all your files are up to date.

1 Software to back up your flash drive is freely available and there's a lot of choice. We've used Allway Sync here, as it is available for users both with and without U3-enabled flash drives. U3 is a company that produces proprietary software for flash drives and it is the developer of Launchpad, a program manager that auto-starts like Windows Start menu when a U3-enabled drive is connected to your PC.

Go to *www.allwaysync.com* and download the installation package. Once the software is installed, you can set up your first

backup profile. Simply open Allway Sync and you'll see the software's opening screen. There are a few manual options hidden in the View and Job menus; just follow the default options and select a folder to be synchronised.

2 With your flash drive attached to your PC, click Browse, expand My Computer and choose your flash drive and the necessary folder. Then do the same for the folder you wish to keep synchronised.

You can rename the Synchronization profile by right-clicking the tab and typing a new name. You can add as many new job profiles as you like; if you want to back up certain files to certain folders, rather than making a complete copy of the contents of the flash drive, you can. Once the profiles are added, you can analyse the differences between the files in the source folder and those in the destination folder. Just click Analyze and the results will be displayed.

3 In our example, none of the files we want to back up exists in the destination folder, and a message appears saying that there is "substantial difference in the folders". This notification is normal, as it is the first time we've backed up these files and folders. You should keep an eye out for this message after future analyses, particularly if you're not in the habit of synchronising the files regularly. Choose the Ignore option and press Synchronize. After a short

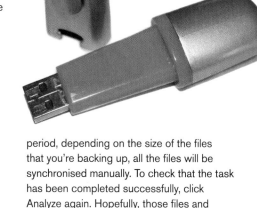

period, depending on the size of the files that you're backing up, all the files will be synchronised manually. To check that the task has been completed successfully, click Analyze again. Hopefully, those files and folders that previously did not exist will have disappeared from the list.

You can also set your backups to synchronise automatically. To see the options choose View, Options from the Menu bar, select the profile that you wish to customise, choose Automatic Synchronization and then simply tick the options that you require. Here you can choose to synchronise when the drive is connected, when file changes are detected and when Allway Sync starts up, and you can select from a number of other options to ensure that your flash media is always backed up and organised. ■

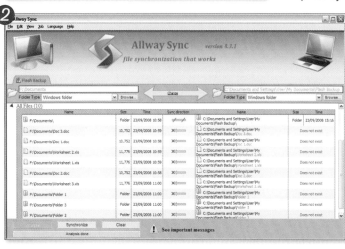

TIME REQUIRED	DIFFICULTY LEVEL	PROJECT	HARDWARE

30 MINUTES

HARD
INTERMEDIATE
EASY

PROJECT 065

Synchronise your mobile with your PC

Keep your contacts and files up to date by linking your phone and computer

IF YOU USE more than one mobile phone, or you change your handset regularly, it is helpful to synchronise data between your phone and your PC. In this walkthrough, we'll show you how to use the Mobile Master application to synchronise contacts and multimedia data between the two, regardless of the model of phone you have.

1 You can buy Mobile Master from *www.mobile-master.com* for €9.90 (around £8) for the Light Edition, with prices rising to €35.90 (around £29) for the Corporate Edition. For this project, we've used the free 30-day trial software.

Once you've download and installed the program, it will ask you to configure your phone connection. Mobile Master will give you the choice of cable, Bluetooth or an infrared connection, and will then begin scanning for your phone. We chose cable, using the USB-to-mini-USB lead that came with our phone. If you don't have the cable drivers installed, it runs through Windows' Found New Hardware Wizard. Once the drivers are installed, click Next to begin the scan for your phone.

2 Once Mobile Master has recognised your phone, click Next again to show the Mobile Master configuration screen. You can skip through this if you want to have a look around the software's options, but we chose the default: to synchronise our contacts with our installation of Outlook. Click Next again. You then need to decide whether the PC overwrites the mobile, or vice versa, in the event of a contact conflict. We chose the option of 'If conflicts: user input', which means that we are prompted to select which is the most up to date. You can then choose specific groups or folders, plus options for synchronising your appointments and calendar, and the conflicts override option for the calendar.

3 When you've finished configuring the software, go to Mobile Master's home panel. From here, you can synchronise anything from your contacts and calendar to photos, videos, music and the organiser.

Say you want to synchronise some images, for example. Select Photos and Videos from the menu. Choose where you would like the files copied to and press OK. After a short while, you'll have your images and videos backed up and easily accessible on your PC. Synchronising other information is just as simple, and allows you to keep your phone and PC organised with very little effort. ■

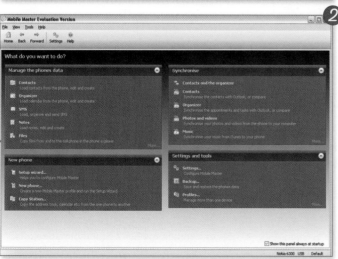

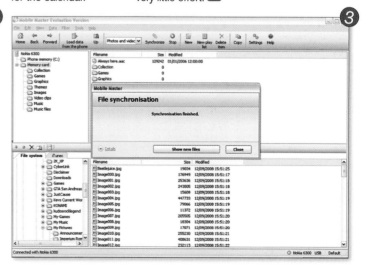

093

HARDWARE

PROJECT
066

DIFFICULTY LEVEL

HARD
INTERMEDIATE
EASY

TIME REQUIRED

15
MINUTES

Add support for Bluetooth

Enjoy the full benefits of Bluetooth by adding an adaptor

IF YOUR PHONE or PDA has Bluetooth, it's easy to upgrade your PC so it can talk to your mobile device without wires. This upgrade lets you add other devices, too.

Bluetooth makes it easy to get photos on to your PC from your phone's camera, or copy MP3s to a music player phone. All the major phone manufacturers have software that will enable you to do this. Nokia has its own PC Phone software, which lets you make calls and manage texts from your PC.

You can also synchronise your PDA or connect to the web through your phone without having to take either out of your pocket. Adding Bluetooth to a PC also lets you connect wireless peripherals such as mice and keyboards.

1 Before plugging in your adaptor, insert its driver CD and start the installation software. If you have Windows XP with Service Pack 2 or Windows Vista, you should be able to use Microsoft's own Bluetooth software instead – simply plug in your Bluetooth adaptor and let Windows do the rest.

Here, we'll be focusing on the Widcomm software that's included with almost all Bluetooth adaptors. If you're warned that the Bluetooth drivers are not signed, click Continue Anyway. When prompted, plug in your adaptor. If you're using a PCI card, you'll need to turn off the computer, install the card and then restart the PC.

2 Open My Computer and double-click on My Bluetooth Places. The Initial Bluetooth Configuration Wizard will appear. Click Next. You'll be asked to name your computer; enter something obvious such as loungepc. Choose Desktop or Laptop in the drop-down menu. Click Next, then Next again.

The following screen shows the Bluetooth services that your computer can provide. Untick any services you don't want to use. However, leave Bluetooth Serial Port selected, as this is used by many Bluetooth applications. When you click Next, the software will install more drivers. On the subsequent screen, click Skip and then Finish.

3 Go back to My Bluetooth Places. The window will be mostly empty. To add a device, click Bluetooth Setup Wizard at the top left. Ensure that your device has Bluetooth enabled and is in 'discoverable' or 'visible' mode. For mobile phones, these options will be in the configuration menus. There's usually an option to make your phone visible for a set period of time. On your PC, select the 'I want to find a specific Bluetooth device' option and configure the way this computer will use its services. The PC will begin searching.

Once your device appears, select it and click Next. If it doesn't appear, check that it's ready and click Search Again. Bluetooth Security Setup will appear. Enter a PIN into the box at the bottom and click Next. Your device will prompt you to enter the same PIN. This allows it to connect to your PC.

After a few seconds, a window shows the services that your device can provide to the PC. Select the one you want, then click Finish. The two are now connected. Disable discoverable mode on the device if you prefer. If you want to use advanced features on your phone, install its software now. ■

CHOOSING A BLUETOOTH ADAPTOR

If you have a laptop with a CardBus (PC Card) slot, there are Bluetooth adaptors to match. For a desktop PC, you can buy an adaptor card that fits into a free PCI slot. Alternatively, many adaptors such as the one pictured above connect to a USB port.

Bluetooth adaptors come in two types: Class 1 and Class 2. Class 1 adaptors can connect to devices at a range of up to 100m, while Class 2 devices have a range of around 10m, which is suitable for most purposes in the home or office. A PC Bluetooth adaptor will work with most devices, but you'll need one with stereo audio support (Profile A2DP) if you want to transmit music to Bluetooth speakers.

SOFTWARE PROJECTS

It's amazing how many possibilities a new piece of software can open up. We've got projects that involve installing Linux, converting your old VHS tapes, donating your spare processing power and a whole lot more!

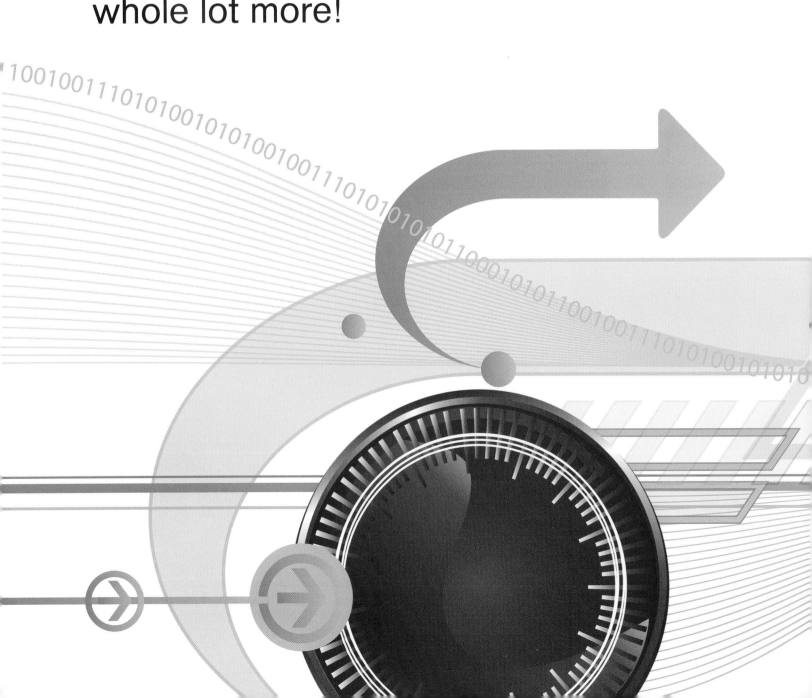

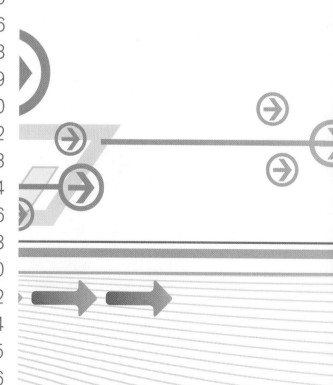

PROJECT
067

DIFFICULTY LEVEL

HARD
INTERMEDIATE

TIME REQUIRED

1
HOUR

Edit video with Windows Movie Maker

Splice and dice your video clips with ease

MICROSOFT HAS BUNDLED its Windows Movie Maker application in with most versions of Windows since the Me edition. Many of you running XP or Vista should have it installed or on the installation disc ready to use. If it's not on your PC, then it can be freely downloaded from *www.microsoft. com/windowsxp/downloads/updates/ moviemaker2.mspx*.

1 After you've launched Movie Maker, load all the footage you wish to use. To do this, click on Import Media, navigate to the folders where your clips are stored, and select the pieces of video you'd like to include. For this example, we've used the demo videos installed by default on Vista, which are all wildlife-based sequences.

2 Once you've imported the video clips, you can drop them onto the Storyboard at the bottom of the screen in the order you wish to see them presented. If you want to reorder them at any point, drag them around to where in the chain you want them. Movie Maker has some intelligence, and if you import a video containing multiple scenes it will break it down into selectable clips for you to work with.

3 Often you'll want to alter the clips by removing footage from either the start or end, or both. To do this we need to enter Timeline mode, by selecting it from the View menu. In this mode you can see exactly long each clip runs for, and the size of each in relation to the total running time.

4 Play the clip in the side panel until you get to the point where you wish it to start in your movie, then pause it using the video-style controls. A green vertical line on the Timeline shows where that marker is, and you can drag it to make adjustments. To remove the footage prior to that time, select Trim Beginning from the Clip menu. Conversely, the Trim End command will remove footage from the current position going forwards. If you make a mistake, don't worry; there's an option on the clip menu to reset the start and end.

5 We've added the clips and adjusted their start and end points; now for some light music. Use the Import Media button again – this time one of the default musical files is picked. Movie Maker can handle all manner of audio file types. Our chosen one is a Windows Media file suitable for our production.

6 After the music is imported, you can drag it from the media collection on to the timeline, to the section marked Audio/ Music. When it appears there, you might notice that it's longer than your production, so you'll need to fix that. Position the pointer over the end of the music and it will change shape. Click and drag to move the audio track to end at the same point as the movie.

7 Next, it's titles and credits. The title generator is available under the Edit menu for both Titles and Credits. You select which you want and then enter the text that will make up the wording. Once you're happy with the words, font and colour, simply click Add Title and they'll be inserted into the timeline at the front of the clips.

8 The credits are added using the same technique, except obviously they're placed at the end. This extends the running time of the movie, so you'll need to make adjustments to the length of the audio accordingly. You also might want to right-click on the audio and select 'Fade out', too.

9 You've tweaked your video and audio to perfection, and played it through to make sure it's exactly what you want. Now you can choose to publish the movie, which will take all your work and assemble a finished production that you can distribute. Selecting Publish offers you these choices, allowing you to make highly compressed versions for the internet, or high-quality DVDs.

UNDERSTANDING RESOLUTIONS

All digital video has a 'resolution' – the number of picture elements or pixels that make it up. A DVD is made up of a grid of these coloured dots, and in the UK has a resolution of 768 horizontally by 576 vertically. Digital cameras will have their own resolutions that they will record at, and some might be greater than DVD (if they're labelled HD) and less if they're in an 'economy' recording mode. It's possible to shrink higher resolutions down, but stretching them upwards doesn't yield as good results. It's best to shoot at the highest quality settings, as you can then edit and output the finished movie for optimum results.

10　If you choose to output a compressed file, Movie Maker informs you of the important details about the movie it's going to generate, including the resolution, running time and aspect ratio. If the video has to fit on a memory stick, then you can select the option to compress the output to a specific size. That said, this might impact quality if you opt for too small a file, so try and use this option sparingly.

11　Saving the file allows you to enjoy the movie just by opening it, and to reload the edited version if you want to add new scenes and make adjustments. It took a couple of minutes to create our file, although a longer, DVD production will inevitably take a good deal longer.

The strength of Windows Movie Maker is that it's really easy to use, and that it also provides enough features to give you basic, functional video editing facilities. Certainly even beginners should have few problems with it. It also has the ability to import video from a good number of different sources, including video capture cards and USB/FireWire-connected cameras.

The high-definition (HD) version of Movie Maker that comes installed with Vista Premium and Ultimate can handle high-definition HDV camcorders, although that

release has also had the ability to import analogue material removed from it. All versions of Windows up to XP can run version 2.1, available from Microsoft, and a very similar version 2.5 is available for those versions of Windows Vista that don't come with it.

Movie Maker will only create movie files in Microsoft's Windows Media formats, although it's possible to make it output in a

number of different file types if you're prepared to learn how to use the Windows Media Profile Editor (which is part of the Windows Media Encoder 9 Series), and understand how the different video codecs work. However, most people who want to create movies using DivX, H.264 or MPEG-2 codecs usually resort to commercial applications that will support these technologies out of the box. ▬

ONLINE MOVIE MAKER

The latest version of Movie Maker isn't a conventional PC tool. It's a web-based application called Windows Live Movie Maker, and it's currently in the beta stage of development. Due to the performance limitations of the internet, this version is primarily focused on editing low-resolution video destined for

online distribution, but with the same functionality as you've now experienced with the installed version of Movie Maker.

To use it you'll need Windows XP or Vista on your machine, and a broadband connection. If you're interested in experimenting, it can be found at *http://download.live.com/moviemaker*.

SOFTWARE

PROJECT
068

DIFFICULTY LEVEL
HARD
INTERMEDIATE

TIME REQUIRED
1
HOUR

Print your own T-shirts

Fancy yourself as a designer? Then why not wear your work?

SOME SPECIFIC KIT is needed for this project, including:

- Art package software for designing the print or editing the photo
- Transfer paper
- A printer
- Iron or heat press
- Tea towel or pillowcase
- T-shirt

If you've got all that, then transferring a home-made image to a T-shirt is a relatively easy process, providing it's done with care and attention – otherwise it'll be a big mess!

The first step is to choose a design and produce it to a quality suitable for the job. Blowing up a small image won't work (unless nasty-looking pixellation is the aim, where the picture looks fuzzy and blocky); it needs to start big, at a high resolution, and get smaller as you shrink it to your requirements, not the other way around.

It's vital to look at the print preview, and preferably to print on paper, before committing to anything. The printer margins may cut off part of your image, colours will probably look different to how they appear on your monitor, and there may even be a glaring error (remember the story of the man who brought some shirts home from Thailand with 'Endlang' emblazoned across the front?).

Also note that printers don't print white. This could cause all sorts of problems with a complex image and make the overall effect very strange without getting special paper for dark shirts. Remember that any detail work, such as airbrushing, probably won't look the same as on screen and may turn out to be a disappointment. Keeping things reasonably simple is never a bad idea.

Once the image is finished, flip it. It will need to be printed backwards onto the transfer paper. Using a specialist piece of

AVOID PRINTER MELTDOWN!

It is absolutely essential for the sake of the printer that the right paper gets used. Putting paper for an inkjet into a laser printer will produce the unpleasant result of having to buy a new laser printer.

software such as T-Shirt Maker Deluxe might remove the need for this, but all text has to be the 'wrong' way around for it to come out properly on the material.

Now comes the fun part. For starters, the transfer paper needs to be loaded into the printer the correct way, so ensure it's got the right side facing downwards. It's worth running a plain sheet through for testing just to be on the safe side. Once the image is printed, stay away from it for a few moments; it should be fine, especially coming from a laser printer, but it's not worth the risk of smudging it.

Because the sheet is likely to be A4, or at least not the exact size of the printed image, trim it down to avoid having excess clear plastic on your garment. Place the T-shirt on a hard, flat surface – preferably

not an ironing board for heat-dispersal reasons – with the pillowcase underneath. Make sure everything is smooth, lay the transfer out and then read the transfer instructions carefully. No two kinds of paper are alike, and the exact instructions at this point should be obtained from the manufacturer. It's worth taking time to do that, rather than wasting a transfer by cutting an unnecessary corner.

Pay attention to the edges, apply plenty of pressure and heat, and the transfer should be successful. After it's complete, it's worth putting the T-shirt through the wash, inside-out, on a cool setting.

Results vary wildly. Some people report cracking problems after the first wash, while others say their shirts have lasted for more than 100 washes with no damage. Patience is the key, and it may take a few goes to get it exactly right.

Scan and archive household documents

Keep important paperwork safe and secure with the aid of your scanner

EVERY HOUSEHOLD ACCUMULATES masses of paperwork, including contracts, bills, statements and receipts. It's almost guaranteed that every person reading this has a drawer packed to bursting with such documents – things you don't want to throw away, just in case.

The problem with this is the sheer amount of space that all of this paperwork takes up, and how disorganised it can therefore become. Finding that gas bill from just a few months back becomes a veritable archaeological expedition, such is the searching that tends to be involved.

Luckily, with a scanner and Windows' built-in scanning wizard, you can put an end to this often tedious task, and by scanning and archiving your documents to your computer or to CD/DVD, you'll never struggle to find anything again.

First, you'll need to get your paperwork to be scanned together, and then fire up your scanner. Then you'll need a directory set up on your PC for your paperwork. Create a descriptive folder, such as Bills – 2008 and, if you wish, create subfolders for the months, and so on. Once you've done this, slip the first page in your scanner, and you can begin.

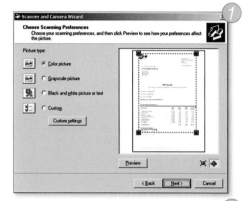

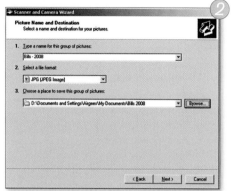

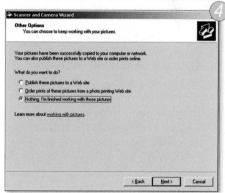

1   To start, go to Start, All Programs, Accessories, Scanner and Camera Wizard. This will open the wizard, so click Next on the welcome screen. Now, pick the type of picture you want and click Preview to scan a test image, so you can get the orientation right, and select the scan area by dragging the image handles. Click the Next button to continue.

2   You now need to give the picture group a name. Do so and then select an image format. JPG is fine for most home documents, but GIF files have smaller file sizes and can also display text more clearly. Finally, choose the location to save the scanned image to (the folders you set up previously) and then click Next.

3   The scanner will kick into action and scan your image to your chosen destination. If you need to stop scanning for any reason, click Cancel.

4   After the scanning is complete, you can choose to publish documents to a website (which is not recommended for home documents, obviously), order prints or do nothing. Select the latter and the folder containing the scan will then open automatically for you.

Once you've done that, you then need to repeat the process for each individual document. What you'll ultimately end up with is a full document archive, split into the folders that you created earlier. You can now burn all of these to a disc for safe keeping, which is always a good idea where important financial data is concerned.

Archive documents to disc with Windows' built-in CD-burning tool

RESCUE DISC

Burning discs in Windows XP doesn't require specialised software or expensive tools, as the operating system comes with its own built-in CD burning engine. While limited, this is very useful for basic tasks, such as copying household documents to disc.

All you need to do is insert a blank disc, and when prompted, select Open writable CD folder. You can now drag and drop files and folders into the new window, and can then burn the disc by clicking Write these files to CD. You'll then need to name the disc, and the recoding process will begin. Once done, your important documents will be on the disc.

SOFTWARE

PROJECT
070

DIFFICULTY LEVEL
HARD
INTERMEDIATE
EASY

TIME REQUIRED
30 MINUTES

Sort out your household accounts

Use your computer to keep your finances in order

MANAGING YOUR FINANCES used to involve lots of paper and hard work. These days, the computer can step in and do what it was intended for: sums. Instead of calculating polygons here and ragdoll physics there, it can finally get down to the pure and obvious maths of income versus expenditure, tax percentages and what's left over after deductions.

There are two ways of approaching this project, and it's entirely dependent on the level of detail required and the expenditure allowed. The traditional method is to a use a simple spreadsheet, such as Microsoft Excel or OpenOffice Calc, and the newer option is to buy a specialist application, the best known being Quicken, Personal Accountz and MoneyDance (which is probably more familiar these days in its guise as Tesco Personal Finance). The top, professional accounting package is SAGE, but this is aimed at businesses and can require training. There are some older products that are no longer supported, such as Microsoft Money, and less 'famous' applications such as Ability Accounts and BankTree.

Prices vary enormously depending on what is purchased and which version – and, indeed, if it's charged for at all. A spreadsheet application can be had for nothing with OpenOffice, whereas a copy of Microsoft

ONLINE OPTIONS

These days, there's another way of organising your finances: an online system. Mint.com provides a free service that actually accesses financial accounts automatically, saving the data entry, and does all kinds of natty things like finding a better credit card and showing expenditure versus the average for the rest of the country.

It's currently available only in the USA. However, it also requires a lot of faith in internet security systems, requiring the input of account details and passwords. Although the site promises security, given the current climate it may take a while for such a thing to catch on in the UK.

Excel is closer to the £200 mark. However, a spreadsheet will require setting up from scratch, because it's not designed for this exact purpose. In turn this gives a large amount of flexibility, but requires an initial outlay of effort. See the boxout for an idea of retail costs.

Let's go, for the purposes of our example, with the free and simple spreadsheet option by using OpenOffice Calc (downloadable from *www.openoffice.org*). It needs a basic knowledge of formulae but will do all the calculations easily and comes with no added bells and whistles.

1 Open up a new workbook. At the top, input all the necessary categories:

- The date of the transaction
- The payee
- Category of payment
- Expenditure
- Income
- Balance

Once this is done, highlight the whole row by clicking on the 1, then go to the Window menu. Click Freeze. A slight division should appear between this row and the next.

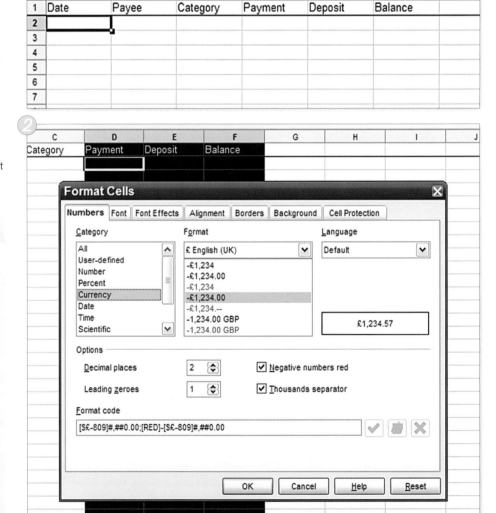

2 Next, select any columns that will contain monetary amounts, and then go to the Format menu. Selecting Cells will show a number of ways of formatting them – under Category, choose Currency. This can be adjusted according to your personal preference, including options for decimal points or commas, and having negative numbers in red.

The same can be done with the Date column, dependant on personal preference.

3 Payees and categories of payments can be turned into a drop-down list to avoid having to type the same things over and over again.

Select all of the cells in a particular column, go to the Data menu and click

Validity. A box will appear with the category Allow. This should be set to list. Make sure Show selection list is checked and then input the names (employer, HMRC and so on) one per line. Then click OK.

On clicking any cell in the column, a drop-down menu should now appear containing entries that correspond with what was typed into the Validity box. This can now be used for easy selection of names. In theory, this could be for monetary amounts if they were constant.

4 Now it's time for the actual figures, and setting up the calculations. On the first line of the Deposit category, enter a starting balance. In the Balance column, in the cell next to the amount, type the formula E2-D2 (deposit minus payment).

5 On the line under this, the first entry goes in. In this case it's a deposit of £180 made by an employer. In the Balance column, place the formula =F2+E3-D3 (cell plus deposit minus payment). The new balance will automatically appear in the Balance column.

6 Now, every time a new entry goes in, all that needs doing is for the previous balance to be copied to the cell below and it will magically become the correct balance again, regardless of whether the new entry is income or expenditure.

It will be obvious if anything is wrong because an error message, likely "#NAME?", will appear. Check all formulae, and that nothing has been copied from the wrong place (forgetting to enter an equals sign before the formula is a very common mistake).

Something this simple can now afford control over any basic financial transactions, and all the spreadsheet graph functions can be used to get a pictorial overview of where money is going.

SOFTWARE PRICES

To give you a comparison, here's what each option costs:

Option 1: Spreadsheet
Microsoft Excel: £208
OpenOffice Calc: Free
Google Docs: Free

Option 2: Specialist software
SAGE: £199
Ability Accounts: £80
Personal Accountz: £40
BankTree: £26
TurboCASH: Free

PROJECT
071

DIFFICULTY LEVEL

HARD
INTERMEDIATE
EASY

TIME REQUIRED

45
MINUTES

Clean up your hard disk

Follow these simple steps to help keep your hard drive healthy

WITH PROLONGED USE, all PCs, no matter how powerful, will start to show signs of sluggishness. Programs will take longer to load, and files will take that little extra time to open. This can be down to many things, with one of the most common being a cluttered and unruly hard disk.

As the PC is used, programs are added and removed and all manner of data is copied to the disk. Your PC has more and more searching to do to find what it needs at any given time. Data becomes jumbled and fragmented, and in some worst-case scenarios, it can be corrupted and unusable.

To combat this, it's wise to take care of your hard drive, and make sure your data is kept clean and tidy. This makes for speedy file access, as well as a much reduced chance of data loss.

A vital step that should be performed on a regular basis is disk cleanup. This task can remove all unneeded files from your hard drive, such as temporary files, installation files and other items that you can get along fine without.

1. Windows features its own disk cleanup tool, found in Windows Explorer. To get to it, go to My Computer and then right-click the hard disk you wish to clean. Select Properties and then click the Disk Cleanup button.

2. In the new window, you'll see a list of possible items to be cleaned, along with the disk space they're currently using. Place a tick into the box to the left of each item and click OK. The disk cleanup tool will then perform its duties and will remove the unwanted files. Another essential Windows-based task is disk defragmenting. This

function analyses your hard drive(s) for fragmented data and then methodically moves data around, tidying it up and placing groups of data together. This then speeds up access to that data.

A heavily fragmented drive won't simply become sluggish, but it could also cause crashes and further complications, so running a defrag once or twice a month is a good habit to get into.

3. Defrag comes as part of Windows and can be found by going to My Computer, right-clicking the drive you wish to defragment and clicking Properties. Go to the the Tools tab and then click the Defragment Now button.

4. Defrag will open, and you should first click Analyse to check to see if the drive needs to be defragmented. Once done, the tool will inform you of the state of the drive. To defragment it, simply click the Defragment button and sit back while the process is run. This can take a very long time, depending on the size of the drive and level of fragmentation.

While it's not an actual disk cleanup application, Windows' disk-checking tool is another task that you can run to further ensure that your hard drives are in good health. To do so, go to the drive properties as you did with defrag and, under the Tools tab, click Check Now. You can choose to automatically fix errors and to scan and attempt recovery of bad sectors. Selecting these options is a good idea, but will take longer to scan. Click Start to begin the error-checking process.

Windows' own disk cleaning tools are useful, but as is often the case, having a dedicated tool for the task is even better, and one of the best free titles around is CCleaner (*www.ccleaner.com*). This is a very powerful and thorough disk-cleaning tool that can not only clean out temp files and other unwanted files, just as Windows' Disk Cleanup can, but it can also remove junk files from a range of other programs, including Internet browsers. It

INTERNET EXPLORER CACHE

You may not consider Internet Explorer when cleaning your hard disk, but this frequently used application can contribute heavily to hard disk clutter. As you browse the internet, you'll amass all sorts of temporary files, such as images. These are stored in a cache to aid faster browsing, but aren't needed afterwards.

To clear out these files, open Internet Explorer 6 and click Tools, Internet Options. In the new dialog box, click the 'Delete' button under Browsing History.

For Internet Explorer 5, click Tools, Internet Options and click the 'Delete Files' button under the Temporary Internet Files section.

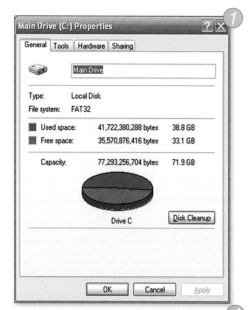

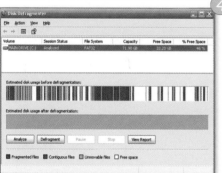

can scan and remove broken system Registry entries and can even uninstall programs. Using the program is easy too.

5 Download and install CCleaner from the website and run it. Before you perform a disk cleanup you'll need to configure the program. In the left-hand panel, select the items you want CCleaner to tackle. Advanced items are possible, but observe any messages that CCleaner displays when you activate these. It's probably best at first to keep things simple.

6 Next, perform an analysis to see exactly what CCleaner is going to remove. Click the Analyse button and the application will return with the list of changes to be made.

7 As long as you're happy with the list of changes (and take a little time to ensure that you are), click Run Cleaner and CCleaner will rampage through your system's junk files, and remove all items. Once it's completed this task, the program will inform you of its success. ▬

NIPPING IT IN THE BUD

By far the best way to combat disk clutter is to stop it happening in the first place. If you don't fill up your hard disks with files, then your drives will have less work to do.

If you've got masses of photos or other media files, it's a good idea to store them on a disc. This keeps them safe and keeps your hard disk clean. Keeping your main system drive clean is a good idea, and storing files on another drive or external hard disk is an effective way to keep your system happy.

The best way to make sure that files you delete are actually removed, and not merely placed in the Recycle Bin, is to press Shift+Del when getting rid of them. This bypasses the Recycle Bin entirely, and deletes the file outright. Be careful when you're doing this, however, because it's nowhere near as easy to recover files that have been deleted using this method if you later decide you need the file.

SOFTWARE

PROJECT
072

DIFFICULTY LEVEL
HARD
INTERMEDIATE
EASY

TIME REQUIRED
15 MINUTES

Add new fonts to your computer

Increasing your typeface options couldn't be easier

IF THE FONTS that came with your PC are starting to feel old, it's time for a change. Many that come with operating systems and word processing software are uninspiring and simply not ideal for fancier projects.

Some applications will install fonts relating to how they work, and there are interesting ones to be found this way. Music-scoring programs, in particular, use ornate and unusual fonts that aren't necessarily on the 'popular' list. However, you can also install new fonts yourself.

There are huge numbers of fonts available, either from the internet or commercial packages. It's not unusual to find titles, such as ClickArt 10,000 Fonts, for less than £10, and with that many it's hard to see a situation that won't be covered.

Fonts are simply stored as files on a PC and accessed by applications from a central folder. The most common is the TrueType font, a .ttf extension, which ensures that what appears on the screen is what appears on the page. You can view your font files by simply looking in the Fonts section of your Windows folder, where they'll be listed like any other type of file.

The best thing about this is that installing a new font really can be as easy as dragging and dropping a new file into that folder. Let's take an example from *www.1001freefonts. com*. The featured font is called Badaboom, and has a comic-book-style appearance.

Clicking on Download Win Font brings up a standard archived file to be saved. Opening it up with WinZip shows three files: two are text files relating to the copyright and distribution, but the key file is the one marked .ttf. This is the font file itself.

Unzip the file to the desktop, or another place it can be easily located. Then, from the Start menu, choose Control Panel and then

Fonts. This goes straight through to the folder mentioned earlier. Under File choose Install New Font. Locate the font file, press OK, and it's done.

All the resident applications on the PC should now recognise the new font, although they may need to be restarted first. Note that it will only work on the computer the font was installed to, and won't be available to any other machines on a network.

The contents of the font file dictate what is available to a word-processing or presentation package. Although it's common for fonts to be capable of being resized from 8-point size all the way up to 100-point or more, some will only come in certain sizes and will look wrong if pushed beyond their limits. Also, don't expect all the standard formatting, such as bold, italic or underline, to be available – they will only be there if you've downloaded the correct versions. A quick glance in the Fonts folder will show that Times New Roman requires three separate files for three separate formats, for example.

One word of warning, though: a sure-fire way to slow down any system is to install too many fonts. Delete those that you don't use, and your computer will thank you for it.

All fonts can be found through Control Panel

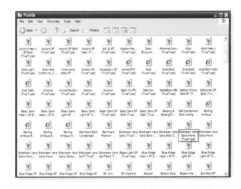
The Fonts folder. Double-clicking any of these will show the font itself

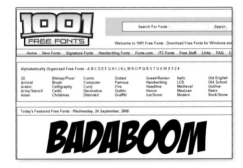
1001 Free Fonts offers a wide selection of fonts for download

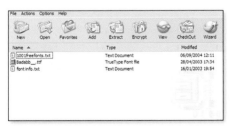
Fonts commonly come packaged in a Zip file

CREATING YOUR OWN FONTS

If you can't find what you want, it's possible to create fonts yourself entirely from scratch. Fontifier (*www.fontifier. com*) will do it all for you automatically; all that's required is to download the template provided, write the alphabet out in a creative way and let the software work out the rest. For $9, a professional-standard font (dependent on original input, of course) will be produced, and the downloading and installing process is exactly the same as above.

TIME REQUIRED   DIFFICULTY LEVEL   PROJECT   SOFTWARE

45 MINUTES

HARD
INTERMEDIATE
EASY

073

Produce a PowerPoint presentation

Get your point across with a good presentation

ALTHOUGH IT LOOKS far more fancy, Microsoft PowerPoint is essentially Microsoft Word with some bells and whistles added on. Anybody with a basic grasp of how to use a word-processing package can get to grips with making a presentation that looks reasonably impressive, and it won't take much time to do.

1 Opening PowerPoint, or any equivalent such as OpenOffice's Impress, will bring up a screen asking whether it should use any templates. It's generally easier to go for a blank presentation and start from scratch.

2 Likewise, there's an unnecessarily large menu with lots of content-placing templates. Choosing the blank one is actually the most useful, but anybody not wanting to think about it too much could go for one of the pre-set ones. More slides can be added through Insert, New Slide.

3 Next up is to pick a background for the slides by choosing Format, Apply Design Template. The one chosen here, Neon Frame, uses a nice dark background with simple patterning and white text. It's important not to have loads going on in the basic template, because things can get very cluttered later on.

4 Adding text and pictures is exactly the same as in Word, by using text boxes and the Insert function. They can be moved around by dragging or resizing.

5 Now comes the part that makes PowerPoint famous: adding movement and transitions.

Each object on the page can be made to 'fly' in or appear by right-clicking and selecting Custom Animation. PowerPoint comes with many different ways of making people jump, and it's worth using a handful rather than all of them to avoid the presentation looking amateurish.

Objects can also be made into hyperlinks, which is useful for times when external content is required or viewers need to be directed elsewhere once the presentation is finished.

6 Using too many colours, fonts or animations is off-putting and should be avoided, however tempting it may initially be. Ideally, only one or two images should be used per slide, and they should be big enough to serve their purpose.

Remember that there may be blind spots on the display when it comes to your presentation itself, especially if the screen is behind a desk. Also, if your audience are sat in rows, the people at the back of the room might not be able to see the screen.

The biggest mistake tends to be using too much text on one slide. Don't overwhelm the audience by giving them too much to read.

7 An understanding of the page concept is important in PowerPoint. Ask yourself where does the text appear from? Is this a logical approach? Do the text and images sit well together?

8 Some colour combinations can be very hard to read. Red has been known to cause problems, and using a light colour on a light background is eye-damaging at best and unreadable at worst. ■

CREATING FILMS

With a bit of imagination it's possible to do some very impressive things in PowerPoint. Use of the Zoom In function on text can produce the effect of a page being 'stamped', and Crawl can give the *Star Wars* scrolling effect. Cars can drive across the slide, staggered arrow animations can produce the effect of an animated neon sign pointing to a doorway, and so on.

A nice effect...

Bad presentations BANNED!

This effect was created by rotating the text box and using the 'Zoom In' animation.

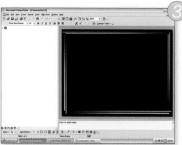

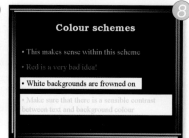

SOFTWARE

PROJECT
074

DIFFICULTY LEVEL
HARD
INTERMEDIATE
EASY

TIME REQUIRED

45
MINUTES

Organise your images

Keep your images in order with simple, free tools

WITH DIGITAL CAMERAS now available for a far more reasonable price than ever before, and with the massive popularity of mobile phone cameras, people are increasingly taking advantage of flexible, money-saving ways to take pictures.

Unfortunately, this can lead to a surplus of images and, once they're transferred to your PC, you'll have folder after folder of holiday pics, birthday snaps and wedding photos, all scattered around in no real order, making them hard to view, and even harder to show others. With the right tools, however, this problem can be solved in an instant, and your once-cluttered image collection can become an ordered album of memories.

There are plenty of programs available on the PC to take care of such matters, and one of the best free options is Picasa 2, now owned by internet giant, Google (*www.google.com*). Picasa 2 is a powerful image organiser, packed with features that let you get the most from your stored images.

The core of the program is that of an image library. This has a full list of all folders on your PC that contain images, and catalogues them by date, making it easy to find any image, including holiday snaps from years gone by. Any of these images can then be gathered into special photo albums, and organised into attractive slideshows for showing your snaps to others.

The Timeline feature is an interesting way to view and search your images. It presents a full-screen scrolling menu organised along a simple timeline from which you can perform a range of tasks, such as viewing items and setting up automatic and manual shows.

Picasa 2 is a powerful program, but there's an even easier option for organising your images. Adobe Photoshop Album Starter Edition 3.0 is available free of charge, and is attractive and easy to use. It gives you

access to a wide range of tools, including the ability to view all photos in a single library or the more attractive option of a slideshow if you'd prefer. There's a timeline that can filter images by date created, and you can easily upload items to the web, or email images to friends and family.

However, it's in organising photos where this application is most useful, and if you need to catalogue your snaps, it's as easy as dragging and dropping files where you want. Here's what you need to do.

WINDOWS' PICTURE FOLDERS

Using dedicated image-organising software is the best way to manage and organise your images, but Windows also includes its own basic image management capabilities.

Simply placing photos into a folder is enough for Windows to recognise that the folder in question contains images,

and thumbnails of some images will be shown on the folder icon in thumbnail view. If you right-click on a folder that contains images and then select View as slideshow from the left-hand panel, you'll instantly see a full screen slideshow of the photos in the folder for you to quickly look through.

1 To organise your images quickly in Adobe Photoshop Album, first you need to create a new Collection. To do this, click New… under the Collection tab, give your new group a name and description, and then click OK. The new empty group will be created in the right-hand panel, ready for you to use.

2 Now, select the images from the library that you wish to include in the

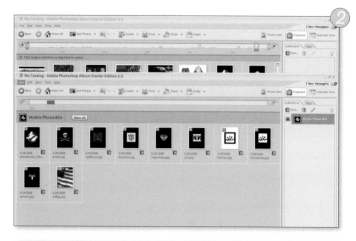

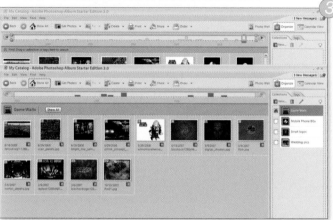

collection. You can drag individual images into the group, or you can hold down Shift or Ctrl to select multiple items and drag them over all in one go As you drop the images in the new collection, the program will then update automatically.

You can create multiple collections for all sorts of themes, such as holiday snaps, weddings and so on. Once created and populated, all you need to do is double-click a collection to view only the photos contained within it.

TWINS VISIONS

A flashier option for organising and displaying images is the free application Twins Visions (*www.twins-solutions.com*). This image organiser and viewer uses DirectX to display your picture folders in a real-time three-dimensional display.

Once it's installed, the program then needs to search through your entire system for your images. When the program opens up, you can then add various picture folders to the 3D view.

Images can then be organised by dragging and dropping files from each 3D folder into another, complete with impressive graphical effects as you do so! Slideshows can also be run, and you can go on a tour of your images, with the 3D view panning around each folder in turn.

XP IMAGE TAGS

It's possible to organise JPEG and TIFF images in Windows using tags, which can then be filtered via the standard Windows Search function. Here's how:

First, right-click an image you wish to tag and then click Properties, Summary (Simple menu). Now, in the Keywords box, enter specific search words, separated by a semi-colon. These words will be used as search criteria, much like internet search terms, so try to make them as specific as you possibly can.

Now, go to Windows' search function and select Pictures, music or video and click Use advanced search options. In the A word or phrase in the file box, enter one of your search words and then click Search. Only items with the matching tags (as well as filenames with the matching word in) should appear.

SOFTWARE

PROJECT
075

DIFFICULTY LEVEL
HARD
INTERMEDIATE
EASY

TIME REQUIRED
2 HOURS

Transfer your VHS tapes to DVD

Preserve those memories by copying them to disc

THERE ARE RELATIVELY few people still recording onto VHS tapes, simply because there are far better (and cheaper) alternatives. Yet there are literally thousands of tapes lying around, containing irreplaceable recordings of family occasions, or other memorable events that are slowly deteriorating.

The best way to preserve them is to transfer them to a new medium that doesn't degrade. DVD is the obvious choice, because it's relatively cheap and, using modern equipment, is reasonably quick to do.

By far the easiest method is with a dual VHS/DVD recorder that will simply do the whole job internally. Just pop a blank VHS tape in one side and a blank DVD in the other and press the record button. However, this method doesn't give you any editing facilities, and this type of recorder can be quite expensive, all things considered.

Alternatively, you could use a stand-alone DVD recorder; these can normally interface directly with your VCR via a SCART-to-SCART cable, or some other combination of SCART and composite/audio phono connectors. In fact, some of the later models are also fitted with a hard drive and 10/100 network connector; this means you can download video, or digital photos to the onboard drive and then burn them directly to DVD. They can also provide a limited degree of linear editing; for example, you may be able to remove superfluous material.

However, if you want to take things to a different level and create proper DVDs from your VHS recordings, and perhaps edit the

A typical VHS and DVD combo

data before burning it to DVD, you need to get the contents of your VHS tapes on your PC.

There are a number of ways to get VHS content onto a computer. The simplest (and possibly cheapest) method is to capture the data using your PC's video card. Many new graphics cards come with this capability (but not all), and it's called VIVO (Video In/Video Out). Be aware, however, that the quality is not always of a particularly high standard.

A better proposition is to use an external capture device such as the EasyCap USB 2.0,

This standalone recorder has a built-in hard drive

If your VCR is fairly modern, it should have the necessary connections

Many modern video cards also include VIVO

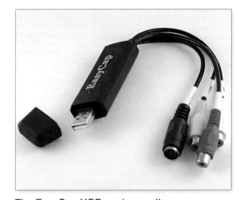
The EasyCap USB capture unit

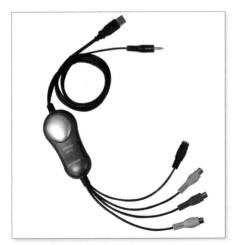
Avermedia Ezmaker Capture unit

Plextor USB Capture

Pinnacle's Dazzle DVD Recoder

the Plextor PX-AV200U, or Pinnacle's Dazzle DVD Recorder. These are all USB 2.0 devices capable of capturing VHS or SVHS video, and they're also able to convert video data to the MPEG-2 format needed for DVD.

These are, of course, not the only products available that have this capability, but are merely cited here as examples. A bit of shopping around should help you find something that's best suited for you.

The final option to consider is an internal video capture device. These tend to be the more expensive choice, but they will usually produce noticeably better results. They will probably have more input output options as well, so could prove useful after you've archived all your VHS tapes.

Typical cards available include the PCI-based Studio Movie Board, again from Pinnacle, or perhaps the Osprey 100 from Viewcast. Hauppauge also has a couple of cards that will capture video, but this is a secondary feature, and their main purpose is to provide TV to your desktop.

The majority of these devices provide four connections, made up of one composite video, two audio and an S-video. To connect them to a VCR you'll need a cable with a SCART plug on one end and three RCA or phono plugs on the other. Your capture device will normally provide more specific requirements.

QUALITY CONTROL

Sadly, VHS is just about the worst quality medium you can record on. Consequently, if you're expecting to transfer the data and somehow miraculously get DVD quality, you're going to be disappointed. However, archiving them to DVD before the tapes start to degrade is certainly a worthwhile exercise, because it converts them to a digital rather than analogue format. That means that like CDs, they can be copied again and again without any subsequent loss of quality.

Some of the hardware options discussed here will also include a software solution too. In many cases these are quite basic but, for the most part, may be sufficient for your needs. Once you've captured your video and started scanning through the files, you may feel that editing would improve the final DVD. In that case there are literally dozens of products to choose from. Typical choices are Pinnacle Studio, Magix Video to DVD, Adobe Premiere Elements and Sony's Vegas Movie Studio.

You'll find that the latest version of Pinnacle Studio has an Instant DVD Recorder option. This will transfer your video files directly to DVD, but still provides full editing facilities if you want to go in that direction. The Magix company also produces a product called Rescue Your Videotapes. This package includes a small USB video converter that will capture and convert a video stream in real time, providing more of an all-in-one option.

Having transferred your video files to the PC and converted them to MPEG-2, the next step is to load them into your chosen DVD authoring program. This will allow you to edit the footage, determine the order in which each clip will appear, and perhaps add a few titles and some background music to the production.

Then comes the creative bit where you can design the layout of your DVD menus, which can be as simple or as complex as you wish. We've talked about that elsewhere in this book but, for example, you can have a single button that will launch the DVD programme, or you can have pages of animated buttons that lead to individual clips.

The final stage will render the menus and convert your video clips into the special format needed for a DVD. The physical process will depend on the software you use, but they're generally similar.

Avermedia Ezmaker DVD PCI version

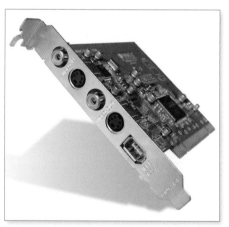

Studio Movie Board PCI Version

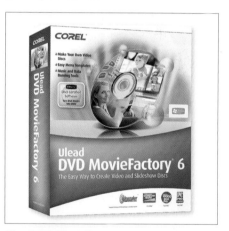

Ulead DVD MovieFactory, a first-class, easy-to-use solution

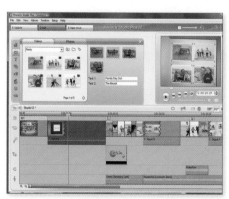

Pinnacle Studio 12 Album screen

Pinnacle's Score Fitter will create a score to fit the length of your DVD

The Smart Movie option in Studio 12 will automatically add a predefined theme

HARD
INTERMEDIATE
EASY

30 MINUTES

Set up iTunes to manage your music

Get the most from Apple's music player

FIRST THINGS FIRST: if you haven't already got a copy, you can download iTunes from *www.apple.com/itunes/download*, and install it on your computer. Just follow the installation wizard and, when you're done, run the application. If you already have music on your computer, iTunes will find it and add it to your iTunes library during the initial set-up.

Now it's time to add some more music. Importing MP3s is simple: just drag and drop them into the application. It's easy to import CDs too; insert the CD into your computer, and you're asked if you want to import it. You don't have to, and you can click the No button to play your CD through iTunes without importing it. If you want to import the entire CD, click Yes and it will be added to your library. If you only want to import a few tracks, select No and untick the songs you don't want before pressing the Import CD button in the bottom-right corner of the application. If your computer is connected to the internet, album and song titles are added automatically.

If you've got an account with the iTunes Music Store, you can add album art

automatically too. Select the option in the Advanced menu. If you haven't, or the store can't find your album's artwork, add it manually. Find the sleeve on the internet, highlight every track from that album, then drag and drop the sleeve onto the window in the bottom-left corner.

You can also edit song titles and other metadata from here. Highlight the song you wish to edit, and select Get Info. By highlighting more than one track you can edit several songs at once, which is useful when adding info like Artist, Album, Year and Genre – you can do the entire album instead of editing each track individually. Music imported from a CD or bought from the iTunes store shouldn't require editing in this way, but MP3s obtained from other sources might not offer the information you want.

Finally, there's the iTunes Store. Click on iTunes Store in the left-hand column, and then Sign In in the top-right corner. If you don't already have an account, you're invited to sign up for one. Do so, even if you don't wish to purchase online, because you need an

account to automatically download album art for your music collection.

This brief guide can only get you started. To get the most from your copy of iTunes, experiment a little, and if there's anything more you need to know, check out the tutorials at *www.apple.com/support/itunes*.

SYSTEM REQUIREMENTS

iTunes' system requirements aren't particularly demanding, but your PC must meet the following minimum specs:
- 1GHz Intel or AMD processor
- Pentium D or faster for iTunes videos
- 2.0GHz Intel Core 2 Duo
- 512MB of RAM, or 1GB for HD videos
- DirectX 9.0 video card with 32MB video RAM (64MB recommended)
- A QuickTime-compatible audio card
- Broadband internet for the iTunes Store
- CD or DVD drive to import or burn CDs
- Windows XP SP2 or later, or Vista
- 200MB HDD space

Importing CDs is easy

Adding album art manually is a drag-and-drop procedure

Drag and drop your music into a playlist

The iTunes Music Store

TIME REQUIRED   DIFFICULTY LEVEL   PROJECT   SOFTWARE

45 MINUTES

HARD

INTERMEDIATE

EASY

077

Use voice-recognition software

Let your PC do the typing. Here we show you how

WITH WORD PROCESSING and sending emails a common activity for many of us, it's perhaps unsurprising that lots of people are typing more than ever. However, if you're not a fast typer, or are looking for a more convenient way to get words on your screen, then speech recognition can be a useful alternative to tapping words on a keyboard. That's because it converts spoken words into written text.

Setting up such a system is quite straightforward, but requires a PC with sound capabilities, a decent-quality microphone headset (preferably a noise-cancelling one) and a speech recognition program like Dragon Naturally Speaking, which we'll be using for our examples.

Before beginning the installation, you need to attach the microphone to your PC. In most cases, the required socket is at the back of the machine (although it can be mounted at the front), alongside the headphone/speaker and aux sockets. Usually, it will have a pink surround, so it's fairly easy to distinguish from the others. If your headset includes earphones, these should be connected to the socket with the green surround.

The first part of Dragon Naturally Speaking's installation will test the quality of your microphone to determine if it's suitable for speech recognition. Then you will be required to read a few passages from a selection of subjects (these are normally provided); this allows the system to adapt its recognition algorithms to your particular voice patterns. During this phase you should speak slowly but clearly, because the initial 'training' (as this process is called) will establish the accuracy of the recognition engine.

The system naturally continues to learn as you dictate, but if you find the accuracy is unacceptably low, you can always go back and do more training. Generally, the more you do, the more accurate the program becomes.

In order to personalise the speech-recognition engine to your vocabulary, Dragon Naturally Speaking will also take some time to analyse the content of your documents folder and emails.

Using the system takes a bit of getting used to, because the program (on a reasonably fast computer) is able to produce text almost as quickly as you can speak. For this reason, you need to adopt a different way of working to how you'd approach things if you were using a keyboard. Rather than dictating words and phrases that have to be constantly refined, most people find it's more productive to form whole sentences in their head before they begin to speak.

It's also easier once you become more familiar with the various commands needed to navigate, or carry out corrections. These commands can be accomplished without touching the keyboard, because dictation is only one facet of speech-recognition software. Most programs allow quite comprehensive control of the PC as well, all in response to the sound of your voice!

There are other benefits to voice dictation. For example, if the system recognises what you say, it will almost certainly spell it correctly. On the odd occasion when it misunderstands you, simply say 'Select', followed by the mistaken text. The correction menu will then open up and offer a list of alternatives, and it's not often that the list doesn't contain the text you need.

In addition, you can use voice commands within a wide range of other applications. So you can, for instance, navigate websites via voice dictation, which is far easier than using the mouse and keyboard. ■

The microphone socket is normally fitted with a pink collar

After installation, you need to position your microphone and begin training

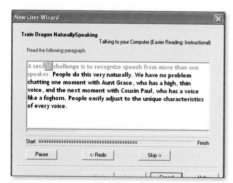

The system tells you what it understands

If you use Vista, you already have a very powerful speech-recognition program

WINDOWS VISTA SPEECH RECOGNITION

Although Dragon Naturally Speaking Preferred is featured in this article, there are other options available. In fact, Vista users have a similar (yet less sophisticated) speech recognition system built into their operating system. It's found in the control panel under an icon that looks like an old fashioned microphone, which unsurprisingly is labelled 'Speech Recognition Options'. You set it up in much the same way, by optimising the recording levels and reading some text, to give the program a sample of your particular variety of spoken English.

HARD
INTERMEDIATE
EASY

1 HOUR

Benchmark your system

Comparing your PC with others can reveal how best to improve it

SINCE THE EARLY days of computing, benchmarks have existed. Initially, benchmark software was introduced as a means of judging the relative performance of systems for promotional material, but now they're commonly used by reviewers and experienced users to evaluate new hardware and software.

Some applications are very general, testing all aspects of the PC. Others focus on specific hardware, such as the graphics card or hard drive. Sometimes it's simply just useful to know how one PC compares with another.

To benchmark your system you'll need some benchmarking software. Depending what it is you wish to test, and to what extent, this might be free download or a commercial tool.

Those running Windows Vista have a simple but informative benchmark application already built into their operating system. The Windows Experience Index scores processor, memory, graphics and your primary hard disk with a series of tests, and then delivers an overall score.

BENCHMARKING GAMES

Synthetic tests don't always tell the whole story about a computer or video card, especially when gaming is involved. Therefore, many games now come with integrated benchmarks that play through a previously recorded gaming session and capture the frame rate over the running time. Crysis and Call Of Duty are among the many games with this feature.

The exact details and commands for each game are different, so refer to the software creators' websites for more.

1 To access the test, open the Control Panel and click on Performance Information and Tools. Here you'll be given a number for the overall system score, and told if you've added any new hardware that might change that score. To run a new test, simply push the Refresh Now button.

2 It takes only a few minutes to perform the tests, and you're informed how it's progressing with a visual guide. It's generally a good idea that you leave the computer alone during the testing, and shut down any running applications beforehand.

3 Once the test is complete you're given an overall score and a breakdown of how this was concluded. Generally, the overall score is actually the lowest number of the subscores, as the system is considered only as quick as the slowest part. It also appears that the scores are arbitrarily out of six, so that's the highest possible score you can attain on any part and therefore total. However, the Windows Experience Index does tell you if a new part you introduced had any impact, positive or negative.

Graphics Benchmarks
Video card performance is one of the most common forms of computer benchmarking. These tests will usually focus on a particular video API, which on Windows computers will be DirectX or OpenGL. Some are exclusively designed for Vista and DirectX 10. Most are commercial tools but offer time-limited evaluation versions. There's quite a broad selection to choose from, and here are a few you might want to experiment with:

3DMark 06 by FutureMark
3DMark06 isn't FutureMark's latest test, but this one works on Windows XP. It's a 580MB download, so it's best to have a fast connection. Try *www.FutureMark.com*.

3DMark Vantage by FutureMark
An exclusive DirectX 10 test for Vista video systems. It's a massive 655MB download and only runs once in the trial version. The Basic Edition costs $6.95 if you want to see it more than once.

Lightsmark 2008
An interesting test that emulates light and shade in a 3D world. It's free and, at 29MB, is relatively small. Find it at *dee.cz/lightsmark*.

General Benchmarks
These tests target either all of the computer or specific functions, and most of them are free or have demos.

Sandra by SiSoftware
This is a comprehensive testing and system-information tool that comes in a free 'Lite' version, and also a range of commercial paid ones. It tests almost everything in the computer, and is a very popular benchmarking application. Download and buy from *www.sisoftware.co.uk*.

HD Tach by Simpili Software
This tests hard drive performance, and builds a database from the results for comparison. The free version tests reading, while the commercial release costs $49.95 and tests write speed also. Available from *www.simplisoftware.com*.

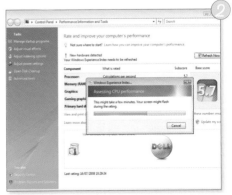

Extend your laptop's battery life

Get more working hours out of your notebook computer

THE COMMON FRUSTRATION with the modern-day laptop is that the battery life of the machine rarely matches what you need. And how frustrating is it to find that you're watching a two-hour DVD on the train, only for the battery to run out of juice just as you get to the all-important ending?

However, while the power a battery can provide is finite, you do have some influence over how quickly your machine demands it. And there are some simple things you can do to ensure that your laptop's battery endures that little bit longer.

First and foremost, one of the biggest drains on a laptop battery is powering the screen itself. While you obviously need a display to look at, there's still an adjustment you can make here to help prolong battery life. That's because virtually all laptops now allow you to adjust the brightness of the screen and, as you'd expect, the brighter you set the display, the more power it will require. It's surprising how much difference to battery life it can make if you reduce your screen's brightness to a more modest level. You can do this usually via shortcut keys on your laptop's keyboard, or you can click on the battery icon in your System Tray and adjust it from there.

Clicking on the battery icon also brings up a further selection of options. You may, for instance, be offered the choice of Balanced, High Performance or Power Saver when you do so. If you plump for High Performance, your laptop will run at full power and run as fast as it can, and inevitably drain the battery a lot quicker. However, investigate the Power Saver option or, at the very least, take a look at Balanced. These scale down the performance of your laptop, but shouldn't make too much difference to the way you work. Unless you're doing some heavy multimedia-editing work, or

EXTRA BATTERY

Of course, if you can afford it, you could always buy a second battery for your laptop, which could be useful for long journeys. Also, many companies sell universal laptop batteries; they tend to be quite bulky, but can provide some much-needed extra juice.

playing an intensive game, you're unlikely to need the full grunt of your laptop's processor, and it makes sense to slow it down and save some power if you're doing something simple such as word processing or meandering around the Internet.

You can also make adjustments to just how hard you push the machine. After all, by its very nature, the more you make a computer do, the greater its power demands will be. While on a desktop computer it might make sense to have a lot of programs running, it's always best for power-conservation purposes to keep running applications to a minimum on a laptop. The less work you give the laptop to do, the longer your battery life will be. So only run what you absolutely need to run if you're looking for maximum battery performance.

One of the most power-intensive jobs you can give to a laptop is to play music or movies directly from a CD or DVD. Operating the drive itself has a sizeable power demand to it, before you factor in the processing power to read the data itself. Where legally feasible, it's in your battery's best interests to rip your audio and video files to your hard drive.

One more piece of advice: even the most modest of USB devices have a power drain on the system that they're attached to, so choose carefully what you actually need to keep connected and what you don't. Be it a wireless mouse, USB flash disk or MP3 player, they'll all combine to speed up battery drain, so where possible, keep usage of them to a minimum. ▪

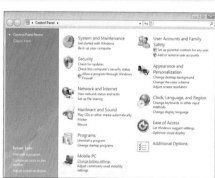

Windows has its own power management tools built-in

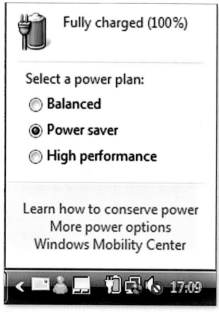

Power saver means maximum battery life

SOFTWARE

PROJECT
080

DIFFICULTY LEVEL
HARD
INTERMEDIATE
EASY

TIME REQUIRED
30
MINUTES

Make your own business cards

Create unique, impressive business cards from your own printer

THE MOST FUSS-FREE way to make and print business cards is to use software supplied by a card stock manufacturer. You'll find a copy of the Avery Wizard software at *www.avery.co.uk*. This application installs into Microsoft Word, transforming the plain word-processing program into a full step-by-step business card designer.

1 When you've installed the application, open Word and click the Avery Wizard icon. Use the Product Category drop-down box to select Business Cards.

2 As you choose a card type, the proper orientation is set for you. If your style isn't listed, pick one that matches the dimensions stated on the card packaging. Click Next and tick Create a sheet of identical layouts. The next window that appears looks similar to a scaled-down image-editor plus word-processing program. The options are very basic, but are all you'll need to design an impressive card.

The blank work area is properly proportioned to match the business card stock you'll be using. A box on the top options bar indicates the scale the card is currently shown at, and you can change the zoom factor with the drop-down arrow, should you need to. You'll also see a small graphic that represents your card layout – in this case, it's eight cards in two columns of four rows.

You fill the perfectly sized empty canvas with the text and images you'd like on your card. You can choose from any font installed on your computer. Choose a style that's easy to read at small sizes, rather than ornate, fancy styles. You can add flair to your card in

your choice of colours and by adding a small graphic.

The most professional look is one that's matched to your other stationery and becomes familiar at a glance. If you have a logo, use a small version of it in a corner of the card. If not, use the tools to add colours that match your website, product or service. For example, for a landscaping business, use greens and other garden colours. Two or three well-chosen colours are often all the punch a card needs to make a good impact.

Be sure to include the important information you want potential customers to have such as name, mailing address, both landline and mobile phone numbers, and email and website addresses.

3 Create coloured stripes and boxes with the rectangle and paint-fill tools. It's best to keep the design as simple and clean-cut as possible. Avoid a cramped layout by leaving ample space and margins around text and images. When all artistic and informational elements are complete, press Next then Print Preview to check your work.

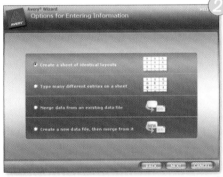

4 Pressing Finish closes the wizard and opens the document in Word. Save your card design as a normal .doc type file. You're now ready to print out your unique business cards. You'll soon spot the benefit of designing cards in this way, as each is spaced to fit your sheets, including fold lines. You can minimise waste by printing only what you need, and make new cards should your contact details change at any time. ▪

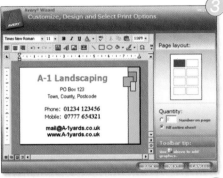

VCARDS FOR EMAIL

You can also create digital business cards for email attachments or to make available for download via any websites you may run.

Recipients simply click to add your details to their email contact list. This information can contain much more than your name and email address. You can include a website, reachable through a

click on your card, and details such as business hours, driving directions and even a map.

In Outlook Express, add yourself as a new contact in your Address Book. Then go to File, Export, Business Card (vCard) and Save. When composing mail, go to Insert, My Business Card to attach your details.

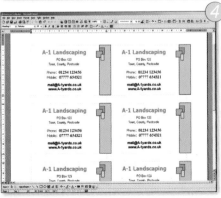

TIME REQUIRED   DIFFICULTY LEVEL   PROJECT   SOFTWARE

15 MINUTES

HARD
INTERMEDIATE
EASY

081

Rip a music CD to your PC

Transferring your CD collection to your computer couldn't be simpler

FOR THIS GUIDE, we're going to use Windows Media Player, since it's probably already on your system. If for some reason it's not present or you haven't got the latest version (11), a quick trip to *tinyurl.com/lkvp5* will remedy the situation, as you can download a copy direct from Microsoft.

While the following guide doesn't show the only way to rip a CD with Media Player, it does show a simple method, and one that works. In fact, it can be boiled down to four straightforward steps:

1 Start Media Player by either clicking on the relevant desktop icon, the Quicklaunch icon, or by going to Start, All Programs, Windows Media Player.

2 Click on the tab that says Rip. As the instructions in the white part of the screen suggest, To begin, insert an audio CD into the CD drive.

3 You might at this point see a pop-up window regarding copy protection. Click Do not add copy protection to your music and click in the tickbox by the disclaimer. Next, press OK.

4 Depending on how it's set up, Media Player may now proceed to rip the entire album, track by track. If it doesn't begin, click Start Rip. As each track is being converted, you can see its progress, and when completed, it will read Ripped to library. Your ripped songs are stored in the My Music folder on your PC, or you can play them via the Library tab of Media Player itself.

You might not want to rip every track on the CD, in which case you should click the Stop Rip button. Now remove the ticks from the songs that you don't want, and click Start Rip to convert just those tracks you want.

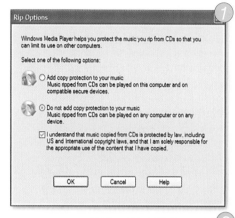

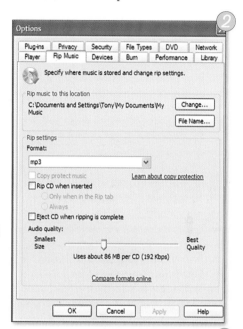

This is a basic way to get your music on your PC, and doesn't take into account some of the more advanced features. For example, you may want to store your music somewhere other than the My Music folder. If so, all you have to do is select Tools > Options, and when the Options dialog opens, select the Rip Music tab. Where it says Rip music to this location, click Change. You'll be given the option to browse your PC for the folder of your choice or even create a new one. From now on, all of your ripped music files will appear in this folder by default.

Also in the Rip Music part of the options, you'll see a section entitled Rip Settings. Here, there are settings for how Media Player behaves when a CD is inserted, and whether it will eject the disc once ripping is finished. However, the really important feature is the Format drop-down menu. By default, it will be set to Windows Media Audio. Although this is a pretty good format for audio files, for the sake of compatibility with portable devices, it's best to select MP3.

Obviously, Windows Media Player isn't the only software that rips CDs. Among the more well-known alternatives are iTunes and RealPlayer. Although the process inevitably differs slightly from program to program, it's nearly always just as straightforward. The best approach might be to try a few programs to see which one suits you best.

SONG INFORMATION

You may find that when you insert your CD, the names of the songs are missing, as well as other information such as the album and artist names. Windows Media Player needs to download this information from the internet, so there could be a problem with your connection. If you want to, you can enter all the information manually, but this is time consuming and probably unnecessary.

Touch up your photos

Remove red eye and minor skin blemishes in a photograph

THE TWO MOST common obstacles to a really great casual photo portrait are the 'red eye' effect that occurs in low-light, and minor skin blemishes. Automatic red-eye removal is now common in Adobe Photoshop, Paint Shop Pro and other image editors. Here, we'll use Photoshop to give a portrait a finishing touch, without overdoing. The same principles apply in most image-editing packages.

1   On the right is an almost perfect portrait, but we need to remove the red eye, as well as the redness around the cheek and jaw area, and to clean up a few blemishes.

2   In Photoshop, select the Red Eye tool from the tools palette (or press J) and draw a square from the top-left corner around the pupil area, ensuring that the pupil remains roughly in the centre of your selection. Let go, and you'll see that Photoshop has substituted a natural pupil colour for the affected red area. If the boundaries of the recolouring are too wide or narrow, undo the step (Ctrl+Z), change the Pupil Size parameter in the Options panel, and try it again. If the results are too dark, undo the step and experiment with lowering the Darken Amount setting from its default 50% in the Options panel. Getting authentic results with an automated tool can be difficult. If you're not happy with automated red-eye removal in your image editor, try a manual approach instead. First, we need to save a selection only for the affected area.

3   Press Shift+M to choose the circular marquee tool, position the cursor in the centre of the pupil and drag out a selection with Alt+Shift held down. This will force the selection to move out from the centre and also keep it proportionally even.

4   The easiest way to add a selection for the second pupil is to save your current selection and put it to one side for now. With your pupil area selected, choose Save Selection from the Select menu, and call the selection Pupil 1, or whatever you like. Press Ctrl-D to deselect everything.

5   Now repeat the selection process from before with the second pupil. When you're happy with your selection, choose Select, Load Selection... and tick Add To Selection in the Operations category. Non-destructive editing of the original will give you more choices in case you need to go back, so press Copy (Ctr-C) and Paste Into (Ctrl-Shift-V) to make a new layer on top of the picture that just contains the red pupils.

6   Sample a suitably dark colour from the eyelash area with the eyedropper tool (Ctrl+I) and paint the colour freely on the pupils. In the Layers palette, select the mostly black mask in the pupils' layer and apply a light Gaussian blur to it in order to soften the edges of the retouched pupils.

7   It's important for realism that the natural gloss of the eye shows through any corrections, so set the pupils layer to 50% transparency and use the Eraser tool (at 50% hardness) to remove sections of retouching that obscure highlights. Now set the pupils layer back to 100% transparency. If you're happy with the correction at this point, you can merge the layers down to a single image (Ctrl+E) and move on to the skin.

8   Before addressing the minor imperfections of the skin, there's an area of redness around the subject's left cheek bone that we need to match with the paler skin on the rest of her face.
Select the Lasso tool (L) and draw an area that comfortably takes in the blotchy skin. Choose Select, Feather and give your selection a Feather Radius of about 15 pixels, depending on the size of the picture. This will ensure that your adjustments don't give themselves away with hard edges, and thus look more natural.

9   Select Image, Adjustments, Hue/Saturation and move the Hue slider up by five to 10 degrees until the cheekbone area matches up. Here we've indicated the effect by including the cheekbone area before and after the adjustment. The clone tool, now a common feature in any worthwhile image editor, needs to be used with great caution, as it will carry with it not only information about texture but also about hue.

10   In Photoshop, the Clone tool (S) should only be used at very small brush sizes to patch up small and distinct areas. After selecting the tool, hold down Alt and click on an area of unaffected skin that you would like to clone onto a small blemish, then let go and click on the blemished area. Try to select a source area that is fairly far away from the target area and yet retains the same hue and lighting, or it will be very clear to others what you've been up to! Here our portrait presents the added problem of very narrow depth of focus, making it hard to get any distance between the source and target area.
Luckily, Photoshop's Patch tool has the answer. This tool transfers textural information but strips it of hue or lighting channels, blending the target area very effectively with the source area. Also, it can use any selection you make as a brush, giving greater flexibility.
With the Patch tool selected (J), draw a marquee from a suitably clear area to cover a blemished area. Make sure that Destination is selected in the Options panel.

11   Drag the Patch tool's selection over the blemished area and let go. Within a few moments, Photoshop will have calculated the mean texture between the two sections to

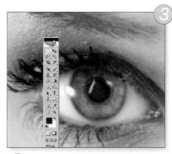

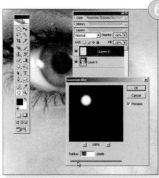
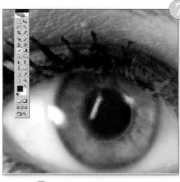

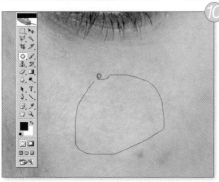
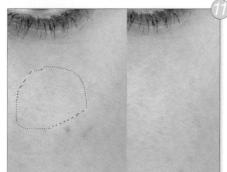

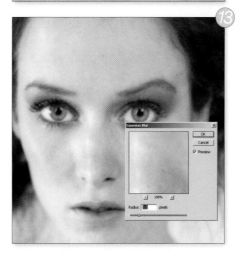

cover over the imperfections, and the results are usually far more effective than the clone tool for large areas of retouching.

12 Having worked away the specific areas of imperfection in the face, a popular retouching technique is to unify the texture of it with a blurred overlay. Taken to extremes, this can give your subject the android-like sheen evident in many glossy magazines, but in moderation it lends the skin a glowing and flattering appearance. To do this in Photoshop, go to the Layers panel and drag your current layer image of the face onto the New icon at the bottom. This will give you a duplicate layer to create the cosmetic mask with.

13 Time to blur the cosmetic layer. Go to Filter, Blur, Gaussian Blur and apply a blur of about three pixels to the cosmetic layer (you might have to experiment to find the right level of blur for your size of picture).

Now we need to remove all the parts from the cosmetic layer that won't look good blurred, including defined features such as eyes, lips, eyelashes and eyebrows, as well as the surrounding frame of the head, hair and shoulders. Think of the cosmetic layer as a face-pack, and you'll have an idea of what

needs to be left behind. Using the Eraser tool for this task could leave you out of options if you run out of undos and want to reclaim some earlier information, so rather than destroying the information in the cosmetic layer, we'll mask it off with a Layer Mask. This is effectively a stencil that we can chop and change at any point, and we make one by selecting Layer, Layer Mask, Reveal All.

Now you can click on the white layer mask next to the cosmetic layer and paint areas away (white will reveal, black will hide) without losing any information in the layer.

Toggle between revealing and hiding the layer by pressing X, which switches the brush colour from black (hide) to white (reveal). Keep the brush sharpness very low and vary the brush transparency to suit the area you're working on in the Options panel.

14 If the cosmetic layer is now too intense, reduce its transparency. To give a glowing effect, set the transparency mode of the layer to 'screen'. If you do this, the lightening effect will be very intense, so it's worth further reducing the layer's transparency. ▪

SOFTWARE

PROJECT
083

DIFFICULTY LEVEL

HARD
INTERMEDIATE
EASY

TIME REQUIRED

15
MINUTES

Put together a playlist

Save time and effort and play your music the way you want

A PLAYLIST IS essentially a set of instructions for a media player to open a pre-chosen selection of multimedia files, and play them. The ability to do this is one that even the most basic of media-playing software possesses. Depending on the player you're using, the files in the list can be movies, photos or music. However, it's the last of these that is the most common, and which will be the focus here.

For this guide, we're going to use Windows Media Player 11, because it's likely to already be present on your system, and it's a very powerful, feature-rich program. The principles are similar across alternative applications, however.

1 First, start by bringing up the classic menus, by right-clicking on the black bar at the top of Media Player, and selecting Show Classic Menus'

2 Now, go to File, Create Playlist. Media Player opens a new box on the right-hand side, where a flashing cursor prompts you to name your playlist. Name it what you want (Playlist 1 or Party tunes, for instance) and press Enter.

3 In the playlist box, you'll see 'Drag items here to add them to your playlist'. Indeed, that's all there is to it. Navigate through your music library as normal, and drag over individual tracks, whole albums or even the names of artists to include everything by them. You can even add whole genres of music, provided the tracks have that information attached to them.

4 When you're finished, simply click on the Save Playlist button at the bottom. From now on, your playlist will available by going to Library, and selecting it from the list on the left-hand side.

To create additional playlists, just repeat these four steps. If at any time, you wish to add more songs to one of your playlists, all you need to do is right-click on the song, album, artist or genre you want to add. In the context menu, select 'Add to', then click on the relevant playlist.

Of course, other media player software will require a slightly different approach, but the basics are usually the same. Be aware, however, that many media programs use proprietary formats for playlist files, so they won't be compatible with other media players. For example, Windows Media Player creates files with the extension .wpl. Some applications, however, are more open, and create playlists as .m3u files, which should work in any media player. These are basically text files and, as such, can quite easily be edited manually in a simple application such as Notepad. Another popular playlist format is the .pls file. It doesn't work in Windows Media Player without downloading an extra plug-in first, but works by default with many other players, including iTunes.

If you don't plan to use your playlists in more than one program, these file formats shouldn't be anything to concern yourself with. Just follow the instructions here, and you'll be able to spend less time choosing your music, and more time listening to it. ▪

AUTOMATIC PLAYLISTS

If you go to File, Create Auto Playlist, you can have Windows Media Player take some of the work out of making a playlist. Here, you can set a number of criteria for Media Player to use, so it can create a playlist for you. For example, you can set it to include, or exclude, a certain artist, album, or genre. You can even set it to filter files by their bit rate, the date they were added, or how many times you've played them. Usefully, you can limit it to a certain amount of items, or a particular duration. This means you could select just an amount of time to play music for, then when you press OK, it will randomly select songs from your library to fill that duration.

Burn your home video to DVD

Take your own movies and put them on a disc

CAPTURING A FAMILY event such as a wedding or holiday on video is only the first stage of a bigger process. If you want others to experience those events you'll need to convert it to a format that most people can accept: a DVD.

Helpfully, Windows Vista contains an application, Windows DVD Maker, that's made specifically for the job. Before you begin, though, you'll need to locate all the content you wish to put on the DVD. That can include video and still images. If you want to trim scenes or reorganise the video, you can use Microsoft Movie Maker 2 – as we're about to – or any commercial video-editing application.

1 Opening Windows DVD Maker for the first time, it explains what it does, but unless you clear the tick on Don't show this page again, that's the last time it'll tell you.

2 Loading the video and images is just a matter of clicking Add Items and then navigating to where they're stored on your hard drive. A list of included items is created, the order of which you can change. Here you

can also give the DVD a title, which is used by the menu-generating stage of the process.

3 Greater control over the DVD you will create is available by selecting Options. Here you can set the aspect ratio, the playback settings and the video standard (PAL or NTSC) that will be used when the DVD is burned.

4 The final job is to choose the menu style that the DVD will use. Each item you loaded in the Add Items phase is presented on the menu, so you can jump directly to that scene or image. Further menu controls are available under Customise menu, and you can preview how the DVD will look.

5 The final action is to burn the DVD, for which you'll need a blank DVD and a drive capable of burning to it. Inserting a disc will initiate the burn, which, depending how much material you have and the speed of the drive, could take anywhere from minutes to over and hour. After it's complete you're given the option to save the project as a file,

allowing you to quickly generate another copy should you require one in the future.

COMMERCIAL TOOLS
If you use Windows XP or another operating system, then there are a large number of commercial tools available that do the same job as Windows DVD Maker, often with much more control over the end results.

Most DVD writers come with an entry-level version of Nero, a multi-purpose disc authoring suite. The latest full version is Nero 9, which includes complete video-editing and disc design applications. Using Nero, it's possible to create professional-looking DVDs. With the right software tools, you can re-create anything you've seen on a commercial disc. The downloadable version of Nero costs £50. Other DVD-authoring tools cost less, but they contain fewer features. Many also support the creation of video CDs, and the latest versions offer new high-definition movie generation on Blu-ray discs. However, to burn onto high-definition media you need HD-quality source video, a Blu-ray writer and expensive BD-R media.

DVD MEDIA

There are numerous types of DVD media available. For home use, either DVD-R or DVD+R single-layer discs are usually fine; they contain enough space for about two hours of high-quality video. You can also get dual-layer media in both flavours that can store twice the capacity of single-layer discs. Rewriteable discs are also available.

PROJECT	DIFFICULTY LEVEL	TIME REQUIRED
085	HARD / INTERMEDIATE / EASY	2 HOURS

Install Linux on your PC

Install a free operating system on your PC alongside or instead of Windows

REPLACING YOUR PC's operating system (OS) is a fairly advanced task that should only be attempted by those who are confident in their own ability to deal with any potential problems. If you do it right, your PC should at least respond a little faster and feel less cluttered. At best you can save your machine from the scrap pile entirely. However, if you do it wrong, there's almost no limit to how much of your data you could lose, so it's essential to pay attention and make sure you know what you're agreeing to.

Warnings aside, installing a new operating system is, ultimately, a step that many computer owners will want to take. The first part of the process is always to ensure that you have backups of all the data you feel is essential. Perhaps even consider using an entirely new hard drive to install the new operating system on. Once you're sure that your data is safe (or you have decided you don't care about it), then you can begin the installation of your new operating system.

For the purposes of this guide, we've chosen Linux rather than Microsoft Windows. Linux comes in hundreds of different versions (called 'distributions' – see the Linux Distributions boxout), and the version we will use for this guide is called Ubuntu. It's generally regarded as the best version of Linux for beginners.

First, you need to download the installation disc from *www.ubuntu.com*. At the time of writing, the current version is 8.04 and the OS comes in two versions: Server and Desktop. Download the Desktop version, and burn it to a CD using whichever software you are comfortable with. Be aware that you're

downloading an entire 700MB CD, so it may take some time, even on fast connections. If you prefer, it's possible to get a free CD of Ubuntu sent to you, or you can buy it if you want faster delivery.

Either way, you now have a Linux boot CD. Put the disc in the PC you want to install Linux onto, and reboot it. If all has gone well, your computer will boot from the CD rather than the hard drive, and rather than going into Windows, you'll get to the Ubuntu install program. You'll then be asked to select a language; for this article, we'll assume you chose English.

On the next screen, you can choose your next step. In this case, we want to choose Install Ubuntu, but feel free to play around with

the other options. You can, if you like, boot Ubuntu from a CD without installing it, to see whether you get on with the operating system or not. Once you've chosen the Install option, you have to wait for it to load itself into memory to run. The installer will then appear.

The instructions for the installer should tell you all you need to know for the first few steps – the hard part comes during the step entitled Prepare Disk Space.

This step will partition a new 'virtual' hard drive from whatever free space may be available (it'll siphon off the free space and give it a 'pretend' drive of its own).

Since the installer will be modifying the partition table on your hard drive, any data currently stored on it is at risk, so ensure that the PC does not switch off at any point and that you follow all instructions carefully.

If you want to install Linux alongside your current operating system, select the option Guided – Resize the partition and use the freed space. If you want to replace your operating system, select Guided – Use entire disk. Beware that the second option will format your hard drive, and wipe any data stored on it. The third option, manual, should only be selected if your hard drive is empty.

Select the drive partition that you want to format, and click Delete partition. This will allocate the drive's contents as free space. Select the free space and click New Partition. This will create what's known in Linux as the 'root' partition.

Select Primary for partition type, and enter the size in megabytes (do not use all the space). Select the mount point as / and leave the other options at their defaults. Click OK and the primary partition will then be created.

Next you will need to create the 'home' partition. Select Free space and New partition again. Set the partition type to Logical, and then set the size (again, do not use all of the free space). Select a mount point of /home and leave the other options at their defaults. Click OK, and the home partition will then be created for you.

Finally, you'll need to create the 'swap' partition. This should be twice the size of the amount of RAM you have installed. Repeat the process as before, creating a new logical partition. This time, set the Use as option to

WHAT IS LINUX?

Linux was developed as a free clone of the popular UNIX operating system. It's open source, meaning that the software is written by a community of developers rather than a central company. There are many versions of Linux available (called distributions), each of which contains its own software that may not be compatible with the others. Linux itself is capable of

running some Windows programs, though it isn't technically Windows-compatible, and will realistically require its own set of applications (lots are available, though).

The choice to use Linux is usually motivated by the fact that it's less prone to instability and viruses compared to Windows, though the fact that it's free is also a popular reason.

Choose a language for the installer; there are plenty to pick from!

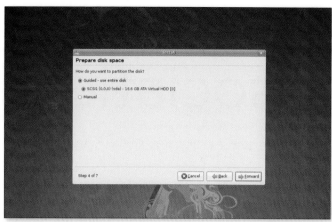

Choose a disk partition to install to, and format it if necessary

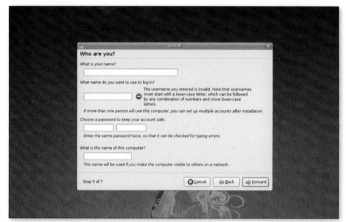

Here's where you enter your user details

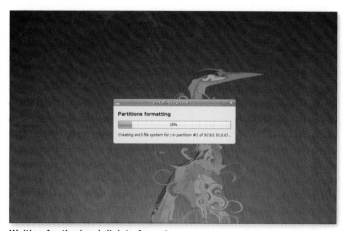

Waiting for the hard disk to format

Eventually, you arrive at the Ubuntu login screen

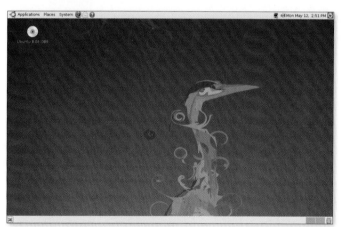

The Ubuntu desktop, ready for action

'swap' and leave the other options at their default settings.

Click the 'Forward' button to continue. The dangerous part is now behind you!

You'll need to fill in your new user details as prompted, including a login name and password. You will then be ready to install the operating system on your newly partitioned drive. The installation process itself should take about 10 minutes (it's a lot quicker than something like Windows Vista), after which you'll be asked the reboot the computer.

Once your PC has rebooted, you'll find yourself able to access your new Linux installation. Remember to remove the CD from the drive, otherwise you might simply boot back into the install menu again! Depending on your choices, you will now either find yourself with a new Linux OS, or a 'dual-boot' system containing both a Windows and Linux operating system.

WHAT'S A DISTRIBUTION?

A Linux distribution is a term for a software package that traditionally contains Linux, a front-end graphical user interface (GUI) and a set of applications. There are over 300 distributions, though the most popular are those run by commercial organisations such as Fedora (Red Hat), openSUSE (Novell) and Ubuntu (Canonical Ltd.).

Recommending a Linux distribution is difficult, as each is tailored with a specific type of user in mind – novices, however, are encouraged to choose Ubuntu due to its superficial similarity to Windows and the lack of technical knowledge required to use it. Other distributions may not be quite as forgiving!

SOFTWARE

PROJECT
086

DIFFICULTY LEVEL

HARD
INTERMEDIATE
EASY

TIME REQUIRED

15
MINUTES

Set your file associations

Change which programs open particular file types by default

THE ABUNDANCE OF software choices at our fingertips invariably means that most users install and try a selection of applications for a given task, before deciding on their favourites. Downloadable software, cover DVDs and free, open source applications have put more programs into our grasp then ever before.

But what if, when you double-click on the icon of an image file, for instance, you find that Photoshop Elements opens up instead of Paint Shop Pro? Or why won't your MP3 files play by default through VLC Player, rather than Windows Media Player?

Installing lots of programs inevitably means they each battle to become your default for a certain file type, and it can all become a bit of a muddle.

Fortunately, setting default applications for files isn't that tricky a job, and a useful project to help keep your system running just as you want it to.

This is what you need to do.

1 First things first, we're going to isolate a file we want to open. So meet our test MP3 file, 'Singalong'. As you can see, there's an icon to the side of it, which here means its default application is VLC Media Player. Let's switch that back to Windows Media Player instead.

2 Here, we've right-clicked on the file, and one of the options that appears is 'Open With' (we're using Windows Vista here, but it's a similar process for Windows XP). That's the one we want.

The submenu then offers some installed default programs for you to choose from, but we want to change the file association permanently, so instead click on Choose Default Program.

3 As you can see, one of the options here is Windows Media Player. So for the purposes of this example, we simply choose that, and make sure the tickbox marked Always use the selected program to open this kind of file is checked. But what if you program isn't listed? That's when things can get a little fiddly, but it's still quite simple to sort out.

4 For an unlisted program, you need to manually locate the relevant application's .exe file on your computer. So let's assume we're looking to link up our 'Singalong' file to VLC Player again, and pretend for the purposes of this example that it's not listed. At step three, instead of selecting a program, we need to hit the browse button in the bottom right.

5 This is where you may have to do some exploring. By default, you're left in the Programs directory, so you need to search for a folder that correlates to the name of your intended program, or its publisher. In the case of VLC Player, it's published by VideoLAN, hence this is the folder that we want to select.

6 In the VideoLAN folder, we've located the program's .exe file (which we could check by right-clicking on the file we suspect is the one we want, and selecting Properties). Highlight the file, click 'Open', and then make sure the 'Always use the selected program to open this kind of file' box is ticked again. And that's the job done!

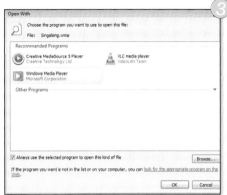

Manage your system sounds

Ensure your PC makes only the noises you want it to

THE STANDARD SET of sounds in Windows can become irritating after you find yourself listening to the same clunks and dings for the hundredth time. If you wish your computer made noises that were a little more soothing or interesting – or even stayed quiet entirely – then you're ready to make some changes to the system sounds. So let's take a look at what you need to do.

To change the system sounds, you first have to navigate to Control Panel (either through the Start Menu or My Computer). Once there, you need to find the sound configuration dialog. Most commonly, this will be found in the Sounds, Speech And Audio Devices category, so left-click on that, and then on the icon for Sounds And Audio Devices that appears.

You should now see the Sounds And Audio Devices Properties dialog. The tab you will find yourself looking at first concerns only volume controls. To find the correct page for this task, you now need to left-click on the Sounds tab, which is second from the left.

If you have Windows Themes installed, you will now be able to choose a Sound Scheme from the drop-down menu. Sound Schemes are a quick way to change all the sounds on your system to an entirely new set.

Sound Schemes are professionally compiled and use sounds that complement one another, so they're usually the best choice for a beginner looking to make changes. Here, you can also choose the No Sounds option, which will remove all of Windows' audio notifications, or Windows Default to get everything back to normal.

The box below Sound Schemes is entitled Program Events. This will allows you to find out exactly what sound is associated with a particular event.

For example, the first is entitled Asterisk – this is the 'event' that accompanies a dialog box designed to accompany an error in Windows. Pressing the play button at the bottom will allow you to hear the sound associated with it, as you would if an error occurred in Windows.

If you want to change an individual sound, rather than all of them, you can bypass the selection of a sound scheme and do it here. Select the sound you want to change by left-clicking on it in the Program Events box. The current file associated with this event will be displayed in the Sounds box in the very bottom-left of the dialog. By clicking the down-arrow on the far right of the Sounds box, you can select any preinstalled sound to associate with that event. If you want to get rid of the sound entirely, scroll up to the top of the Sounds box, and you'll see the option [none] – selecting this will mean Windows no longer plays a sound for that event.

Furthermore, if you've downloaded or recorded a new sound and would like to add it to your system, left-clicking the browse button on the far right will bring up a file dialog, which you can then use to navigate to where the sound is saved and select it for use. Note that Windows sounds must be in Wave (.wav) format, so MP3s won't work.

Once you've made changes to your sound scheme, you should left-click the Apply button in the bottom right. If there are no further changes you want to make, then left-click on OK. Your changes will now be saved, and you should start hearing your new sound choices shortly. If, on the other hand, you decide not to keep any of your changes, left-click on Cancel and any unapplied changes will be discarded. ■

WINDOWS VISTA SOUNDS

Note that this procedure as documented here is for Windows XP and may be slightly different on other versions of Windows.

In Windows Vista, you can change sounds and sound schemes by going into the Control Panel, left-clicking Hardware and Sound and then left-clicking Sound. Open Audio Devices and Sound Themes and left-click on the Sounds tab. This will present you with similar options to those available in Windows XP, as described in the main article.

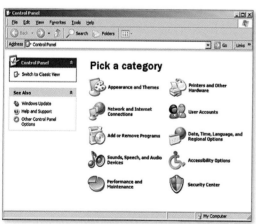

The Control Panel is where you'll find the tools to alter your system sounds

Here is the Sounds, Speech And Audio Devices category of the Control Panel

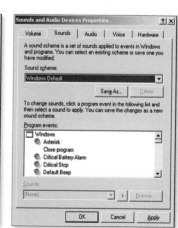

The Sounds And Audio Devices Properties dialog

SOFTWARE

PROJECT
088

DIFFICULTY LEVEL
HARD
INTERMEDIATE
EASY

TIME REQUIRED
30
MINUTES

Produce your own podcast

Become a star from the comfort of your own living room

A PODCAST IS a radio programme or recording designed to be downloaded to an MP3 player or MP3 playback software, rather than transmitted over the airwaves. Fortunately, it's not too tricky to make one.

A good podcast needs a theme and a purpose driving it. Like any PC project, before diving head first into the fun, technical bit, some thought should be given regarding what the goals of the podcast are. What is the podcast going to be about? Who is the intended audience? How often will it be uploaded? How long should each broadcast be? Writing down all the ideas on paper is a great way to plan the podcast before going ahead, and will eventually make for a smoother, more professional-sounding product at the end.

A script can also be a good idea with certain podcasts, depending on the type of broadcast you're aiming for. This will help to ensure that any key information is included and that the amount of waffling or veering off course is kept to a minimum.

Podcasting software can be bought or obtained for free online. Audacity (*audacity. sourceforge.net*) is a good example, great for beginners and expert users alike with its simple-to-use interface.

As for hardware, a headset with a microphone attached, plus a decent sound card in your PC are the very basic tools required to record a podcast (the sound

PODCASTING TIPS

● **Prepare beforehand. With a script and a few ideas at hand, the recording will sound far better.**
● **Research other podcasts on the Internet. Listen to others' efforts and learn how their podcasts are structured to gain useful tips and ideas.**
● **Be natural. A podcast that sounds awkward is difficult for listeners to engage with. Enjoy yourself and the chances are those listening will as well.**
● **Use the editing and post-production tools available with Audacity. An unedited podcast won't sound half as good as an edited one.**

facilities build into the modern-day PC by default are usually up to the job). These can be bought from numerous suppliers at varying price levels. Budding podcasters should be wary of spending too little on such devices, because poor-quality hardware will make for a poor-quality podcast.

For an even more professional-sounding recording, you should think about getting a mixer and a separate microphone. These can be purchased as part of several podcasting-specific solutions on the market, and if spending money on such hardware, you're well advised to first search on the internet for reviews of products, and checking magazine tests, before making a purchase.

Finally, an area with little to no sound interference should be used when recording your podcast. Eliminating background noises and hiss can be dealt with to a large extent during the editing process, but by keeping this at a minimum from the start, the clarity of the recording will make it easier for the user during post-production. At the very least, it could save you an awful lot of time.

Download Audacity (choose from the ongoing beta release or the stable version, which is 1.2.6 at the time of going to press)

and open up the software. Once the main interface opens up, it's important to get to know the software before recording begins. The software's interface is simple to get to grips with, and with a good look around the various tabs and options available first, you're likely to feel much more confident about what's what.

Also, you should make sure the default sample rate is set as 44100Hz and the Default Sample Format is at 32-bit float rate (both fine for most podcasts). These settings can be checked within Edit, Preferences. Of course, you can alter these preferences if you'd like to experiment a bit.

If using a mixer, it should be set up correctly prior to plugging it into the computer, because connecting it before doing so could damage your sound card.

Most mixers should come with a tutorial, and it's a good idea to to read any instructions carefully before setting them up. It's particularly important that the input sound level on the mixer is not set too high before setup, because otherwise the sound quality of the recording could be negatively affected as a result. You want your podcast to sound as good as possible, after all.

Once all your software and hardware is installed and configured correctly, podcast recording can begin by clicking on the red recording button on Audacity's main interface. The sound levels of your recording are easy to monitor via the meter toolbar, at the top right of the main interface. The green meter monitors output levels while the red one monitors input/recording levels. You should ensure that input levels do not peak at the 0dB limiter levels, as there's a danger that sound interference will occur if that happens.

When you've finished recording, click on the yellow Stop button on the main interface. Alternatively, the blue Pause button can be used if a mistake is made or a break in recording is needed (recording can then be restarted by pressing again on the Pause button). However, it's often best to continue through any perceived errors or momentary lapses so as not to disrupt the podcast's flow. After all, mistakes can always be edited out later if needs be.

To edit a recording down, then, you simply have to highlight a section of it and press the delete key on your keyboard. It's a fast, simple process.

Zooming in on a recording is possible by clicking on the magnifying glass to the left-hand side of the main interface. This will ensure the exact section of the podcast that needs editing out can be selected first. These are just some of the options. There are lots of other editing tricks that can be carried out in Audacity, and you should feel free to experiment with the progam's capabilities if you want to get the most from it.

Post production in any podcast recording is vital, and there are several steps that can be taken to improve sound quality and make for a much cleaner-sounding recording. All are accessible via the Effect tab, found at the top of the screen.

After first clicking on the left-hand side of the recording to highlight all of it, clicking on Effect and then Noise Removal will remove any background noise that might be heard; for example, a loud hissing sound from a PC. This is done by recording only the noise that you wish to remove, and the application then uses that sample to filter it out of the recording.

Following this, clicking on Effect, Normalize will increase the general audio level across the recording to make it as loud as possible without distorting the audio quality. Finally, clicking on Effect, Compressor helps to compress the dynamic range of the podcast, softening the louder peaks while maintaining the volume of the softer parts. It makes it sound that little more polished.

There are many other editing effects that can be added to the podcast, including fading in and out the recording (or selected

Planning a podcast will help when it comes to the actual recording process

A good microphone will improve sound quality greatly

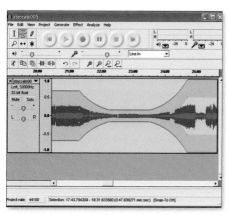

Audacity is a free tool to help produce podcasts

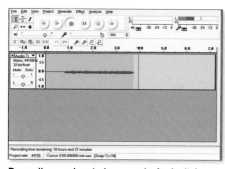

Recording podcasts is easy via Audacity's interface

sections of it), adding echo and altering the tempo. However, by applying the three effects mentioned above before editing, the podcast will be of a much better sound quality, and will reward the time you've spent on it.

Once the recording is edited, it's ready to be saved. Audacity files can be saved in MP3, OGG Vorbis or WAV format. Any of these is perfectly acceptable for good audio output, although MP3 is arguably the more popular with many media players (and certainly with those who might download your work). WAV files are notably bigger in size, and so aren't ideal for distributing across the internet.

To export the podcast into one of these formats, select File, Export As. Next, select the file type required, choose the file name and press Save. ▬

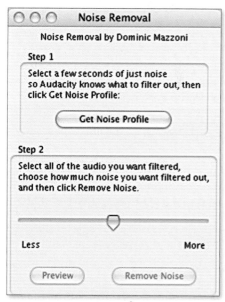

Using Noise Removal in Audacity will help to remove any background noise

USEFUL LINKS

Here are a few links that might prove useful when carrying out research:
iTunes *www.apple.com/uk/itunes* (repository of several audio and video podcasts)
Podcast Alley *www.podcastalley.com* (podcast directory plus forum)
Juice Receiver (formerly iPodder) *http://juicereceiver.sourceforge.net* (podcast aggregator that downloads podcasts in various formats)

SOFTWARE

PROJECT
089

DIFFICULTY LEVEL
HARD
INTERMEDIATE
EASY

TIME REQUIRED
30 MINUTES

Sort out your system security

Protect your PC from viruses and malware for free

PC SECURITY IS crucial, but it needn't cost a packet. To secure your PC without spending a penny, simply install a free anti-virus application, such as AVG Free Edition, and complement this with ZoneAlarm, one of the best free PC firewalls.

Let's begin with anti-virus, and AVG. Visit the website *www.grisoft.com*. Finding the free version can be tricky, so scroll to the bottom of the page and select Site Map. Then select AVG Free Edition from under the Home Security section. You should see the download link on the next page.

Once you have the setup file, all you need to do double-click it to install, and follow the onscreen instructions. Once installed, you should always check for the latest updates, and make sure that your copy contains all of the latest virus definitions. To do this, open up AVG (double-click the flag icon in the bottom-right taskbar next to the clock) and from the main menu, select Update Now. AVG will connect to the online service and will download all the latest software updates and virus definitions. AVG will be set to check for future updates automatically each time you boot up the PC, and it's advisable to leave this setting as it is.

ZoneAlarm is a powerful, free firewall that prevents unauthorised access against intruders, and also controls your own access to the internet, blocking programs or applications until you let them through.

You can download a copy from *www.zonelabs.com* but, like AVG, you'll need to hunt for it, so use the site map again. Once you find the correct free link, download the setup file and then run it. The program can be installed using a streaming installer, or you can opt to download the full setup. The second of these options is advised, because then you'll have a copy on disk should you ever need it again.

Once installed, you'll need to follow the onscreen instructions to finish configuring the firewall. These are straightforward, and once done the firewall will be activated automatically.

Most standard programs will be granted automatic access to the internet, such as Internet Explorer and email apps, but others will need to be given permission. When a program that requires such permission is used, ZoneAlarm will pop up and ask if you wish to grant internet access or not. Select the Allow option if you wish to grant access, or select Deny if you're unsure and want to block access.

Other features of ZoneAlarm include basic intrusion-monitoring, which lets you view the IP addresses of anyone who attempts to access your computer (both legitimate and otherwise), and you can use the emergency stop button to cut off all access to the net.

AVG is a fully featured anti-virus package, and it's completely free

MALWARE PROTECTION

Malware is the collective name for such things as spyware and adware, which can cause all manner of problems to your PC.

To combat this threat, it's highly recommended you install and use a malware scanner. One option is SpyBot Search & Destroy. This is a powerful scanner that will detect and remove offending files with ease.

To get hold of it, visit *www.safer-networking.org*. Here you'll find the free download. Once installed, run the update option to make sure the most recent definitions are included, and then run the scanner. Afterwards, select the 'Immunize'

Ensure you're free of malware with SpyBot Search & Destroy

option and you'll have a good level of malware protection.

ZoneAlarm Free is a powerful firewall

TIME REQUIRED	DIFFICULTY LEVEL	PROJECT	SOFTWARE

30 MINUTES

HARD
INTERMEDIATE
EASY

090

Use your spare processing power

Put your computer's full potential to use on worthwhile projects

MODERN PC PROCESSORS are very powerful. A processor that's capable of heavy-duty video encoding or games playing won't be taxed when you're merely browsing the web or checking your emails. A lot of processing power will be left unused, so why not put it to good use on scientific and humanitarian projects?

Distributed computing is a means of harnessing the spare processing power of computers all over the world. Organised by a central server, when you download and run a distributed computing application, your computer receives and analyses small packets of data over the internet, and then returns the results to the researchers. It does all this in the background, and only uses your spare processing power – they never prevent you from doing other things with your PC. If you arrange for it to be opened whenever you start your computer, you'll make a contribution to one of these worthwhile projects, yet barely notice you're doing so.

1 Folding@Home
http://folding.stanford.edu

One of the oldest and most established collaborative computing projects, Folding@Home analyses the way proteins fold, a data-intensive task that would take decades without the help of home computer users. Incorrectly folding proteins cause diseases such as Alzheimer's, cystic fibrosis, BSE, emphysema and some cancers, so understanding how they fold might one day help us find a cure. Folding@Home is available for Windows, Linux, Mac OS and even the PlayStation 3.

2 SETI@Home
http://setiathome.berkeley.edu

SETI is the Search for Extra Terrestrial Intelligence, a project hosted by the Space Sciences Laboratory in California. It uses radio telescopes to search the universe for transmissions which may have been made by alien life forms. Identifying radio transmissions from the background noise of deep space is an incredibly data-intensive job, which is where the collaborative project comes in. SETI hasn't found any aliens yet,

but who knows what the future may bring? It could be your PC that finds ET.

3 FightAIDS@Home
http://fightaidsathome.scripps.edu

The world's first biomedical distributed computing project is organised by the Olson Laboratory at The Scripps Research Institute, California. It uses computer simulations to predict how new drugs will function, and analyse how HIV builds resistance to current treatments. FightAIDS@Home is available for Windows, Mac OS and Linux.

4 Climateprediction.net
www.climateprediction.net

We spend approximately £1 billion a year on trying to predict the effects of global warming. This project aims to go through predictive models hundreds of times each, investigating how minor changes affect the way the Earth warms and cools. This allows the researchers to explore how our climate may change in the next century under a wide range of different scenarios.

5 Einstein@home
http://einstein.phys.uwm.edu

Einstein@home searches for spinning neutron stars (also called pulsars) using data from the LIGO and GEO gravitational wave detectors. If Einstein is to be believed, these stars are creating ripples in space-time. But was he right? This cutting-edge physics project aims to find hard evidence for Einstein's theoretical predictions. You can run it on a Windows PC, Linux or Mac OS.

6 GIMPS
www.mersenne.org

A prime number can only be evenly divided by itself or one. Thus seven is a prime number, as only divisions by one or seven result in whole numbers, but nine is not, because it can be divided by three. But what's the highest prime number? Is there a highest, or is it infinite? No one yet knows, but in the summer of 2008, a UCLA computer discovered a prime number of 12,978,189 digits. Could this distributed computing project for Windows, Linux, OS/2 and FreeBSD find one higher?

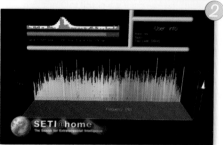

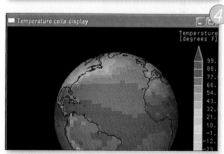

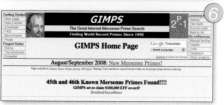

SOFTWARE

PROJECT
091

DIFFICULTY LEVEL
HARD
INTERMEDIATE
EASY

TIME REQUIRED

1
HOUR +

Catalogue your collections

Keep a record of your collections and their whereabouts with a database

THE TROUBLE WITH large collections of anything is that it's easy to lose track of what you've got. Books, CDs and DVDs get moved from room to room, left behind at a friend's house or lent to a neighbour or relative. It's not hard to forget where you last saw that case containing your favourite movie.

You can use your computer to keep track of the things it's helped you acquire. Software is available that helps you record and organise your collection. It'll take a bit of effort to enter what you own so far, but after that, it's simply a matter of a few clicks to add each purchase to your personal database.

The visual organisational tool Libra is available free of charge and can be downloaded at *www.getlibra.com*. It handles books, audio CDs, film DVDs and videogames, and provides thumbnail images of each title, with an easy search function to start building a record of your collection.

You need to download and install the program, but before you begin, visit *www. getlibra.com/node/181*, then download the file named ItemSoftware.xml and copy it to the C:\Program Files\Libra\plugin\item folder. This extends the functionality of the Libra program, letting you add and organise your software titles, in addition to the preinstalled categories.

SPECIAL COLLECTIONS

When hunting for programs for cataloguing your collections, you'll find some that make an inventory of household property, such as appliances and jewellery, which is great for insurance purposes. Other collections have a much more specific focus, such as coins, wine, even comics, and there are applications made just for them.

Another free program makes keeping track of comic books easier. Called Comicster, it's found at *www.madprops. org/comicster*. Like Libra, it links to a database to fill in the important fields and provide thumbnail images for your issues,

Open Libra and select the Default Library to start your database (or you can get to know the program with the Sample Library.) You'll see blank shelves to be filled with your personal collection.

1 First, go to Menu > Preferences > General tab and alongside Select the default currency: choose GBP from the drop-down box.

2 On the Amazon tab, select all entries other than Amazon UK and move them to the right-side box by clicking the '>>' button. You can then move them back if you'd like, where they'll be placed beneath Amazon UK. This ensures that Amazon's UK site is the default choice. Now the program is customised for UK users. You can add your first title to your library.

3 Click Add and choose the category for your item from the drop-down box. You'll notice that Amazon UK is already selected in the next box. For this entry, we've used Games. If we enter Halo 2 in the first blank box and then press Enter, the page fills with examples that Libra has retrieved from Amazon.co.uk, with thumbnail pictures and title details.

Comicster helps to keep your comic book collection at your fingertips

series, characters and creators, this time provided by a global fan community. Great for serious comic collectors.

Scroll through the selections and click on the item that corresponds to yours, making note of the platform and other specifics for the best match. Now click Add to Library and Clear results. Your choice is added to the shelf on the right.

4 Click Library and you'll see the start of your customised collection. Clicking on a title's thumbnail fills the right and bottom panel with information, again gathered from Amazon.

Libra includes a feature to add items by scanning the barcode of your titles using a webcam connected to your computer. If this is difficult, or you don't have a webcam available (or can't find a barcode), then finding item details by the title is almost always just as fast.

If your title isn't listed on Amazon, or you'd prefer to enter details yourself, click on Add and then the Manual tab. Use an image you've scanned as the thumbnail by clicking the Unknown cover and browsing to the relevant image file. Then add the details you'd like included by filling in the title, description and other fields. You can also edit any of the information, descriptions, purchase price, notes and such like of any item at any time by clicking on the relevant field and typing in replacement text.

5 Switch between Icon and Tile views and sort by any field, such as Platform for games or Rating for DVDs.

You can further customise each entry by adding tags. This can be anything that's important to you, that isn't covered in the other fields. It also helps in another way.

To keep a record of your collection you can produce reports for Excel, plain text (CSV), or web pages by going to Menu > Export, choosing a file type and selecting which libraries to include. The database options are useful for importing into other programs, while the Web Export choice produces attractive, linked pages with a handy image-zoom feature, along with all your database details.

6 The Web Export offers a close-up look at each title. You can also further

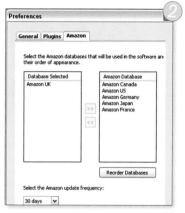

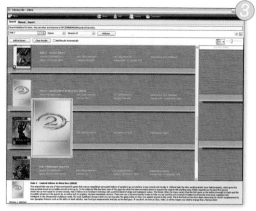

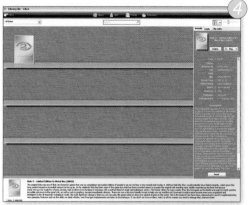

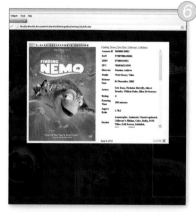

limit the listing to items that contain certain tags. So, if you wanted to keep track of who purchased what, or which titles were gifts, adding this information to the Tag field helps you produce reports based on those tags, such as listing all titles received as gifts. Or you may like to make a note of where the title is stored. There's no need to worry about running out of space; the My Info tab lets you leave more detailed notes about any title.

You'll also see a Loan tab, which is one of the most useful reasons for recording your collection. With a few clicks, you can keep track of items that you've lent to your friends and family.

7 First, add your friend to your Friends list by clicking its button. Next click the Add Friend button and enter their name and optional e-mail address (the Username isn't implemented).

Now return to the Library and click the title your friend has borrowed. Then click beside Borrowed by to select their name. Click the arrows to bring up a calendar to set a Due Date and Check Out date, enter any Loan Notes and click Check Out.

The borrowed title is then marked with an orange Out band placed across its thumbnail. If it's not returned by the determined due date, the band changes to a red Late banner. When the item is then returned, you then just need to click on its thumbnail and select Check In to clear its loaned status.

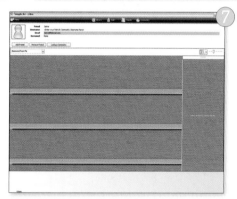

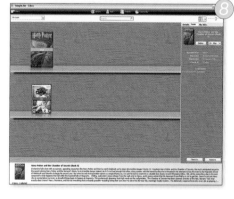

8 You can see which of your titles are on loan at any one time from the Library view. You do this by clicking Menu and ticking only the On Loan selection in the drop-down box below.

Also, you can limit the views to individual categories in the same way by ticking only those boxes, or you can search and organise by tags.

Some people prefer to organise collections using text-only dattabases, but images make it easier to see your collection at a glance.

Whatever your preference, there are plenty of programs to choose from and most make the process of adding and updating painless. And you need never lose track of your prized collection ever again! ■

MAKE LIBRA WORK HARDER

Libra has an additional, often underused, option. The Play button defaults to finding the title on Amazon's website, allowing you to update or view information about it. You can also add other functions to the button, however.

To do this, right-click the drop-down arrow and choose Add/Remove Play Actions. An Edit Play Actions window

opens. Click Add to define a new Play Action. Enter a name for the action, choose a file, and the application that handles the file. It could be a text or PDF critique of a book, a screenshot or video clip for games and movies, or interactive web pages, granting multimedia capabilities to your collection-cataloguing application.

HARD
INTERMEDIATE
EASY

30 MINUTES

Make your own greeting cards and invites

Make your printer work harder by creating custom cards and invitations

MANY HOME PRINTERS perform limited tasks; printing an occasional web page, PDF document or series of photos tends to be the extent of their exertions. Under those circumstances they rarely save a household money, but instead sap budgets with paper and ink expenditures.

Printing greeting cards and party invitations at home can actually save money, and the more family and friends you have on your yearly card and invite list, the more you can save. Pick the right program and you can choose, modify and print cards, invitations, stationery and envelopes, and other projects that rival store-bought versions for less cash. An added advantage is being able to customise cards to include your own sentiments or to incorporate your photos into the designs.

Programs that include a wide range of templates are best. It's like having a complete card shop as close as your computer keyboard and screen. And with pre-designed templates you can easily create the ideal card for any occasion in minutes.

Open a program like Greeting Card Factory Deluxe (although the majority of its ilk work in a similar way) and click Choose a Template from the splash screen.

Click the small plus sign by Greeting Cards to view the occasion types, and again by Birthday.

Scroll through the card styles for the category you need and choose a style you like. For example, select Just For Kids and pick the Cat & Cupcake style (as we've done in the screenshot in the top right-hand corner). Double-click the thumbnail to open it up to work on.

Begin by clicking and dragging the edges of the card – left, right, top and bottom – to meet the thin print area guide lines shown.

Customise the card by clicking on different elements and making changes. Click on the background colour of the card and click the Color tab at the top of the right panel. Clicking on a colour square changes the background colour, in this case to green. Click and drag a corner of any element in or out to resize text or images.

Now click on the greeting text and change its colour to complement the new

Many specialised programs are available

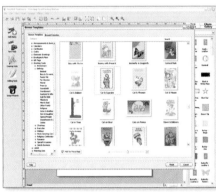
Selecting from an existing template

background. You can do the same with the shape object behind the text as well.

You could make any change even more significant by clicking the drop-down arrow by Solid and choosing gradient fills or a texture.

Move to the card interior by clicking on the Inside tab below the card. Again, match the edges of the design to the guide lines. Then click on the various different elements – that's background, shape and text – to modify the colours of each to ensure they complement the new card front.

You can further customise the card by double-clicking in the text area and personalising with the recipient's name. You can change the font style, size or spacing at this stage, or click the Text tab in the right panel at any time to alter fonts.

To make the card really special, click the Back tab at the bottom of the screen and from the Effects tab, select a 3D text style. Then, you need to enter the Gallery tab to choose an Accent image to create a unique logo or brand for your design.

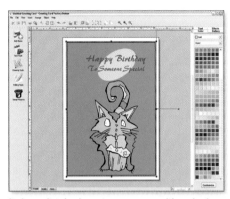
It doesn't take long to come up with a design

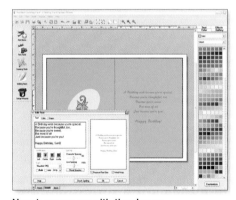
Now to come up with the rhyme...

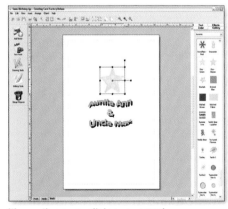
It's worth personalising your card

When your card design is complete, go to File, Save As and name your greeting card project. You can then save your design as a graphic (JPG), PDF document, or HTML page as you prefer.

Then all you need to do is print your card using the Print and Fold wizards in the program, or create digital versions to email or post online.

Configure your system bootup

Is Windows slow to start? Here's how to speed things up again

IT'S SAID THAT nothing in this world is certain except death and taxes. But that's not right. Something else is certain, too: as a Windows installation gets older, it also gets slower. Windows is like an animal, and once you start feeding it from the never-ending buffet of new and exciting software, it can become bloated and sloth-like.

One way this sluggishness can manifest itself is in long bootup times. The problem is that too many programs like to configure themselves to launch automatically as soon as Windows starts. Such programs often show up as icons in the notification area (where the clock is). Clearly, you want your anti-virus software to start running right from the off, but where's the good in having your bootup crippled by the likes of QuickTime, Adobe Reader, and Dr Einstein's Sudoku Jewel Training Quest Deluxe? It's best to start

programs like these manually when you actually want them.

Some programs that auto-launch do so from the Startup folder on the Start menu. Have a look at what's in yours. Click 'Start', and go to All Programs, Startup. Any entry here can simply be ditched – just right-click them and select Delete. Doing so won't delete the program itself, of course, but just the shortcut that makes the program launch.

Other auto-launch programs like to hide their settings in the registry. To put paid to this sneakiness, you need to open the System Configuration Utility. For XP, go to Start, Run, and type 'msconfig' in the text box (omitting the quotes), then click OK. For Vista, click Start, type 'msconfig' in the Start Search box, then hit Enter. In both cases, when the new window pops up, select the Startup tab.

You'll now see a list of all the programs currently configured to run when Windows boots. Now just untick the entries you don't want. The titles of some entries might be slightly obscure, so if you need help in determining what programs they represent, simply expand the Command field to reveal their full file and folder names.

Nothing in the list is needed for Windows to run properly, but even so, it's wise to untick entries one at a time. That way, you won't get in a muddle if you disable something you find you actually want – you can just go back and tick it again. Whenever you make any changes, you'll need to reboot, and after the first occasion a window will appear and remind you that you've altered your boot settings. To stop this from appearing every time you start your PC, put a tick next to 'Don't show this message…' and then click OK.

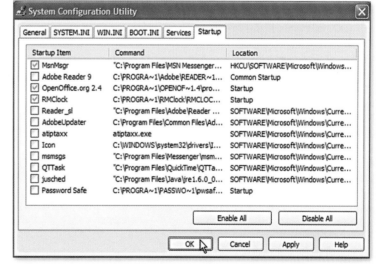

EDITING THE REGISTRY

To prevent Windows from getting bogged down in unnecessary settings, entries disabled with 'msconfig' should ideally also be removed from the Registry. To do that, open the Registry Editor. For XP, go to Start, Run and enter 'regedit' in the text box, then click OK. For Vista, click Start, type 'regedit' in the Start Search box, then hit Enter. To remove an entry, locate it using the path shown

in the Location field of 'msconfig' (or, sometimes, go to HKey_Local_Machine\ Software\Microsoft\Shared Tools\ MSConfig\StartupReg), right-click it, then select Delete.

Before messing with the Registry, you should always back it up first. To learn how to do that, visit *http://tinyurl. com/6j8xa* and read up on the free tool called 'ERUNT'.

Keep the Registry ship-shape by clearing out those unwanted auto-launch settings

PROJECT	DIFFICULTY LEVEL	TIME REQUIRED
094	HARD / INTERMEDIATE / EASY	30 MINUTES

Run emulators and play older games

Use your PC to run software designed for classic computers and consoles

IF YOU'VE BEEN into computers for longer than you care, or are even able to remember, then you'll have fond memories of machines like the Commodore 64 and Sinclair Spectrum. And if you were a console kid, then the mere mention of the Super Nintendo and the Sega Mega Drive is sure to trigger pangs of warm nostalgia.

These retro machines are long gone, and if you want to relive the days when memory was measured in kilobytes rather than megabytes or – shock! – gigabytes, you can always scour car boot sales or online auction sites for some dusty old retro kit. There is another way, however. A much simpler, cleaner and cheaper way.

Using emulation software, you can coax your PC into running software written for other machines. In simple terms, an emulator takes unfamiliar code and converts it into a format that your PC can understand and execute. There are emulators available for just about every computer and console ever released, from the humble Sinclair ZX81 to the Sony PlayStation, and the best bit is that 99 per cent of emulators are completely free to

download and use. Pop along to either Emulators Unlimited (*www.emuunlim.com*) or Zophar's Domain (*www.zophar.net*) and you'll find dozens available to download.

As with any free software, emulators usually come with limited instructions, making them tricky to get working in some cases. Fear not though, because regardless of which program you're trying to use, there are several general steps that are required to set up any emulator program.

WHAT YOU NEED
First, you must ensure that everything you need is included in the download. Most modern emulators come bundled with the native system software (such as the Sinclair Spectrum BASIC ROM), so all you need to do is double-click the executable file and the emulator will run. If you receive an error message telling you that a system file is missing, refer to the accompanying Readme text file included in the download for more information. The reason that system files are sometimes not included is because they are (or once were) licensed to the original

You can bring back the glory days of classic gaming to your PC – although you'll have trouble getting the old joysticks to work!

manufacturer and distributing them can technically be in breach of copyright. As a result, it's up to you to source these system files by searching the web, although you do need to be sure of the legality of the file you're looking for first.

Once the emulator is up and running, the first thing you need to do is configure the display. When first run, it's likely that the emulated machine will appear in a tiny window on your desktop, as it's set by default to display its native resolution.

Most emulators allow you to drag the window to a more suitable size. If not, check the menu for a View or Display setting – it may be available under Options or something

EMULATING A PC

One of the ironies of PC emulation is that it's easier to run software for long-dead platforms than it is to run PC games designed for DOS or earlier versions of Windows. XP and Vista users will often find that older PC titles will run at the wrong speed, or without sound, or won't

run at all. The solution is DOSBox, a program which faithfully emulates DOS on your current OS. DOSBox is available for free from *www.dosbox.com*, and while it's not the easiest emulator to set-up, it's definitely worth it if you're a fan of classic PC gaming.

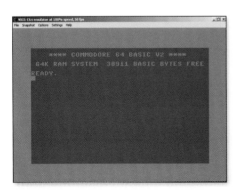

The Vice emulator is one of the most versatile around as it emulates all of Commodore's 8-bit computers, including the VIC-20 and C64

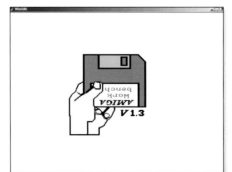

UAE is the Amiga emulator of choice, although it can be tricky to configure. An Amiga Kickstart ROM file is also required

There are several Mega Drive emulators available but Gens is the best. It includes support for the Mega-CD and 32X add-ons

similar. There will almost certainly be an option to switch to full-screen view too. Depending on how advanced the emulator is, there may be a whole host of additional display options. For example, you should be able to select from a variety of rendering options to give the graphics a smoother look (so they appear as they would on a TV set). For that added touch of retro realism you may even be able to add a scanline effect!

The next step is to sort out input methods. By default, most computer emulators will map the native keyboard to your PC's keyboard. If you're emulating consoles, you'll usually find that the joypad has been mapped to your PC's cursor keys, with the Ctrl and Shift keys acting as the fire buttons. There will often be an 'input' setting where you can define the controls and possibly configure peripherals like PC mice or joysticks.

Once you have the display and input settings configured, the final step is to run some software on your emulator. Obviously you won't be able to load up your original tapes and disks, so you'll need to convert these to a digital format which is supported by the emulator.

Thankfully, the vast majority of programs (particularly games) have already been converted, and there are established software archives for most classic platforms. When you've downloaded some software (and again, you need to check to legalities of the file you're downloading before you do so), you should be able to drag and drop the file into the emulator window and it will run.

If not, open the File menu and look for an 'Open' or 'Load' command. With some older emulators, you may be required to copy software into a certain folder for them to run, so check the Readme file again if you encounter any problems.

That's it! You should now have emulated software running on your PC. Most emulators have lots of advanced options which you can tweak and configure, but as you've no doubt seen, the key settings are often selected by

default so there's no need to worry about them. One option you might want to tweak, though, is the speed settings. Older programs may run quite slowly due to the primitive hardware, but you can address this problem by configuring the emulator to run quicker.

At the other end of the scale, if you're trying to emulate a more modern platform, your PC may struggle to replicate the original clock speed, so you may need to look at the frame-rate settings and add a frame skip to improve its performance.

EMULATE A SINCLAIR SPECTRUM
If you're about to dabble with emulation for the first time, then the Spectrum is an excellent starting point. There are several very good Spectrum emulators available (our recommendation is ZX Spin, which you can grab from *www.zxspin.co.uk*), and you can access thousands of Spectrum programs and games at the World Of Spectrum archive (*www.worldofspectrum.org*).

Here's what you need to do:

1. Having downloaded ZX Spin, extract the archive to an empty folder and double-click the ZXSpin.exe file. The Spectrum Basic screen will appear in a small window. To increase the size of the window, either drag it with your mouse or click View, Window Size. You can press F4 to toggle full-screen mode on and off.

2. The Spectrum keyboard has been mapped to your PC's keyboard so you can start entering Basic commands. By clicking Tools, Options, Controllers you can select which Spectrum joystick is emulated by the cursor keys (with the Ctrl key as fire). Alternatively, you can choose to define your preferred keys.

3. ZX Spin supports drag and drop, so you can load a Spectrum program by simply dropping it into the emulator window. Alternatively, you can click File, Load File. The program will then load in seconds.

For more detailed information on using ZX Spin, you can access the Help Topics from the Help menu. But you should find that the basic configuration of the program is ample for what you need it to do. All you need to do now is play a few games!

RECOMMENDED EMULATORS

For some computers and consoles there are a number of different emulators available. So which one should you use? Here are our recommendations, based on ease of setting up, accuracy of emulation and software support.

Machine	Emulator	Webpage
Spectrum	SPIN	www.zxspin.co.uk
Commodore 64	WinVICE	www.viceteam.org
Amstrad CPC	Caprice32	www.caprice32.cybercube.com
BBC Micro	ModelB	www.modelb.bbcmicro.com
Atari ST	STEem	www.atari.st
Amiga	WinUAE	www.winuae.net
Mega Drive	Gens	http://gens.consolemul.com
SNES	SNES9X	www.snes9x.com
GameBoy	VirtualBoy Advance	http://vba.ngemu.com
Arcade/Coin-ops	MAME	www.mame.net

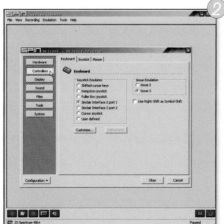

SOFTWARE

PROJECT
095

DIFFICULTY LEVEL
HARD
INTERMEDIATE
EASY

TIME REQUIRED
1+
HOUR

Back up your entire system

Secure your whole system from catastrophic failure

COPYING A FEW important files to disc is enough for many people where backing up is concerned, but if you use the computer for work or rely on it in other ways, then it needs better protection.

The most likely disaster than can befall your data is a hard drive failure. If this breaks, then all your data, applications and system will be beyond reach. The only way to protect against that loss is to create a complete backup, one that can be restored to a 'bare metal' installation. That term describes a PC where the hard drive is entirely blank.

To make a backup of this type you'll need appropriate software and sufficient drive space, not including the one where the system currently resides. Having this type of backup handy can enable you to rebuild a system quickly, and avoid the arduous task of reinstalling all of your applications, along with the data they use.

COMPLETE BACKUP: WINDOWS VISTA

1 Microsoft very kindly made the Vista backup utility more powerful than the tool it included in earlier versions of Windows, in that is can now back up an entire PC. To access this feature, open the Control Panel and locate Backup and Restore Center. In here you can select to backup or restore both files and folders and entire systems. For a thorough backup you'll want to click on the button marked Back up computer.

2 All backups need somewhere to store the files, and this solution offers two possibilitie: a hard drive or DVD. The quickest and easiest option is a hard drive, although you can't select the same drive that you're trying to secure.

Backing up to DVD media will require you to feed the computer new discs throughout the procedure, and depending on how big your system is it might take lots of DVDs to complete the operation. In this example, an external USB drive called Duo is called into use.

3 The system will then ask you to identify which drives on the current system you wish to back up. In this example system there are three drives, but the operating system and applications are on a drive called Vista_32. If you're unsure which is your system drive, look for the one with a little Windows logo on it.

Once this has a tick against it, you can click Next and prepare to back up if the target drive has sufficient space on it to make a compete copy.

4 The confirmation panel details what's to be secured, how big a backup it will make, and where the backup will be saved. If you're entirely happy with your choices, feel free to click Start backup and the contents of the computer will be written to the target location.

5 You're given a progress bar to show you where in the backup cycle your system currently is. At this point the

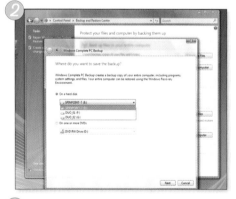

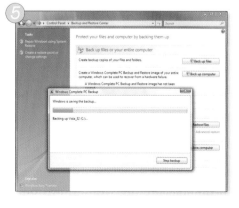

computer should be left alone, because any changes you would make might not be copied to the backup, and you'll slow things down if you give your computer other things to do.

Exactly how long it takes is very dependent on the speed of the drive system you're using and how big the system is. In this example, the system was approximately 100GB, and took roughly 50 minutes to be secured to an external USB drive.

RESTORE VISTA

6 There are two ways to get the backup you just made back onto the computer, and the one you use will be dependent on if your operating system is actually working or not.

If Vista runs, then you might be tempted by the Restore Computer button that's visible within the Backup and Restore Center. If you click that you'll be given more information about how this can be done.

Before you proceed to follow these instructions, please stop and consider the implications of a full restore. The entire computer will be wiped and any files or software added since the last full backup will be erased. This isn't a task you want to undertake unless you've no alternative.

To initiate a restore you'll need to get into the Windows Recovery Environment. If the system is semi-functional you can press F8 when the computer boots up and select the Recovery Environment from the menu

that pops up. Alternatively, you can boot from the Vista DVD and select the Repair your Computer option from the second page, after you've selected your language and nationality. Do not click Install on this page!

7 The System Recovery Options can fix a range of problems, but they also give you access to Windows Complete PC Restore. This is the feature you need to take a backup and restore it over the existing system, in whatever condition it is.

8 The system records the last known full backup and offers you this as the default option. If you want to regress the system to a prior or alternative backup, then you choose here to Restore a different backup and identify the one you want.

9 This is the confirmation window, giving you one last chance to cancel the restore before proceeding. If you tick Format and repartition disks the hard drive will be wiped of all information, including the partition details, before the restore operation is carried out.

Once you've clicked Finish, the restore will begin, so be sure this is what you really want to do before taking that step.

COMPETE BACKUP: WINDOWS XP
The built-in backup routine in Windows XP only supports file and folder options. Therefore, if you wish to make a copy of your entire system, you'll need to resort to a third-

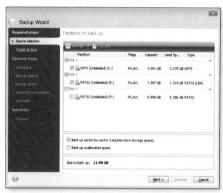

True Image can perform a complete backup

party application. The two best known for this facility are Acronis True Image and Symantec's Norton Ghost, although a simpler tool has now been launched by Symantec, called Save & Restore, which can also perform this task.

Acronis True Image Home 2009 is a complete disk-management tool that includes a complete backup among its many features. It can also back up your system in the background as you work with a 'set and forget' feature. This peace of mind costs £39.95 and there's a free trial available from the Acronis website at *www.acronis.co.uk*.

Symantec, through its Norton brand, makes both Ghost 14 and Save & Restore. They both cost £39.99 and curiously do much the same job for those wanting a complete backup. However, Ghost has a few options to secure the data across a network that makes it slightly more tempting. Both offer bootable discs that then can be used to initiate a restore on a damaged system.

You'll find both and more information on them at *www.symantecstore.com.*

HOW OFTEN SHOULD YOU BACK UP?

The answer to that entirely depends on how much you use the PC, and the work involved in restoring or replacing that work. However, the best strategy is often to combine a complete snapshot of the system each week or month with daily incremental changes. Then if the drive dies you can restore the snapshot and then bring the system up to date with the most recent file changes, too.

If you use your system for home working you might want to consider backing up twice a day, so that the most you can lose is a few hours of work. Some commercial applications will back up all changes in real time, although your system needs to be quick enough for this not to reduce the running performance noticeably.

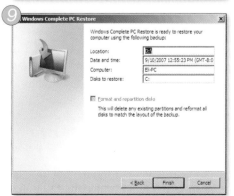

SOFTWARE

PROJECT
096

DIFFICULTY LEVEL
HARD
INTERMEDIATE
EASY

TIME REQUIRED
60
MINUTES

Tweak your system settings

Use Windows' hidden features to speed up your PC

FACTORY SETTINGS ARE fine for most users, but if you want to take full control of your PC, you can manually tweak some settings to improve your system's speed and stability. Here are just a few possible tweaks that you can make.

Please note that in order to make some of these adjustments, use of the Windows Registry Editor is required. Editing the Registry incorrectly can lead to problems and system damage, so you do so at your own risk. Back up the Registry before making any changes.

BOOST THE WINDOWS PREFETCHER

The Windows prefetcher is a system that can 'prefetch' data and store it, thus leading to faster load times. However, the default setting of this is 3. Increasing this to 5 or even 9 grants the system more space to prefetch data, meaning even faster load speeds.

To tweak this setting, open the Registry Editor (see 'The Windows Registry' box below) and navigate to HKey_Local_Machine\System\CurrentControlSet\Control\SessionManager\Memory Management\PrefetchParameters. Double-click the setting called EnablePrefetcher and set Value Data to a higher number. You'll need to reboot your computer before the changes take effect.

MOVE YOUR PAGEFILE

The Windows pagefile is used by most programs to speed up data access, and the larger the page file, the more data that can be handled, thus speeding up access. But, as well as changing the size of the Windows page file, it's also wise, if you have more than

one hard drive, to move it from the main system drive (where Windows is installed) to another drive entirely. This should result in a faster system.

To perform this change, right-click My Computer and select Properties. Click the Settings button under Performance and then the Advanced tab. Under the Virtual Memory section click Change. The Virtual Memory window will open. Highlight the system drive (usually C:) and select the No Paging File option and then hit Set. Now, select the drive you wish to move the page file to, click Custom Size and enter the same value the lower section recommends (you can use more

if you wish, but for now select the recommended option).

Click Set and then you'll need to reboot the PC. The page file will now be located on the new drive.

OPTIMISE YOUR BOOT FILES

Bootup files are, unsurprisingly, loaded when you start your PC. But if these are fragmented, boot times may be sluggish.

You can set the system to defragment these files during bootup, which should increase performance. To do so, open the Registry Editor and navigate to HKey_Local_Machine\Software\Microsoft\Dfrg\BootOptimizeFunction.

You'll see a setting called Enable. Double-click this and change the value to Y. Reboot for the changes to take effect.

FINE-TUNE STARTUP

A great way to speed up boot times and the PC in general is to cut down on programs that load up when Windows starts. You can control this by going to Start, Run and typing msconfig into the text box. Click OK or press Enter to open the System Configuration Utility. Click the Startup tab and you'll see a list of programs that boot up when Windows starts up.

THE WINDOWS REGISTRY

Many system tweaks involve the use the Windows Registry. This is an essential part of your operating system and, as such, should only be approached by users confident in their abilities.

To open the Registry Editor, go to Start, Run and type 'regedit' and click OK or press Enter. Once the editor opens, you'll see the various sections of the Registry down the left pane. Clicking on the folder navigates through each

sublevel to the settings and values underneath. The right-hand pane contains these values, and you can double-click entries to edit them.

Be very careful when editing the Registry. A wrong move can cause major problems with the PC. To be safe, click File, Export and save a copy of the Registry. This can then be double-clicked at a later date to restore the previous, working version.

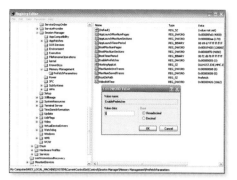

Increase Windows' prefetcher capacity to speed up load times

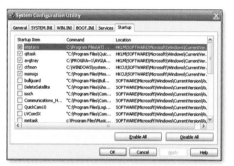

Msconfig can be used for many tasks, including streamlining your system's boot-up

Browse through the list and uncheck any items you don't want. If you're not sure what an item is, either perform a search online to find more information, or leave it be. No items listed should damage the computer if removed, but it's best to be careful anyway.

Once you've removed all the items you don't want, click 'Apply' and then reboot your PC. The removed items should no longer boot up with Windows, and should no longer use precious resources.

TURN OFF INDEXING SERVICE

The Indexing Service is used to boost the performance of the Windows search engine.

TWEAKUI

Microsoft has released Power Toys to complement Windows. These bestow a range of extra features and abilities. One of these is TweakUI. This is a tweaking tool that grants access to a selection of useful tweaks and settings that can let you take full control of Windows, without having to venture into the Registry.

The program is free and can be found at *www.microsoft.com/ windowsxp/Downloads/powertoys/ Xppowertoys.mspx.*

With this you can customise Windows features, including menu animations and other visual features, Start Menu items, installed drives and

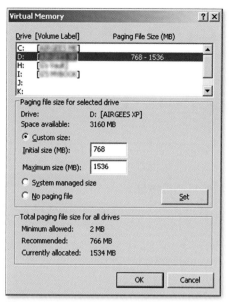

Place your pagefile on a separate hard disk to give Windows a speed boost

However, this can take up masses of hard disk space, as well as system resources. Fortunately, it can be disabled.

To do so, open up My Computer and right-click the drives on which you wish to disable the Indexing Service. Then you need to select the Properties tab, and you'll see a box called Allow the Indexing Service to index this disk for fast file searching. Remove the tick from this box and click Apply. This must then be done for each of the disks that you wish to alter.

FORCE WINDOWS TO UNLOAD DLLs

Dynamic Link Libraries (DLL) are files that are essential to the running of a PC, but Windows often keeps DLLs loaded in memory, even when they're not being used.

To recover resources and force Windows to unload them, open the Registry Editor

TweakUI is an easy-to-use and powerful free tool from Microsoft

drive letters, icons included in the Control Panel, and much, much more.

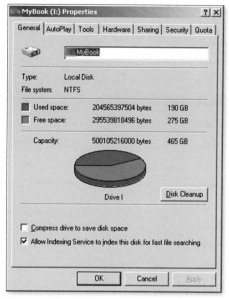

Turn off the indexing service to help increase system speed

Force Windows to unload DLL files for increased resources

and navigate your way to HKey_Local_ Machine\Software\Microsoft\Windows\ CurrentVersion\Explorer.

You'll now need to locate the setting AlwaysUnloadDLL, or create a new DWORD value if it doesn't exist. To do this, right-click in the right-hand window, select New and pick DWORD. Name the value 'AlwaysUnloadDLL' and then give it a value of 1.

Windows should now start to unload unused DLLs after a reboot.

DISABLE THE THUMBNAIL CACHE

Thumbnails of images can be useful for scanning through images to find the one you want quickly, but Windows' thumbnail cache, which is used to store thumbnails for future use, can use up a lot of space on your PC's hard disk.

To disable this feature, if you don't need it, navigate to HKey_Current_User\ Software\Microsoft\Windows\Current Version\Explorer\Advanced in the Registry Editor, locate the setting called Disable ThumbnailCache and set the value to 1. If the key doesn't exist, you'll need to create it (DWORD). ■

SOFTWARE

PROJECT
097

DIFFICULTY LEVEL
HARD
INTERMEDIATE
EASY

TIME REQUIRED
1
HOUR

Get started with scrapbooking

Master the art of scrapbooking with your family photos

WHILE INTEREST IN other crafts and hobbies may have dwindled in the digital age, scrapbooking has grown in popularity. Many of us have large collections of photos thanks to inexpensive digital cameras and mobile phones with photo features.

Scrapbooking goes beyond a conventional photo album. It reflects creativity and artistic expression using frames, stickers, and novelties, along with notions such as buttons and ribbons, all on specialty papers to produce highly textured, three-dimensional pages to showcase photos and commemorate occasions and celebrations.

Just as digital imaging is the modern equivalent of photographic film, computer scrapbooking is the digital version of traditional physical scrapbooks. While 'digi-scrapping' will never have the tactile characteristics or charm of traditional books, it does have a number of distinct advantages.

Most serious scrapbookers design their pages in graphics programs such as Photoshop or Paint Shop Pro. However, even with some graphics editing experience, novices may find them hard to use for scrapbooking, because the craft requires keeping track of many layers and working with multiple items on each page. Instead, beginners may do better to download a dedicated program such as Scrapbook Flair, which is available for free from *www.scrapbookflairsoftware.com*.

To try your hand at scrapbooking, you'll need digital photos and an optional scanner and printer for adding documents and printing pages. Before you begin your first scrapbook page, organise your photos into folders. If it's an occasion or event you're recording, consider what scanned items you might include. You could add tickets, greetings cards

and postcards, or birth, marriage, sport and academic achievement certificates. You can add these from within the program or scan and prepare them in advance.

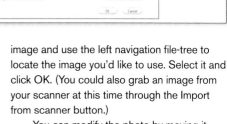

1 To begin your first scrapbook page, launch Scrapbook Flair, choose Create a new project and then click Show me some ideas. Use the Select a theme drop-down box to choose the Baby and Toddler templates. Next, select a paper size and orientation, if available, that most closely matches where you're going to use your completed page.

2 Select the template you like best and click OK. The template opens full screen. In the right-side panel are the layers, with a thumbnail for each image in its own layer. On the left are the options to start customising the template.

3 Click Add Background, then again on the green pattern and finally on the OK button. (You could also change to a solid colour rather than a pattern by ticking 'Use single color background'.)

4 Click on the frame that will hold the photo where it reads Click to add

image and use the left navigation file-tree to locate the image you'd like to use. Select it and click OK. (You could also grab an image from your scanner at this time through the Import from scanner button.)

You can modify the photo by moving it with the nudging buttons on the left. Click the directional arrow buttons under Move Image Within Shape to slide the photo a little to the right. You could also choose to change the shape of the image from rectangular to an oval, hexagon or star shapes by using the Add Shape button.

5 Now you need to click on the Edit Image button to go into the photo-editing window. A sepia treatment might look good on the background of muted colours. Click Effect and choose the Sepia option by clicking Select Effect and then OK.

6 Click Add Embellishment to add more to your page. Select an embellishment you like and click OK. (You could also browse to images you may have collected and stored on your PC.) Drag the digital sticker to where you'd like it and click, hold, and drag a corner out to enlarge the image.

7 There's room for another image on the page. Click Add Image, and Click to add image, and then browse through your folder again. This one is facing right, so move one of the embellishment stamps to the right and then drag the new photo to the left side.

ADVANTAGES OF A DIGITAL SCRAPBOOK

You can try computer scrapbooking with little to no experience or expense. Working with digital additions to your pages, called embellishments, it's easy to experiment with layouts and placements. You can redo a page hundreds of times without fear of ruining your project, and new items can be downloaded for free.

Large communities of enthusiasts exist online, with plenty of places to display your pages and lots of people willing to share their designs and resources with others interested in the hobby.

If you miss the tactile look and feel, create a hybrid, adding traditional embellishments to digital pages.

Next, resize the image to fit the space by clicking and dragging the corner.

8 With the new, small photo still selected, click Add Border and select a frame style. Enter a width and click OK. Drag the framed photo into its final position.

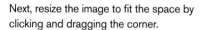

9 Finally, add a journal entry. Click the 'dd Text button, Click to add text and type in your entry. Select a font colour, style and Transparent Text or Drop Shadow (handwriting styles generally look best.) Click OK, and you then drag the text box into place where you want it to be.

You can add more images, text, and even a speech balloon, if you like. When you're happy with everything on your page, go to Save, Save As and choose a name and location to store your creation. You can then print your image or share it online should you wish to.

To make additional pages, click Page, then New Page and select another template style, or choose a background and build your

own. If you have more than one page, use View Layout to see them all and change the order, if needed. For other options, choose Export to save as a JPG image, wallpaper or web page folder and files.

You can save many pages, or entire books, to CD for physically sending to friends and family. If saved in a standard file format such as JPG, then even family members without computers can usually view the scrapbook pages through their DVD players and televisions.

As you become more skilled, you might be comfortable and confident enough to try scrapbooking in your favourite graphics application. Use a program that handles layers easily and allows you to import and work with graphics with transparency. If you get in the habit of naming layers before you begin work on each, they'll be easier to keep track of, and you're far less likely to get in a muddle!

Once you've moved to a full-featured graphics program, you'll be able to do more detailed work with your scrapbook pages, such as rotating individual images and layers and applying a broader range of special effects to the various elements.

Whichever program or method you use, be sure to save your work in a high-quality format, such as the program's native file type, before subsequently saving as a JPG for sharing in emails or posting online. You'll be glad that you did if you ever want to have your pages and work printed professionally and bound as gifts or family heirlooms to be handed down to future generations.

ADDING RESOURCES

A lot of the fun of scrapbooking is adding embellishments. Fortunately, the hobby is so popular you needn't be an artist to have lots of styles to choose from. A search for scrapbooking will yield many sites with tons of resources on offer.

Scrapbook Flair has its own extra templates that you can download at www.scrapbookflair.com/download. aspx. To install saved templates, simply click Show Designer Ideas in the Select Template window, choose a category, click Import My Template, and then browse to the downloaded template (.ptf) file. The new designs will be added to the software.

Record your own music

Produce professional-quality recordings at home

PRODUCING HIGH-QUALITY, professional-standard sound recordings is no longer the sole preserve of recording studios full of expensive hardware and people spitting out technobabble. With a minimum of fuss, a PC and some basic knowledge, anyone can turn a bedroom into a personal musical playground where ideas can be tested, recorded and slowly developed into a song. Here we'll go through what you'll need.

SEQUENCER
A sequencer stores and manages sounds and acts as the hub for both professional and home studios. It allows the user to cut, paste and add effects, as well as overlaying sounds that are recorded into a computer. It simplifies the recording process, too. Every note played or sung can be tweaked separately until the pitch is correct and the tempos match, allowing you to develop your ideas from a simple melody into a completed song.

Sequencers are easy to install and reasonably user-friendly, although its worth spending some time working out what's what. However, you may have to devote a few minutes to managing the various wave files bouncing around on the monitor. It doesn't take long to get up and running, though

GETTING SOUND INTO A COMPUTER
This is simply down to personal budget, but investing a little money can make or break your recordings. Every computer comes with an onboard sound device – which is the cheapest method available – but due to low-quality inputs, hissy mic preamps and having to fiddle around with leads at the back of a base unit whenever you swap instruments, this is the most problematic solution.

By connecting a mixer to your sound card – which costs a few hundred pounds – you can plug in a number of instruments at once and use higher-quality XLR microphone leads. This also makes it easier to adjust the individual levels as they are recorded, lessening any signal peaking (which also removes unwanted distortion).

Other methods you can use include an audio interface that plugs directly into a base monitor and contains any necessary plug-ins. Alternatively, you could use a FireWire-

This is the Tascam 2488mkii, a recording and mixing workstation

compatible analogue mixer and a multi-track recorder. Simply record all your material directly into this unit and then port it to a computer over a USB connection.

MONITOR SPEAKERS
Standard home stereo speakers enhance the sound quality of a recording, boosting the overall mix and making the material more attractive to the ear. In other words, they lie. Professional studio monitors are designed not to varnish anything that passes through them, producing a truer reflection of any recorded tracks and also showing up any noticeable mistakes. For better sound recordings, you should invest in a set of active monitors (powered speakers) for your home studio.

A pair of speakers costs around £200 – but any serious home recording artist should invest this money if they're looking for a fair reflection of their recorded and mixed material. If a final mix sounds good through a set of monitors, it'll sound fantastic when played through stereo speakers, and all the tweaking to get it right will be worth the effort.

CONDENSER MICROPHONES
The only microphone you need for recording both vocals and instruments is the Shure SM-58. This classic, industry-standard mic is robust, reliable and, most importantly, comparably cheap at £69.99. Depending on what you're recording, a few SM-58 mics will fulfil any initial requirements, while instrument-specific mics – such as those designed specifically for drums – can wait until you bring your home studio up to a professional standard, should you choose to do so.

STUDIO LAYOUT
One of the most important aspects of any home studio is the setup. A poorly arranged studio affects both your productivity and the way your creations sound.

The starting point should be the arrangement of the monitors. Ideally, the distance between them should be the same as the distance between each speaker and your head; that is, you and the mounted monitor should make up the three points of an equilateral triangle. This creates a

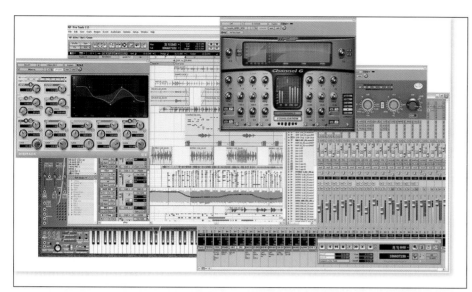

The comprehensive – and initially bewildering – Pro Tools HD7 software

The renowned Cubase 4 music software. Cheaper, less comprehensive editions are available for home users, too

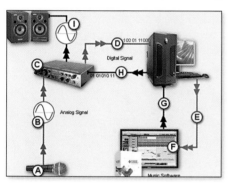

This is an example of how you might route your sound card into a home studio setup

Here's a home studio, up and running and ready to go

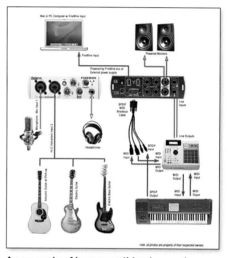

An example of how everything in your home studio may hook up

stable stereo image and allows the speakers to fully project the sound.

Once you have placed the speakers in a suitable position, you can arrange the remaining equipment. Of course, the main hub – and the item you will use the most – is your computer. This should be the centre point of any setup, and the branching-off point for anything you need to plug in for recording. The main aim is to avoid unnecessary frustrations, while not disrupting the flow of your creativity. Items you use frequently should be within easy reach, while those that are least important and rarely used can be kept on shelves or under a workstation. If everything you need is close at hand, it will aid the recording process. However, make sure you keep your working environment comfortable.

SOUND PROOFING
It's possible to fit a band into a good-sized room, ignore the acoustics and record a decent garage-quality demo, but a room can be quietened to create a more productive environment to work in. You should consider this process only when using microphones, as they are easily affected by outside noise. In the long run, cutting down on sound interference could reduce the time you spend

adjusting levels or redoing sections that have been affected by chatter or passing cars.

The most basic method for insulating a room against sound is to create a layer of thick plasterboard with a layer of acoustic foam between the two walls, with all the windows double-glazed and a heavy rubber lining around the door (but make sure you let in some air every half hour so that you don't suffocate). The more costly method – and one that requires a little more effort – is to create a quiet room. This involves using a separate, insulated booth for the sole purpose of recording vocals and instruments that require microphones. By removing low-level background noise, such as that created by the base unit of a computer, this is the prefect environment to record in.

GENERAL ADVICE
The best training any potential home recording artist can have is simply to get stuck in, read everything available and listen to lots of recordings made by others. By starting with the simplest of setups and finding out what other people use, it's easy to start building both your knowledge about the process of recording music and confidence around setting up your home studio.

Learn the basics, make sure you have enough room to work, keep everything laid out, plugged in and ready to go before any creative spark is gone. And be patient, because it'll take a little trial and error before you start knocking out the recordings. ▪

RECOMMENDED EQUIPMENT

Sound card: M-Audiophile 2496 (RRP £48)
Mixers: Mackie DFX-12 (RRP £220)
Audio Interface: Presonus Firebox (RRP £199)
Firewire Mixer: Mackie U 420 Firewire 4 Channel Production Mixer (RRP £199)
Multi-Track Recorder: Tascam 2488 MK11 (RRP £559)

Sequencer programs
Cubase (RRP £239)
Sonar (RRP £219)
Logic Studio (RRP £319)
Pro Tools (RRP £164)

Visit www.dolphinmusic.co.uk for further information.

SOFTWARE

PROJECT
099

DIFFICULTY LEVEL
HARD
INTERMEDIATE
EASY

TIME REQUIRED
15 MINUTES

Change your Windows desktop

Learn how to change your background image in Windows

THE FIRST THING you'll have do before you set about assigning a new desktop wallpaper for your computer is to select an appropriate image. You should be able to find specific desktop images online, although if you prefer, you could always pick something out of your own collection – a digital photo, for example.

The most important thing is to ensure that you know exactly where the file you want to use is saved. Make sure this is a permanent location; if you move or delete the image, you may find your newly assigned background disappears the next time you boot up!

Once you've chosen an image, the next step is to assign it as your desktop background. This is done in the Display properties. The easiest way to access this area of Windows is to right-click on your current desktop, and then select Properties from the menu that then appears. However, you can also reach it by going into the Control Panel and double-clicking on the Display icon.

In either case, this will open up the Display Properties dialog. You'll find yourself on the Themes tab by default. To change your desktop background, though, you need to be in the Desktop tab, which is the next one across, second from the left. You should now left-click on the tab to make the Desktop options appear.

Now, on the Desktop tab, you'll see a list of available wallpapers, together with a thumbnail image of your current desktop background. Left-clicking on any image in this list will show you how the background would look if assigned using the current options.

WINDOWS VISTA

Note that this procedure as documented is for Windows XP and may be slightly different on other versions of Windows.

In Vista, you can change the desktop background by going to Start, Control Panel, Appearance and Personalisation, Personalisation, Desktop Background. This will present you with similar options to those available in Windows XP, as described above.

Pay close attention to the Position drop-down menu on the right of the dialog. If your image does not fill the screen, you might want to select the Stretch option (which resizes the image to ensure that it fills the available space, mostly used for large images) or Tile (which repeats the chosen picture to fill space, mostly used for small images). Center leaves the image at its current size, and using the drop-down below you can also choose the colour that will surround the image if you so wish.

If your image isn't in the available list (which it almost certainly won't be), you need to click on the Browse button on the right. This will open a File dialog box. From there, you must then browse to the location of the image you want to use, and select it.

Once you're happy with the options you've selected, click Apply to confirm your choices. Your background will then

change to your chosen image. If you're happy with your choice, you can then click OK to close the Display Properties dialog. If not, you can choose a new image and try that.

If at any point during the procedure you decide you don't want to change your desktop after all, simply click Cancel at the bottom of the Display Properties dialog, which will close the window without making any changes to your desktop. Note that this is only the case as long as you haven't yet clicked Apply.

Display (bottom right) is accessible from the Appearance and Theme Control Panel

The Display Properties dialog as it first appears. This is the Themes tab

The Desktop tab of the Display Properties dialog is where you select an image

144

Write a movie script

Learn how to simplify the process of writing a screenplay

FOR THIS GUIDE, we're using a useful free piece of software called CeltX. You can download it from *www.celtx.com*. When you consider that commercial alternatives cost hundreds of pounds, it's quite a bargain.

When you first run CeltX, you'll be presented with a list of template types to choose from. Since you're attempting to write a screenplay, the appropriate choice from this list is Film.

When you select this option, you'll be sent to a blank project. The drop-down at the top of the page shows you what the current formatting mode is, and will usually prompt you for the next correct or expected item; for example, with a blank page open, the first thing you type will automatically be formatted as a Scene Heading.

Type the name of the first scene and then hit Enter. You'll notice that the name of the

scene has appeared in the bottom-left box. This is the Scenes window, which will help you organise and switch between the scenes you've written, once you have more than one.

Now that you've hit Enter, you will notice that the formatting mode has changed to Action. This formatting type is reserved for general comments and stage directions. The first thing to do then is establish your scene. Once you've done so, hit Enter again.

You'll notice that the formatting mode will remain as Action, in case you have more to write. If, however, you are ready to move on to dialogue, you can press the tab key. This will change the formatting mode to Character. Type the name of the character that will be speaking, then press Enter. The format will again change automatically to Dialogue so that you can type their speech out.

Once a character has been entered once, you'll be able to auto-complete their name the next time you use the character formatting. Simply type the first letter of their name, then hit Enter. CeltX will now alternate between character and dialogue formatting each time Enter is pressed to make conversations quick and easy to write. You can exit this mode by pressing Enter twice, which will return you to Action formatting.

Once a scene is done, you press Enter twice while in Action formatting. By doing this, you will select Scene Heading formatting, which will let you begin a new scene.

At the bottom of the screenplay window, you will notice several tabs. The default tab is Script. Selecting one of the others will change the overview format of what you've written. For example, choosing Typeset will give you a print preview, while Scratchpad grants you the opportunity to add annotations.

That covers the basics of writing within CeltX. It should be noted that the program also covers project management. In the top left you can see the Project Library, which will help you manage the elements of your project – the screenplay is just one of these. Selecting the Master Catalog will allow you to see all the characters used so far, and what scenes they appear in. On the right, you can add notes about props, effects and make-up.

None of this is strictly necessary if you're just writing a screenplay, but may help you think about the constraints and practicalities of your ideas. ▪

WHAT IS CELTX?

CeltX describes itself as 'media pre-production' software, and is designed to help you manage and create your creative writing projects, be they movies, novels or plays. Unlike other, more mainstream word processors, a program like CeltX will be able to help you automatically format your work specifically for the type of project you're writing.

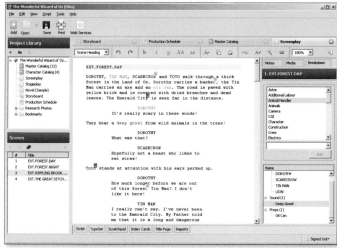

An example screenplay

CeltX's 'Choose a Project' dialog

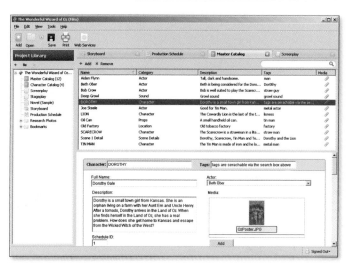

The Master Catalog

145

SOFTWARE

PROJECT
101

DIFFICULTY LEVEL

HARD
INTERMEDIATE
EASY

TIME REQUIRED

30
MINUTES

Burn a DVD with proper menus

Capture, build and burn – make a custom DVD in a few simple steps

WE'VE ALL BECOME familiar with the vast advantages of digital video over older analogue sources, and video cameras are, for many of us, as close as our mobile phones. To make the most of all your captured movie moments with family and friends, it's worth a little extra time to treat your clips to the convenience of chapters and menus, by burning your video to custom-made DVDs.

There are only three main steps to getting a finished DVD from your videos: capture, build, and burn. What's more, with just a little extra planning, you can design your DVD to include photos and your favourite music.

To get started, you need your source video in a digital form, either within your digital video camera or transferred from other sources to your hard drive or discs. You'll need a video editing program that can prepare your video for use with your DVD player, and add interactivity and navigation features through chapters and menus so you can go jump to any part of your video easily. Lastly, you'll need blank DVD discs and a DVD writer. It's also worthwhile to invest in a few rewritable DVDs for practice, and to help avoid making 'coasters' (which are unusable discs with errors).

CREATING COMPLIANT FILES

The DVD creation process is easy and quick. However, the major job of your video software is to re-encode the video to the DVD-compliant file types that work with DVD players. For lengthy videos, this encoding (or conversion) process can take hours to complete.

You can write the DVD-compliant files, complete with menus, to your hard drive, where you can test them before burning to discs. Look for this option in the final stages and choose it in place of Burn. Then reuse the compliant files to make changes or experiment with menus, saving lots of rendering (conversion) time.

Most video-editing programs will contain everything you need for each step, including disc burning. Many are available at a reasonable cost, thanks to the popularity and ease of home-made video and the abundance of low-cost cameras and phones with video capabilities. Some also have trial versions to test out before you buy, so it's worth testing a few to see which you're most comfortable with. Many applications also handle other similar projects such as creating slideshows from your photos and mixing music tracks, which you can add to your DVD project.

The program you choose to build your DVD should include a Capture or Acquire step to get the video from your camera and bring it into your PC, ready to work with. Before you begin, plan what you'd like to include on your disc and have your sources ready and waiting.

We're using the trial version of Ulead DVD MovieFactory for these examples. You can get it from *http://tinyurl.com/6cmr6c*.

1 Begin your project by importing your video. Connect your camera following the manufacturer's instructions (commonly USB or FireWire). Click the camera icon to capture video stored on your camera (or choose the Add video files or Import DVD-Video option if your clips are stored on your hard drive, an optical disc or memory card).

2 Your video is added to the timeline, which is found at the bottom of the screen. To add points in time that you can move to with your DVD remote, click Add/Edit Chapter and click or drag the jog bar to a time period or scene change in the video and click Add Chapter. Repeat the process to the end of the video or click Auto Add Chapters and pick a fixed interval setting and click OK.

3 Click Next and select a menu template from the drop-down categories. You can double-click on text to add your own titles. Right-click on text to change the font style or colour. Click and drag a corner to resize text. It's quite easy to come up with a good-looking menu.

4 Place a blank disc in your DVD burner, click Next and name your project (without spaces) in the Label box and select your drive. Indicate the number of copies, DVD-Video and click the Burn icon to create your disc. ■